THE SPIRE AND OTHER ESSAYS
IN MODERN IRISH CULTURE

THE SPIRE

and Other Essays in Modern Irish Culture

Bruce Arnold

The Liffey Press

Published by
The Liffey Press Ltd
Ashbrook House, 10 Main Street
Raheny, Dublin 5, Ireland
www.theliffeypress.com

A catalogue record of this book is
available from the British Library.

ISBN 1-904148-36-0

Printed in the Republic of Ireland by Colour Books Ltd.

CONTENTS

PART 2: LITERATURE

PART 3: ART

ABOUT THE AUTHOR

Bruce Arnold is Chief Critic of the *Irish Independent* and a regular political commentator for the paper. He has worked for Independent Newspapers for thirty-five years, first for *The Sunday Independent*, joining the *Irish Independent* in 1973 as parliamentary correspondent and political columnist. He has been the newspaper's art critic, theatre critic, and in 1986 became its literary editor, a position he held for thirteen years.

He was born in London, educated at Kingham Hill School and then at Trinity College, Dublin, where he read Modern Languages. He has the postgraduate degree of Doctor of Letters from the National University of Ireland and is an Honorary Fellow of Trinity College.

He has published fifteen books and has made several films on artistic and literary subjects. He has written three plays for children and the libretto for an opera about the life of Jonathan Swift, *A Passionate Man*, the music composed by James Wilson.

He is a Fellow of the Royal Society of Literature. In 2003 he was made OBE "for services to journalism and to British–Irish relations".

ACKNOWLEDGEMENTS

My first and greatest debt is to the *Irish Independent*. Most of the essays in this collection appeared first in that newspaper and I am proud to present them again in a more lasting form. I trust also they have not lost the original enthusiasm with which, generally speaking, they were first written. Vincent Doyle was the editor who presided over the paper when most of them appeared and I enjoyed working with him and for him. The control he exercised was light, the encouragement was brief but sincere, and the tolerance for hard-hitting articles was perfectly judged. I also owe a debt to the team that supported him, particularly Gerry Mulligan, Peter Carvosso, John Spain, Paul Hopkins; and also, at an earlier period, Jim Farrelly and Aengus Fanning. The many colleagues I had, across the broad spectrum of politics, art, literature and theatre, were supportive and involved. I worked also, from time to time, for *The Sunday Independent* and this I enjoyed.

Some of the essays in this book were written for other publications, for the BBC, as lectures or talks, or were simply expanded from earlier, shorter pieces. I am grateful to all those who asked for them.

An unfailing source of encouragement and judgement about all the writing published here has been my wife, Mavis, to whom I owe a continuing debt of gratitude.

To colleagues past and present in the Irish Independent

FOREWORD

Paraphrasing Descartes, Bruce Arnold says of himself *"Scriptito ergo sum"*. In the late fifties, fresh from National Service in post-war Britain, he came to read English at Trinity College Dublin. Unlike almost all the others who made the same journey, he decided to stay on after he had taken his degree — in his own throwaway if not totally apposite description, like a remnant of the Raj. He did so, he says, because Dublin was a city of writers and he wished to write.

Write he has for over forty years with an enviable fluency, embracing journalism, learned articles, autobiographical novels, short books, and hefty, well-researched biographical tomes. Art is his great love and his biographies of William Orpen, Jack Yeats and Mainie Jellett are his most acclaimed works and, by common consent, formidable contributions to scholarship. In this volume, he has added some extra snippets on these artists as well as an extended essay giving us a splendid overview of their very different roles in the development of Irish art.

There is more of Bruce himself and occasionally greater insight in his shorter more ephemeral work contained in newspaper articles and addresses. The decision to bring together a collection of these (all from the last ten years) will be applauded by admirers like myself. The topics reflect the polymath he is. They cover politics, biography, literature, art, all illuminated by acute personal and social observation with a little autobiography and occasional introspection thrown in for good measure.

If Bruce has devoted his life to Ireland he has never attempted or wanted to be anything other than God's own Englishman. He can fairly lay claim to the qualities he attributes to his compatriots that they are polite, logical, intelligent and dogged. He regards as preposterous English people who seek to assume an Irish identity. His sympathy is with those English who love Ireland while remaining English, such as Derek Hill, the artist, at whose memorial service Bruce gave a splendid address full of insight that is one of the best short items in this book. Like Hill, Bruce values his detachment from Ireland as much as his attachment to it.

For all the allegations of being a spy or a blow-in which have wounded Bruce down the years and to which he makes glancing reference, he is justified in believing that he is accepted and welcomed in this country in many parts of its diverse society. The reason for this is, I believe, that he pays Irish people and their institutions the compliment of taking them seriously. Never for a moment does he make the fatal error of suggesting that the Irish are great fun. He is never condescending. Because he seeks to appreciate what is good in Ireland, he earns the right to have his criticisms heard.

Some of these criticisms trespass on the sensitive and intertwined areas of religion and nationalism. While he may be a little hard on the Catholic Church in failing to give credit to it for its many positive contributions to Irish life down the years, he makes criticisms that need to be made and confronted honestly. Individualist free spirit that he is, he finds it difficult to understand the family-like ties of loyalty and gratitude that bind Irish people to certain institutions, even when these institutions fail them.

He has the courage to challenge self-delusions about our unique Celtic character and to tell us bluntly that we overrate "our gift of the gab". After years listening to Dáil debates, it is understandable that he should remark that "the Irish gob is no richer than the

English one". He also challenges the nonsense that because something is Irish it must be regarded as somehow better. He speaks with special knowledge when he says that this has led to the acceptance of much that is second-rate in our art and literature.

He is also right to remind us that we are all heirs to the culture of his native country, especially its literature, and that our life is so intertwined with theirs that there is, side by side with an Irish identity, also a common British identity felt in varying degrees by different sections of our population. The current links have, as Bruce points out, more to do with Jack Charlton, Man. United, the Irish in Britain and the omnipresent British media than the lordly landowners or great pro-consuls who once sought to bind the two islands together at the top level.

Yet, for all his questioning of our collective obsession with Irishness and its definition, Bruce appreciates the important role the assertion of an Irish national identity has played as an inspiration not only in political but also in literary and artistic life. He is critical of art historians Anne Crookshank and the Knight of Glin because, in their magisterial work on the history of Irish painting, they do not relate Irish art to the broad sweep of Irish history.

He can be hard-hitting when he chooses and not inhibited by the embarrassment of having to meet those whom he has criticised. Those who guided the destinies of our National Gallery at the time must have smarted at his account of their behaviour in relation to the supposed Leech painting called *The Goose Girl*. Yet Bruce has survived to join the Trustees of that august institution where he is, no doubt, on courteous or even affable terms with those whom he called to book.

His interest in Irish politics on which he has written for some forty years has given him an insight into the more mundane aspects of Irish life. His judgements are balanced and usually perceptive. But occasionally, he likes to trail his coat and deliberately overstate his case so as to startle readers and provoke a response.

He is never displeased to find himself the focal point of controversy.

He has indulged this part of his nature in his 2000 Bloomsday lecture, reproduced in this book, in which he reconstructs the relationship between the Irish-speaking Englishman Haines (alias Chenevix Trench), Buck Mulligan (alias Oliver Gogarty) and Joyce's alter ego Stephen Dedalus in Sandycove Tower at the beginning of *Ulysses*. It is impossible not to admire the audacity it takes to rush into a vineyard peopled with lifetime scholars and assert that one has something new to say and to say it so attractively and with such assurance and style.

Style, sometimes of peacock proportions, is part of the Bruce we know and is, as he confesses, expressed in his dress:

> Dressed in cavalry twill, a waistcoat and
> with a taste for bow ties, mannerisms

These lines are from a moving poem about his Trinity contemporary Brendan Kennelly that concludes an address given in 2002 at a summer school in Kennelly's native Kerry. Of all items in this book I like it best because it encapsulates the openness that is one of Bruce's most attractive qualities. He alone among his English contemporaries saw the value of the Irish country boy and had the sense not to look down on him:

> I looked at his shabby belted coat
> In awe and secret envy and respect

Beneath obvious, and less obvious, differences, Bruce sensed a kindred soul who was, like himself, nothing without words. The rest did not matter. The friendship they formed survived even Kennelly's allegiance to Mr Haughey in his heyday. Anthony Cronin is another Haughey acolyte who has managed to retain Bruce's esteem — "a ragged-trousered thinking man, poet and critic, who carries his research on crumpled sheets of paper stuffed into baggy pockets of corduroy jackets". One does not often read better than that.

Bruce may not be Irish but after half a lifetime here he is certainly of Ireland. He writes with a blend of frankness and mystery of how, as a result of therapy, he came upon the realisation that he had made Ireland a substitute father figure for his real, pub-crawling father about whom he had written four novels in an effort to get the man out of his system. Ireland, Bruce says, became an object of love, criticism, interest, questioning and identity. He claims to love the country and its people not because they are Irish but because he has made them a natural, coherent and integrated extension of himself. As occasionally happens to me with Bruce's writing, I am not sure that I understand all of what he is getting at but I like the general drift.

If Bruce has tilted at many distinctive features of Irish life, he does not welcome the Ireland "of his youthful dreams and fledgling experiences" being watered down and changed, a country whose shedding of history, religion and national identity is symbolised by the meaningless monster spire in O'Connell Street to which he devotes the first article in this book. If that is ever accomplished totally, this would be a far less interesting society than the much maligned one of Bruce's early Irish years that, for its obvious shortcomings, inspired a man of his ability and discernment to remain on in this country to chronicle and to criticise so constructively many aspects of our life.

Charles Lysaght
September 2003

"You cannot hide the soul"
— Herman Melville, *Moby-Dick*

PART 1

CULTURE AND SOCIETY

1

THE SPIRE

When you approach the Spire in O'Connell Street in bright sunlight, the reflection of the sun off the steel is dazzling. But it is only a thin line down the centre, brilliant, glowing, intense. Because the Spire's surface is round, the direct reflection into your eye comes off only a small segment of its circumference. And because it is so bright, the rest of the surface is hardly visible until you get quite close. At that point the full substance, grey where it does not catch the sun, whitish gold where it does, becomes apparent.

Those of us who saw it, during the first days after it went up, in weather of unparalleled perfection, were lucky. Beautiful cloudless days with low bright sunlight showed it to its very best advantage, its brilliant surface and clear lines cutting a shaft through the familiar buildings, the leafless trees, the distant horizon.

It has a slight bend to the north. I could not believe this at first, but stopped two pedestrians in Henry Street who confirmed the fact. The third person I asked was a Guard. At first he said it was straight; as though a bend in it would constitute an irregularity, and he might have to intervene. But with a bit of coaxing he had a second look, and decided, yes, it did lean very slightly at the top towards Parnell Square, at the north end of the street. He looked round for his fellow Guard, who was talking to people a short way off, and realised he would have to stand alone. "Do you think you ought to arrest it?" I asked, and for a fraction of a second he took the remark as serious.

I extended my inspection and found that the grey monumentality of it was clearly etched when one looked at it into the sun. Time will tell what it will look like in the more normal weather of the city, and after time has changed the patina of its surface, the high polish of the steel.

છ

It has a meaning, the Spire, and I will tell you about it. It stands for us, the Irish, now. It has no religious significance, no cross on the top of it. The last spire of any serious magnitude was on a church and dates back roughly a century. Such spires are the main feature of the city skyline, and they tell us what we once believed and where we went to express that belief. The idea of the city and the country wanting to celebrate itself with a spire that had nothing to do with religion represents a new and changed attitude. Not too long ago its conception and its existence would have seemed offensive. Such thinking seems entirely irrelevant now.

The Spire has no nationalist significance. It is not related to our history. It has no association with our past. We might try and attach its meaning to a historic figure, a hero like Brian Boru or Daniel O'Connell. But to do so would be an entirely false attachment of identity to something that is not about them or what they did or what they now stand for.

It is aspirational. Spires are. They aspire. The word has use both as noun and verb. Shoots or sprouts of plants put forth spires; so does grass. A deer's horn culminates in a spire; so does a unicorn's. Tongues of fire can be spires; so can mountain peaks. The tapering portion of a steeple is a spire, pointing towards Heaven and sometimes surmounted by a cross.

Our spire is still, and it points up as well. But quite towards what is something of a paradox. When the idea was conceived, the world was becoming our oyster, economically. The millennium belonged to us. We were a nation triumphant. In that sense the spire was timely. Now, it may not seem quite as appropriate. But whatever may happen in the future, it will remind us of where we thought we stood in 2000, and, vaguely, why we thought of ourselves that way.

The Spire is made of stainless steel. Technically it is a considerable achievement. The person who conceived it is from London. He could have done the same job for any city in the world. It would have been a fine thing in Amsterdam or in Bergen. Rome would not have permitted it, nor would London or Paris. But Berlin, so grievously destroyed sixty years ago, could have accommodated it comfortably in the cultural sense, just as we do.

The meaning of this aspect of the Spire concerns our own internationalism. We are like other cities and we want to be like other cities. We want it quite badly, in the sense in which efficiency and smoothness of operation is concerned. And we are not looking for an emblem of the past, of ourselves as we used to be, of history, of Irish literature or culture or life or identity. We are ready to accept a symbol of our common bond with everywhere else in the world. We are no different. We are the same.

This trend has been with us for a couple of decades. Normal life, not very different from Manchester, or Wiesbaden, or Tulsa, or Bologna, with much the same kinds of supermarkets and crime problems and traffic difficulties, has crept up on our once dear "Irishness", tending to take it away from us, or to challenge the importance it once had. It is reflected in street sculpture.

An overtly "Irish" example of this is the Molly Malone statue at the bottom of Grafton Street. This, in my opinion, is a mawkish display of unreal sentiment. What we are increasingly putting up are neutral statues like the figures of two shoppers sitting on a bench near Liffey Street, or, even more abstruse, works of abstract design which may have spatial or textural appeal, but could live as happily on the streets of any city in Europe.

A warped sense of nationalism destroyed what the Spire now replaces. The destruction of the Nelson Pillar, blown up more than 35 years ago, helped to spoil a wonderful street, one of the most beautiful in Europe. It wasn't an emblem of British power, but of history and of a strange and universal hero worship which that adulterer, Lord Nelson, found in the hearts of English and Irish people two centuries ago. But we were already spoiling the street in many other different ways, turning it into a real "kip" from which €600 million will not necessarily rescue it.

Apart from the stunning technical impact — the smooth, sword-like blade reaching into the sky, the impressive strangeness of the Spire — the most interesting aspect of it has been public acceptance.

The Spire is neither religious nor irreligious. It is not Irish. It stands for nothing at all. It does not express the personality of the people, the dignity of their achievements, the hospitality, the wit, the intellectual energy, the creativity of the city or the country. And nobody minds at all. Nobody knows what is wanted any more. This Spire is impermeable, like the Teflon coat the Taoiseach once wore. And it is as popular as the man himself.

The Spire will stand for a longer period than Bertie will. It may grow straight by the time I next visit O'Connell Street to look at it. It will lose some of its shine. But it won't lose its anonymous appeal. That is something residing within the Irish heart, first revealed at its unveiling, astonishing to me.

Irish Independent, 25 January 2003

2

AN ENGLISHMAN IN IRELAND

The difference between the English and the Irish has a good deal to do with identity. After more than half my life spent living and working in the Republic of Ireland, this seems to me to be an overriding and qualifying issue and in the minds of many it has to be confronted, not once, but many times.

Within Irish public life, perhaps more emphatically within political life, and to a large extent in the private lives of many people, the question is constant. Irish identity has to be put on in the morning like clothing. It is part of the public nature and attitude. It is a defining of style and of action. It is a response to a collective obsession about nationalism. It is the individual's expression of the introverted cultural concern with "Irishness".

Being Irish has to be asserted. It is central to all major arguments. It starts when people wake up; it is relinquished when people go to bed at night. No one says: "Hell, I don't need that today."

In England it is different. The English don't need to assert their identity in quite the same way. This is not an attractive reality, but it is reality. And it derives from the arrogance of them thinking they are the norm. This is perhaps their besetting sin. Their language, in the world, is now dominant. They think the same about their attitudes, culture and beliefs. All other people, in English eyes — the Americans, the Irish, the French, the Germans, the Africans and the Chinese — are defined in respect of this norm.

It is, admittedly, a preposterous view. But for those who hold it, and certainly for those who held it in my early days in Dublin, as a student in Trinity College which was then populated largely by people of British extraction, or Anglo-Irish Protestants, it was entirely logical.

Combined with this set of attitudes is that other inescapable and vexing difference between the Irish and the English. The Irish, obsessed a good deal of the time with being Irish, want to know what the English think about this. They want a reaction to themselves; they want a relationship, good or bad. They want to confront their nearest and much larger neighbour with their existence.

Anger, possibly dismay, and certainly a bit of grieving, result when a comparable interest is not to be found on the other side of the Irish Sea. The English are not only not concerned about identity. For the English it just exists. Moreover, they are certainly not concerned with the Irish pursuit of identity as an obsession. The attitude is not confined to the Irish. The English, except in an academic or an aggressive set of circumstances, are just not concerned about the identity of others, including their nearest neighbour, which they regard as a small, agreeable, quaint place to the west. There is this imbalance. It is a fact.

In my own case, that of an Englishman living and working in Ireland, there was nothing in it to do with identity. I never wavered in being, and wanting to remain, English. I did not come to Ireland to find my identity. I did not come to lose it, or have it subsumed in some strange formula about becoming more Irish than the Irish. I was entirely sure of it.

I came for quite different reasons. The most compelling of all was the firm belief that Dublin was a writer's city, and if I wanted to become a writer, I should live and learn my trade there and nowhere else. That brought me to the city in the autumn of 1957. It kept me in Dublin for the rest of my life. It was always this that attracted me. There was poverty, there was a sense in which Time seemed to stand still; perhaps it was the stillness of stagnation.

These forces, together with the palpable existence of a class of writers roaming the streets and drinking in the pubs, made it an infinitely beautiful place to live and work in during the late 1950s. Its cultural, social, political pretensions, and their impact on me, were to come later.

Long before I understood this, I came to see Dublin as the centre of the universe. This was not because it was the capital of Ireland, the location of its government, the focus for interest and loyalty, but because I lived there. Deciding to stay on was eccentric. The English people who came to Trinity — a Trinity it must be said deprived of Irish students by the ban imposed by John Charles McQuaid — left when they finished. Like a remnant of the Raj, I stayed on. Feeling that I had found the first important place in my life, I began work as a journalist on *The Irish Times*.

So eccentric was the decision that even in those early innocent days, in the mid-1960s, I was seen as an English spy. I remember one strange occasion at a Royal Hibernian Academy opening, when Kitty Wilmer O'Brien, standing with other Council members of the RHA, said in her powerfully strident voice: "Of course we all thought of you as a spy!" The silence and the faint nods of those standing with her represented approval for her words.

I rather liked the idea of being thought of as a spy. It had overtones of Samuel Beckett and of Graham Greene. But no one had sent me; I reported to no one. I had no Control figure. I observed and wrote about the life of the country, some of the time for the *Manchester Guardian*, some of the time for *The Irish Times*, and I was watched.

෴

Soon Dublin, the crucible for my early endeavours, became Ireland. I felt by extending my field of interest, from city to country, from literature to politics and art, that I was asserting a right, no more, no less. I had no doubts about that right. Later, under duress, I was made to feel a measure of doubt. That was in respect of my criticisms of Charles Haughey, leading to the tapping of my telephone, and the more serious charge of being anti-national — whatever that may have meant at the time — and of being a British "agent" or "spy". Earlier, it had been either half-hearted or light-hearted; when this was repeated, in the early 1980s, its tenor was quite different. It was meant to sting and isolate, if not also intimidate. And for me it represented a low point. However, it was never repeated. I was exonerated from any such condemnation, and no other lasting expression of dismissal or negation of my rights to be what I am and to do what I do has been levelled.

Taking the position I did, I saw myself as a rock of fact. I had no doubt about what I was. My identity was clear. I did not want to change it. As I have said, I did not want to be Irish. I have never regarded this remote possibility as other than a denial of one's true origins, and I look askance at those English people who think they need or can achieve the changeover. I am bewildered when otherwise well-adjusted English people living and working in Ireland choose to become Irish and so declare themselves as something different and new.

I felt I was bestowing a benefit by having this alternative view. At the same time, as a journalist, I felt fully entitled to use the word "We" in the discussion of issues. I did not mean "We, the Irish"; I meant "We" as the people living in this place, living under a set of laws and traditions that drew their substance, sometimes in equal, sometimes in unequal, measure from an entangled history, both British and Irish, to which I could give allegiance.

This approach annoyed many people. It was particularly irritating when I gave credit to the legacy left to Ireland by the British administrations stretching back to the seventeenth century. Understandably, most Irish people see oppression at the heart of that legacy. They have been taught that way by the Roman Catholic Church and by nationalism.

The "Rock of Fact" of which I speak was washed by a sea that sought to erode the presumptions of such a foolhardy existence as mine. It was thought, by some at least, that I would become Irish. It was expected of me that I would concede. To what degree, and quite what I would concede was a puzzle. But it was not envisaged that I would make no concession at all.

I made no concession. My love of the country grew as I came to know it better, and the same happened with the people. Without being immodest, since I am now tolerably well known, I can say that there are few places I travel in Ireland where I am not made welcome in the nicest, most discreet and acceptable way. In fact, outside the Pale is often more welcoming than inside it. I think particularly of being in John B. Keane's pub in Listowel, or in Glenties or Roundstone.

So if the sea of expectation swirls in ceaseless bewilderment at such a stubborn refusal to compromise on who I am and what I am, it does so in an entirely natural and cogent way. It is a matter for debate; for polite question, sometimes stupefaction, occasionally scorn and puzzlement, that none of these seem to work the change.

Among close friends, colleagues, critics, enemies, the issue of how I see myself in respect of Britain, in respect of Ireland, in respect of citizenship, nationality, identity, is never far from the surface.

ॐ

I don't love Ireland because it is Ireland or its people because they are Irish. I love it, the country, and them, the people, because I have made them a natural, coherent and integrated extension of myself. They are my life and my life is a part of them.

I cannot extrapolate, from the way I feel, any wider or more cogent answers. But for any satisfactory relationship between two such different peoples with such different attitudes about fundamental issues to work, there has to be less of the past, more of the present. There has to be recognition of the reality that we work together, live side by side, share so much that is common, from the weather, through our groceries and what we drink, to our entertainment and our sporting enthusiasms. We have to recognise the essential logic of this and adapt to it more.

I cannot apologise for what will seem an arrogant statement of belief. Since it is a belief, how can I apologise? In fact, I will now briefly refer to three other matters that may appear to worsen what I have so far said. The first concerns religion; the second class; the third style.

A book recently appeared in Dublin called *Untold Stories* (The Liffey Press). More than fifty essayists wrote about being Protestant in the Republic of Ireland. I was one of them. At the launch, I was surprised when another of the essayists told me that I seemed to be the only person who had written exclusively about faith with not a word about identity. Almost all the other writers — a few were not Protestant — had written about identity.

If Irish Protestantism is a guide to identity, then it is a very feeble creature indeed. I don't need my faith to tell me who I am. I don't want it to locate me in a tribe to the joining of which I am positively opposed. I am inescapably part of it, by being part of a Church. But it is the Church, not the tribe, that matters to me.

The faith that I wrote about in *Untold Stories* has been pretty constant over the past forty years and has had two practical results on my professional life. The first is to have equipped me to write on moral and doctrinal issues, on contraception, abortion, and more recently on clerical child sexual abuse and whether or not the Catholic Church in Ireland should be made to conform to the law of the land. These religious questions have represented a huge issue throughout the forty years of my working life as a journalist. I probably write more than any other journalist in Ireland on the Church–State relationship and its impact on politics. Where I stand on theological issues, on the doctrinal differences between the Churches, and on the law and Constitution as they have been influenced by the Roman Catholic Church in the Republic, has strengthened my capacity to criticise on matters of Church authority, doctrinal teaching and even theology.

Then there is the question of class. A colleague in the *Irish Independent* once said to me, "It's a pity about your accent. If you had an accent like Jack Charlton, it would be different." I said I didn't want an accent like Jack Charlton. I thought my own was good enough. But as my working colleague made only too clear, it was, in his eyes, a handicap. He said he hoped I didn't mind him saying this. I said I couldn't agree with him. I had more people who admired my use of the English language and the accent in which I used it than I had critics. The colleague was a friend, and very diffidently he added: "It makes you sound as though you belong to a particular class."

"But I do," I said. "I belong to the English middle class." And I told him how my father commanded men as an officer in the Royal Navy. My paternal grandfather headed a British shipping line in Calcutta. My maternal grandfather was a Bradford woollen merchant. My great-grandfather was a pillar of Gladstone's Liberal Party and a stout supporter of Irish Home Rule. I did not fill in all the complexities, just the obvious ones.

In considering the question of style, I do not intend to explain or justify the outward appearances I have adopted over all the years of living in Ireland. My dress is an expression of myself. Good or bad, it is what I live with and I would feel uncomfortable if I did not reflect how I feel in what I wear and the way I look.

But style for me is a much deeper issue. I derive my expression of it from Schopenhauer's words: "Style is the physiognomy of the mind, and a safer index to character than the face." One expresses oneself through voice, words, accent, dress, attitude, behaviour. It is an exercise both in revelation and concealment. It is presentation. But the mind and the character are behind it, and must reveal themselves if style is there at all.

I have always been entirely comfortable with the sense of style I project, whatever it may be. I wish to change none of it. I want to be accepted for what I am and not for some imagined perfection, perhaps involving the oddity of becoming in some way more Irish than the Irish.

℘

Much hatred has been bred from education in Ireland, out of extreme expressions of nationalism, and probably out of a certain anger that Ireland's obsession with the British and with being British is reciprocated by blank confusion and bewilderment.

The English and the Irish know each other well. We have centuries of history between us and behind us. We have time ahead when we will be as close together as we have been. We share Europe. We share each other's territory and people. On the whole, we like each other and know how to live with each other. We can find things to disagree about, but there are many more areas of common ground and mutual enthusiasm. Let us build on them.

What I have to say is about "Us". When I use the pronoun "We", I want readers to take it to mean whatever they choose. At the beginning of *Brideshead Revisited*, Evelyn Waugh has an author's note that says: "I am not I; thou art not he or she; they are not they." In what I have written I am always I, but we may be us, or we may be them.

The Dubliner, February 2003

3

HIS POTENTIALITY

I saw his name with a hundred others
In a book in the library
It said he had never fully achieved
His potentiality.

— *from* "If Ever You Go To Dublin Town" *by Patrick Kavanagh*

I came to Ireland in 1957. That's forty-five years ago. I didn't come to Ireland, then, for the first time, go away, and come back again. I came, and I stayed. Though I was a student, I knew I would stay, and I knew the reason. And I knew what I would do. I knew how I would do it. And I knew where it would lead.

It led to journalism. It led to books. And it led to art. Within a few years, as correspondent in Dublin for *The Guardian*, I was writing about politics. And I went on writing about politics, through the sixties, the Arms Crisis, the governments of Seán Lemass, Jack Lynch, Liam Cosgrave, Garret FitzGerald, Charles Haughey, Albert Reynolds and John Bruton. I have written without break about Irish politics for longer than any Irish political journalist, and covered many of the most dramatic events. Yet it is not this that I knew about when I came. And it was almost a surprise to find myself in the role of political commentator.

I wrote also about art. I wrote about it when most people in Ireland believed that their culture was a culture of the word, not of the visual image. I did not believe that, and wrote the first history of Irish art, and then wrote biographies of two of its greatest twentieth-century painters, William Orpen and Mainie Jellett. And I went on writing about art. Yet that was not what I came for.

I came because of literature, words, writing. And I stayed because of that. And looking at Ireland as it is today, I do so through the same magic of its writers and what they do. They are the life. They give the meaning. They shape the desires and the memories. And when Seamus Heaney won the Nobel Prize in 1995, it was seen, perhaps above all, or perhaps in a spirit of associative possession, as another capping stone in the evergrowing edifice of Irish literature.

When I first came, it was all struggle: against censorship, against indifference, against even the basic demands of life. Writers like Seán O'Faoláin, Frank O'Connor, Liam O'Flaherty — all of whom I knew, and talked to about writing, and in one case published — were expatriate. They had periods abroad, usually in America, when they earned the money which made possible a life in Dublin. And the same was so with writers like Padraic Colum, and Ben Kiely. In the sixties, even into the seventies, there remained an ambivalence about whether or not the life of the writer, in Dublin, worked at all. I had come to Dublin, a couple of decades earlier, because I believed that it did. It was a belief founded on no practical evidence, merely on the existence of a literature I had learned to love. The learning, in England, was why I came. It derived mainly from the BBC, as it happens, and its productions, in those days — the mid-fifties — of Irish plays, together with its readings of poetry, its programmes about Irish writing, the presence among its staff of men like Louis MacNeice and W.R. Rodgers.

Hearing the works of Synge, of Yeats, of O'Casey, of Joyce gave purpose and faith to the idea of Dublin as a literary city, a place where one could become a writer. The talent would be absorbed from the walls, from what Louis MacNeice described when he wrote about Dublin:

And the brewery tugs and the swans
On the balustraded stream
And the bare bones of a fanlight
Over a hungry door
And the air soft on the cheek
And porter running from the taps
With a head of yellow cream
And Nelson on his pillar
Watching his world collapse.

That was the Dublin I found. There were many hungry doors in the late 1950s, and the fanlights had lost their glazing. Many were lost completely, pulled down, and no regrets. Others were restored. The air was perpetually soft. The porter did run from the taps, with its head of yellow cream, and I used to drink it in the back bar of Jammet's Restaurant, in McDaid's, in Davy Byrne's and across the road in the Bailey, John Ryan's pub, and in Molloy's on the corner of Upper Baggot Street and Haddington Road, one of the pubs in which Paddy Kavanagh used to drink, the pub closest to where I lived. And I revelled in the business of becoming a writer, learning how it was done, seeing the first stories appear, practising with words and sentences.

Editing a literary magazine in the 1960s, that too I loved, and it opened many doors. It brought literature into my life, even into my home. Padraic Colum, then in his eighties (he was older than James Joyce), used to stay with his sister when he visited Ireland, and she lived around the corner. He would come to tea, his stove-pipe trousers in grey tweed cut above his ankles and showing his carefully polished, well-worn, laced-up boots. And he would give gracious and sensibly reasoned advice about Irish writing, and about writers, while our children climbed over his feet, and pulled his pen out of his waistcoat pocket.

I knew so many writers at that time, all, I think, struggling to survive. Once a week I had an encounter with Flann O'Brien. He used to come to *The Irish Times*, where I worked as a sub-editor, to deliver his copy, and I always took leave of what I was doing in order to talk with him. He was pale and strained in appearance, carefully removing his hat when he came in, but keeping on the dark blue overcoat. He spoke in low tones, and rapidly, about city gossip, never, as I recall, about himself.

On what became known as Bloomsday, in the summer of 1962, I went out to Sandycove, to the opening of the Joyce Tower. A glittering array of literary life in Dublin at the time had gathered to celebrate a writer who, in his own time, had been vilified but was now safely dead. The celebration was a tourist event. Bord Fáilte sent out the invitations, and I remember them so well, printed in grainy brown and black, stylish in an early sixties' fashion; this was the time when the Scandinavian design team was attempting to redirect things in Ireland. Two of James Joyce's sisters posed for photographs, looking severe and disapproving, not sure of where they stood in relation to anything. Sylvia Beach sat and offered nostalgia to a hungry audience.

I noticed, in one corner of the garden below the tower, his eyes closed against the sun, his classical profile lean and clear, and thrown back, as if cutting upward through the air into the blue sky above, Louis MacNeice. He was alone. I approached, and fumbled some awkward words of introduction, telling him what I did, asking what he thought of Joyce. He was calm, relaxed, and kindly. He almost welcomed the intrusion. He was not part of the Dublin set; and though he had done so much to give them access to the BBC, provide much-needed work, and had done even more for Irish writing over the years, no one seemed to know what to say to him. I hardly knew myself, but babbled incoherent sentences, and felt that I was walking in elysian fields, among the gods of high adventure in the art of poetry and life. We never met again. Within less than a year he was dead.

I remember reporting, for *The Guardian* newspaper, Brendan Behan's death. It was a protracted affair; his funeral procession was followed by a greater crowd than any since the death of

Daniel O'Connell. He belonged within a different grouping, was revered by other writers. And the set — if that is the word — was one I moved around with circumspection and caution. I never knew whether I belonged or not. With some writers, like Ben Kiely, I formed a lasting friendship. He invited me in, and made me welcome, because he liked what I wrote, and the way I wrote. That was the only passport which mattered to him. And I revere him for the distinction of this. I think I came to feel the same bond, much later, with a very different author, Maurice Craig, whose fine, incisive mind was always a joy to encounter, and sometimes seemed so sharp that one feared being cut by it.

I had the same sense of precision and sharpness with Elizabeth Bowen. I met her only once, in Cyril Connolly's house, in Eastbourne. I was drawn to her because of the wonderful tribute she wrote, many years before, about the Irish Abstract Cubist painter Mainie Jellett. And I reminded her of those words. She instantly remembered the occasion. She had known Mainie Jellett when the two of them were tiny children, living as near neighbours in the Baggot Street area. And she had known her at the end of that great artist's life, when she was dying of cancer in a Dublin nursing home. Behind the shell of her cool words and calm gaze, there sprang to the surface a sudden flood of warm affection. It made the brief crowded moments in Connolly's drawing room infinitely memorable.

These words embarrass me a little, since they sound a bit like name-dropping. Yet all the comments have been kept more or less secret, by me, over a period of more than thirty years. And it was only when a colleague gasped with surprise when I told her about spending time with Eamon de Valera, and learning from him of his ambitions, as a young man, to be an artist — an ambition frustrated, even then, by indifferent sight — that I realised how rich the rewards had been for that strange determination which had shaped my life, all those years before.

Dublin was, of course, to be much more than a home. It was chosen to be a school, an academy of writing, a forum for creativity, an inspiration. And I would set forth along its streets, and would walk in its squares and gardens, and would imbibe the words and the language, the kindness and the subtlety, the venom and the despair. All were to be found in its streets, and among its writers.

As a student in Trinity, I was contemporary with Derek Mahon, Eavan Boland, and Michael Longley and Edna Broderick who later married. As a literary magazine editor, I found myself reviewing the works of John McGahern and Edna O'Brien, and coming to know both of them. They were seen, in the early 1960s, as two quite different forces in writing and, Dublin, being what it is, the divisive predominated in any discussion about them. It was possible to like the one, not the other. I liked both. I loved Edna O'Brien's first book, and wrote about it, and the second and third as well. In those days of censorship we shared a campaign platform. I reviewed John McGahern's first novel for *The Irish Times*, and have remained ever since a friend. And it seemed then that a new shape, a new spirit, was being designed for Irish literature, which had toiled through enough campaigns and difficulties, and deserved a different environment.

It got it. Literature blossomed, as did publishing. Television had a focus on the arts. The Arts Council had a focus on writers and musicians, dramatists and painters; the battle, if it had been a battle, was won. Or was it? Is it ever?

Today, the enemy is profusion. We live in an age of excess. For ten years I have viewed that same favoured child called literature — that gifted, magical creature I have always loved — from a position not unlike the one I enjoyed over thirty years ago, that of literary editor for the Dublin daily newspaper, the *Irish Independent*. Books are not just published today; they are promoted, celebrated, displayed, discussed. Their authors are interviewed, not once, but many times. And the writer's fund of information is swiftly exhausted. What can they say about what they have written, except to invite us to read it? What can they say about themselves, except how difficult it was, how lonely, how long it took? What can they say about the world beyond what they have written about it?

Yet they do say these and many other things. There is a new accomplishment in self-presentation which transcends the book. Personality is all, and the focus has shifted to coverage, not criticism. We read the writer, and ignore the book.

Good writing survives it. It always has. It always will. But instead of surviving neglect or indifference, it survives publicity and promotion, the tidal wave of books, the inexhaustible taste for anthologies, the 60p books, the 50p books, the illustrated version, the paperback, the omnibus edition.

Where once I looked upon the prospect of talking with Seán O'Faoláin, or Monk Gibbon, or Paul Vincent Carroll, or Patrick Kavanagh with tense anxiety and careful anticipation, now I know that the answers will be there for me, without ever asking the questions. The writer will speak without prompting, his encounter prepared for him by a publicist from his publisher who will have a programme of meetings through which he will move, under guidance, in an unbroken, Mahler-like flow of sound.

And all I can think of, all I can remember, is the indelible image from around 1960, crossing in summer sunlight from Wilton Place to Baggot Street, to buy for five shillings a bottle of Chateauneuf-du-Pape to go with the shoulder of lamb. I got it from the Mooney's on the corner of Haddington Road — it is gone, now, turned into a bank — and it involved passing the supine form of Patrick Kavanagh, one of whose favourite places for an afternoon rest was beside the canal lock on a warm little corner of grass near the bridge. I counted myself lucky if he was awake, his head resting on his hand, his hat on crooked, his bleary eye regarding the passing world with a penetrating sense of life's disasters which then redoubled my own desire to write. And I would think of those marvellous lines from his poem, "If Ever You Go to Dublin Town":

> If ever you go to Dublin town
> In a hundred years or so
> Sniff for my personality,
> Is it vanity's vapour now?
> O he was a vain one
> Fol dol the di do,
> He was a vain one
> I tell you.
>
> I saw his name with a hundred others
> In a book in the library
> It said he had never achieved
> His potentiality.
> O he was slothful
> Fol dol the di do,
> He was slothful
> I tell you.
>
> He knew that posterity has no use
> For anything but the soul,
> The lines that speak the passionate heart,
> The spirit that lives alone.
> O he was a lone one
> Fol dol the di do,
> Yet he lived happily
> I tell you.

November 1995, a broadcast talk for the BBC

4

CHOOSING A THERAPIST

I made no choice about my therapist. My wife, who had helped me through a period of difficulty and felt that something more was needed, suggested a male therapist and named one. I had no thoughts or reservations about whether it should be a man or a woman. I had no inclination to make any choice myself, and no basis on which to make it. The idea of liking, or being suited, to the person in question seemed to me irrelevant. Much more difficult, for me, was the choice of being in therapy at all. I interpret the title in this way.

After eighteen months of therapy, which I see as a cycle, possibly to be repeated, I suspect that I am in the majority over the question of choice. Circumstance generally decides. We are advised to go to an individual; unless there is a very negative reaction, we accept the authority of this. Furthermore, I have no feelings about the issue of gender. Without having any clear reason for the view, I think it would have been, and would be, the same with a woman. Perhaps what follows may in a sense constitute a reason for this judgement, in that the reception I got throughout was so professional that no sexual significance ever emerged.

I have decidedly strong feelings that what went on was a "success", and would return to the same therapist in the event of need, or if a breakdown occurred. I use the word clinically. I think that is what happened, or nearly happened, and I can foresee it happening again. I do not feel "cured" of anything. What happened during the eighteen months was a series of self-discoveries, prompted or helped to the surface by the therapist concerned.

While the therapist came to know a great deal about me, I learned nothing about him. I liked him, but in a neutral, professional way. I breached the professionalism on my side by making him a couple of gifts. But they were, in a sense, germane to our consultations, and were partly given in that spirit.

It would therefore be sensible to identify them as books I had written, and to explain that the problem which had brought me into therapy was a problem directly related to my professional life as a writer. I tried to explain this to him in terms that he would immediately grasp. I write, therefore I am. I offered this modification of the central principle of Descartes's life — *cogito, ergo sum* — which of course he immediately grasped. But I then went on to make the point that, although we all write, and although writing is still the language of communication, second only to speech, what I was speaking of was something completely different.

Explaining this became difficult. What I was telling him about writing was part of an explanation of two sides of my personality, one, the inner spirit, two, the working man. If the love of one's life is the exercise of the purpose of one's life, and it goes wrong, then chaos indeed has come. This was how I felt when I sought help. After fourteen books, forty years of published work, I was confronted by professional, emotional, spiritual gridlock.

Firstly, there was the chaos in which the world of writing, publishing and literature has found itself at the end of the millennium. Highly respected authors, with a string of successful works to their name, are being stopped in their tracks by publishers not even wanting to see what they will write, and in some cases refusing to take notice of what they have written.

Secondly, I was also confronted by another, perhaps more subtle, undermining of confidence: the partial breakdown of trust in myself as a commentator on politics. This represented something akin to a new virus affecting one's health, unpredictable, unforeseen, possibly untraceable.

I had lived very publicly indeed as a writer. Over the forty years, on the basis of a fairly careful calculation, I have published about 5,000,000 words, and written a further 2,000,000. Since the average novel is about 100,000 words in length, that represents a huge output. It is hard to define, but at the centre of it, in terms of frequency, lay political journalism, a good deal of it controversial. The future for this seemed a bit in doubt.

There were additional problems connected with these blockages. If what we do is vocational in its intensity, and if the Cartesian concept is applied to it, we are seriously damaged when it goes wrong. We are probably damaged even when it does not go wrong. My belief in a modification of Descartes — *scriptito ergo sum* — creates anyway a form of schizophrenia in which the writer is divided from the man, and yet is the man. (Hence the idea of the inner spirit and the working man.)

The inner spirit is like the heart, pumping life and vigour into everything. The mere act of writing is like a heartbeat, steady and brave and reliable. The working man lives in response to that, urbane, energetic, confident, active, diverse. But he is also elusive; there is an element of camouflage in all that he does, a camouflage designed to protect that inner spirit.

The writing takes over the life. And all being well, this continues throughout the life. But if it goes wrong, it is like a heart attack.

These confusions and doubts were brought into therapy and developed there in a series of invasions of the past. Central to the investigation was my father, who had also been the subject of the four books that I hold most dear, a tetralogy of novels which fall into the category of *bildungsroman*. Thus, the inner spirit had fed on the past, and on the "working man" concept, not just of myself when young, but also of my father. Exploring him, both in fiction and in therapy, had been painful and was painful.

What I thought had been exorcised in fiction came back to haunt me in the present by creating a guilt, not about him, but about myself. I had used him as material. But I had also discarded him in my mind after the novels were finished. I had written him out of the "inner spirit" and back into family history.

In the process I had not realised just how dependent I was on having him, or something parallel, to govern or dictate what I did. In reality I had created a substitute for my father, and this was the country in which I had decided to settle and write, all of forty-odd years ago. Ireland was humanised for me, and became the object of love, criticism, interest, questioning, identity. In a curious way, Ireland responded. Absurd though it may seem, the people manifested, in hundreds of different ways, a response to what I wrote on questions of politics, art, culture, writing, religion. And the response became inextricably linked to the Irishness of Ireland, and the Englishness of this commentator upon the country.

It took many different forms. Some of them were brutal and abusive in a racist way. Some were indulgent and patronising. Some were welcoming and sympathetic.

It became quite often difficult to extract the logic of a position adopted in writing critically, say, about a politician, from the illogical dimension of writing at all about a subject which in theory I might understand, but emotionally and nationalistically I was supposed to be unable to fathom. This perception of myself working within a potentially alien environment was endorsed on relatively few occasions. In the main, what I did was simply a professional task in journalism and was recognised as such.

So was the problem me or Ireland? Even asking the question seems faintly ludicrous, or seemed so until I put it to my therapist, who led me towards certain answers. The route he took was interesting. His analysis was based on a perception about the central importance of the relationship between myself and my father. What I saw as something which I had got out of my system with the writing of four novels which placed my father at the centre of the action was in fact still there. Only I had found an all-embracing substitute for this giant figure hovering over my childhood, and this substitute — which could not have been a person — was Ireland. I had created a "relationship" — in the current, vogue sense of that word — only not with a person. Here was a territory inhabited by three-and-a-half million people which was standing *in loco parentis* and would do so for as long as it took.

Yet Ireland had changed during those forty years, beyond recognition in many respects, becoming less benign, more divided, more anti-British, more affected by British culture, more republican, more international in outlook. And the transformation was acute within the very profession I followed.

The gradual slipstream which had aided my gentle rise into the field of political and cultural comment in the 1960s, became a stronger wind through the more controversial and troubled 1970s, and dragged me centre-stage with the force of a tempest for a time in the 1980s and 1990s.

What troubled me, to the point of seeking professional help, was the realisation that I was contending with these uniquely oppressive forces, combined with the other difficulties outlined above. What resolved the trouble was a growing sense of the absurdity of this attitude within myself. There grew from that a capacity to laugh at myself and my dilemma, recognising that what I believed to be problems were really quite normal aspects of life, and that, for all the buffeting I felt the inner spirit had received, it was still performing its essential task. I was still writing. The heart attack had not taken place.

I was still delivering judgements in my newspaper on political issues. I was still writing books. I was still hearing the mixed voices of Irish men and women, either telling me that I was wrong or that I was right. And all this was normal, not abnormal. It was what I had chosen. It was more right than wrong.

In general, I get on better with women than with men. If there had been a question of choice, I would probably have opted for a woman therapist rather than a man. But the experience has changed that, making me realise how little of the sexual question matters in the realm of "inner spirit", "working man", or indeed in the field of creativity through writing, or confrontation through polemic.

Turning the idea around, and applying it to the therapist rather than to myself, its seems that the working therapist puts up a series of changing mirrors in which we, the clients, are made to see ourselves and persuaded to recognise ourselves when this becomes difficult, or even impossible. The therapist's "inner spirit" is palpably there in the degree of trust which is created, usually by a flawless reception of the client's self-discovery.

I came away from each session exhilarated by this process. I found another aspect of myself, discovered another loophole in the texture of what protected me, and then repaired it, realising each time that there was more to discover. The coherence came from the therapist. It was drawn from what came from me. If there was human curiosity present, it was muted.

Whether this might have been different with a woman, or indeed what might have been different, I think I have no way of knowing.

March 1999; *Inside Out, a quarterly publication for Humanistic and Integrative Psychotherapy*, No. 36, Spring 1999.

5

ALL THEIR POPPY DAYS
HAVE COME TO DUST

Ireland is becoming more British. And I have to say I don't like it. It is acquiring British culture at an accelerating rate and following British patterns of behaviour, British attitudes and British levels of belief. Despite the fever of excitement which will spread through the country this weekend about the GAA replays, a greater fever, in terms of those who follow sport, will focus on English football. We are gripped by the supposed confessions of Roy Keane, in his memoirs, and by the defeat of Manchester United. This English football team commands countrywide attention here, whatever it does. And when the history of 2002 is written, Ireland playing in the World Cup on the other side of the globe, and being led there by Mick McCarthy will be more memorable for more people than anything else.

Throughout the twentieth century, Christian belief in Britain, as well as church-going as a mark of community feeling and stability, declined. The process accelerated more rapidly in the second half of the century, and although there have been attempts at revival, the impact of them has been relatively short-lived. During that same century, Ireland was wont to look pityingly across the Irish Sea, a bit like the Pharisee, and thank God "that I am not as other men are, extortioners, unjust, adulterers". Of course they were, and worse, as history revealed. And the Church they followed had its cupboards full of skeletons. But this did not stop the State being founded and developed on the belief in the great difference between Christian Ireland and heathen Britain.

It is virtually all gone. What took a century in Britain has taken a couple of decades here. The Church, as a place of worship, has been replaced by the shopping centre. Christian practice has been largely replaced by a material obsession with things. Vocations have fallen away. The former authority of the Church has collapsed. The country bows to other gods and the law has recognised this.

The Irishness of the arts in Ireland used to be one of the greatest of touchstones for national identity. Recently, I was giving a talk about Irish art, and how bad quite a lot of it was, and several young Irish painters said to me they did not want to be described as "Irish artists". They were artists, and their identity was of far less importance, if of any importance at all, when compared with how well they painted. This may have something to do with the changed character of technique and subject matter. But whatever it is, it denies the traditional desire of the Irish people to use almost everything they did and believed in as a means of qualifying or describing who they were. Undoubtedly, the same is so of other art forms.

From a personal point of view, this change is not, as I might have once thought, welcome. Quite the opposite; I see the Ireland of my youthful dreams and fledgling experiences, almost all of which were so enjoyable, being watered down and changed. I never really compromised on what I believed myself to be. Contrary to what so many people say, I did not attempt to become more Irish than the Irish. I deliberately sought to remain as I was, and demanded of others that they recognise my right to do so. But I was conscious of the impact on many people of this inexorable change.

I was brought face to face with it in the course of correspondence recently with a man who grew up in the critical, unchanging and rather mean years of the 1950s and early 1960s. He offered as a pivotal moment the year 1966, when "we" celebrated the fiftieth anniversary of the Easter Rising. Even at that stage there were rebels in the system who poured scorn on the tedious and archaic remembrances that went on at the time. But they were a minority. In general, the moment seemed to confirm that to be "really Irish", as my correspondent put it, one needed to be a Republican, Catholic, GAA and Fianna Fáil-supporting, and a lover of the Irish language and culture, as a minimum. An eight-hundred-year-old persecution complex, a deep dislike or even hatred of all things British, an uncle or aunt in Roman Catholic orders, and a grandfather in either the GPO during the 1916 Rising, or in the Old IRA, were optional extras. As he did not conform to this stereotype he became, he said, something of an outsider, a spectator, in the country of his birth. He was Irish, but not quite Irish enough to be considered "really" Irish.

A substantial part of the population would see this view that I quote as archaic and deeply negative. It has little relevance for Ireland in Europe. It is at odds with modern culture. Young people on the whole have become too sophisticated to give it the time of day. And if older people look back on such an interpretation of their origins and roots, they tend to keep quiet about it, knowing that most of those ingredients are increasingly embarrassing when and if they are used as identity tags.

The unfortunate victims of this process of change are those who grew up in the unchanged Ireland, seeing themselves as belonging to a tradition outside the one identified in the quotation above, and not knowing what to do about it. They were the descendants of that honourable band of men and women, the Southern Unionists, who accepted history's definition of their fate and lived with it, giving to Ireland their loyalty and their work, and yet never being seen as wholly Irish. Their Britishness was used against them. Their war service, their Poppy Days, their working lives in the colonies, their British passports, their pride in a dual identity often stretching back through ancestry, seemed never to give them a proper place.

At times the denial was brutal and unfeeling; and it left a legacy of alienation. What is more serious, however, is the degree to which the attitude still prevails in political circles and in the way we look at Anglo-Irish and North–South relations in the wake of the Belfast Agreement. The whole development of conciliation, aimed at resolving the Troubles in the North, has been one-sided. We make available to citizens of the North a status of citizenship in the South, with passports and voting rights. But the British do not do the same for those in the South who have shared a multiple version of their loyalty.

Those I write of, on the whole, conspire in the denial. Their Irishness is real enough for them to set aside their Britishness. They are too old or too set in their ways to join with the younger generations, who love Roy Keane or Mick McCarthy, are laddish and given to un-Irish beliefs and behaviour. But the British also deny this side of the Belfast Agreement. They deny the numbers involved, belittling or obscuring the figures.

Recently, a senior British diplomat confirmed that 250,000 Irish men and women held British passports. And he was giving details of the numbers twenty years ago. With the Celtic Tiger and the rise in our population, this has almost certainly increased substantially.

Among friends, the idea of "Britishness" in Ireland is mainly seen as historical, and made little of as a result. In fact, it is the modern, contemporary idea of Britishness, spreading into every aspect of Irish life that is the interesting development, and not the sustaining of something once used as a mark of disfavour or an emblem of qualified national loyalty. That period is over and done with. We are not at war, but at peace. The time for hatred has long disappeared.

Irish Independent, 17 August 2002

6

THE CHARLTON YEARS

It took a Brit to do it. With an accent you could stir like porridge, and a voice that shatters glass, with a face that so easily crumples with emotion, and a temper supported by a toughness that has become a by-word, not just in football, Jack Charlton has stamped his name and his achievement on a generation. He did the remarkable, the incomprehensible, thing to most Irishmen: he introduced the new and original national concept of teamwork. He made a group of Irish men work together. It is the key to his brilliance. It is the reason for his success. It is the explanation for his fame, and for the fact that his name in this country will live forever.

And he learned it during those other Charlton years, on the football fields of the north of England, playing for Leeds United, while his even more famous brother, Bobby, was helping to win all those games for Manchester United, and in world football. When I was at school, Charlton was the name to conjure with, when there were cigarette cards to collect, and we kept scrap-books with sporting pictures cut out of the daily newspapers. A fine kick on the football field was a fine thing altogether. And in those days I played in goal, and trembled before the approaching horde of mad schoolboys, inspired by Bobby Charlton.

Most of those who revere Jack Charlton never knew him as a player. But they know him as something more important, an inspiration to a generation. His is the name to put on a period of years during which Ireland has discovered that it can do *anything*, and be proud of what it does, and that the anything is not just the effort of the individual, but the effort, shown in Charlton's case, of putting together a team of players to beat the world.

Beating the world has become a national occupation. Running, swimming, making films, writing, acting, snooker, boxing, pop music, golf, Irish dancing, art, we have candidates enough and to spare, and in all these things they have already done it, and we are not yet well-breathed. So what's next? Opera? Cricket? Cooking? When Jack Charlton retires, he could set up a consultancy on where we should go next. Any punter could be reasonably certain that we shall do it again, and again after that. It needs a prophet to point to the sport, or the art, or the discipline.

It ranges over every kind of activity. Sometimes, the riches have been embarrassing. This certainly happened with Ireland's propensity to win the Eurovision Song Contest, an event characterised by the abilities of different countries in Europe and Israel to offer up music of dreary predictability. We showed we could do that. We also watched the rise of Chris de Burgh, and then of U2. Entertainment also inspired a major world success in film, with *My Left Foot*, opening up the eyes of the film world — never a group of people to open their arms at the same time — and establishing a trend which other brilliant endeavours have followed, perhaps most notably *The Crying Game*.

We won gold medals at the Barcelona Olympics, with boxers Michael Carruth and Wayne McCullough. And this started something big, which Steve Collins followed up with his win against Chris Eubank earlier this year. And it was a year crowned with other successes in sport, most notably Sonia O'Sullivan's gold medal in Gothenburg, and Michelle Smith's two golds in the European Championships. And so it will undoubtedly go on, surprising with new mountains climbed, new victories won, but repeating the story that is becoming part of our national expectation, the pure drug of success.

We think it's new. It isn't quite as new as it sounds. A hundred years ago, when Yeats and Synge and Lady Gregory, and George Moore and Edward Martyn, and Douglas Hyde, shaped a national culture out of their own dreams, they welded a self-confidence which changed the great arts of poetry and drama for the whole world in the twentieth century. They held the key to the future, and with it they opened every door in sight. They affected national understanding of politics, liberty and freedom. They shaped the early years of the State. They told their countrymen what needed to be done, and how it should be done. And they inspired the world.

Yet it undoubtedly went wrong. No one looking with a calm and objective eye upon what happened in Ireland in the 1920s and the 1930s, could be happy that national pride and self-confidence, awakened in the early years of the century with a great and glad cry about independence and freedom, was being fulfilled. Writers were leaving, because their work was neglected or suppressed, because there was no money, because the Church stood in their way. They went abroad, and few came back.

The Second World War made things worse. It took a generation after it for Ireland to recover the bare essentials of survival, let alone any feelings of triumph or achievement. And the traditional fighters on behalf of national self-confidence, mainly the playwrights, poets and short-story writers, had to hack their way through the shameful national curtain of censorship which fell on the stage of their effort with no applause for them whatsoever. And if what we knew we could do well was being suppressed, what chance could there possibly be for making films, or for turning Irish dancing into a glamorous and exciting world-beater? The answer has to be: none whatever.

We expended a lot of time in a profoundly wasteful historical wrangle, which went something like this: the British were to blame for the oppression of the Irish, and the robbery of their national self-confidence. Ireland needed to be different and separate.

The Church supported this view, and since it controlled education, spread the supposedly good news of Catholic nationalism,
which possessed its own sports, its own cultural traditions, and its
own language, Irish.

The Church was also responsible for a particular kind of deviousness. This consisted in laying the blame for Ireland's ingrained
inferiority complex at Britain's door in order to absolve itself from
a large share of that blame. This was dishonest, since it was the
Church, during much of the twentieth century, which did much to
root out or suppress the kind of spirit in a nation which produces
greatness, whether in writing, sport or entertainment. These were
all challenging to the virtuous love of God and of the Holy
Mother, and were frowned upon.

It has to be remembered that it was under British rule, whatever about the politics, that the great early-twentieth-century
flowering of self-confidence, pride, actual creative achievement
and revolutionary brilliance, all came to birth.

How could the kind of music which U2 produce have been
made in the Ireland of the 1930s or 1940s, where the act of a man
dancing with his arms around a woman was frowned on by every
parish priest? How could a play like *Dancing at Lughnasa* have
been written, still less produced, in the Ireland of its time, when
the Censorship of Publications Act had become law? How could a
show like *Riverdance*, with its intense vitality and overt sexuality,
have been produced in an era when the glum, expressionless faces
of children schooled by grim-faced religious, remained rigid, star-
ing directly in front of them as their feet tapped out the magic of
age-old dance rhythms buried deep in the Irish psyche?

All those "possessions" — the national sports, the national culture, the national language — were isolationist, but they were
supposedly pure, and reinforced a state in which censorship of
one kind or another was acceptable. We had our own versions,
and we protected them. Alien things were kept out, and were
somehow specified as "dirty".

The politicians were weak in the face of such a powerful reinvention of Ireland, and took most of this century summoning up the courage to challenge it, and open the doors to Europe, to Britain, to all the freedoms of speech, entertainment, culture, leisure and sport, and finally to freedoms affecting women, the control of their bodies, contraception, and divorce.

Most of these freedoms were dearly bought. And the process is not over yet. The self-confidence is real. It has become an intrusive force. When John Bruton met with John Major, and they jointly announced the accord which preceded Bill Clinton's visit, many people looked upon the event and were amazed to see the greater wisdom, the better presentation, the finer sense of reality, the more honest use of language and ideas, all in the hands of our own leader, and not in John Major's hands. And this, despite the fact that John Major is by far the best British leader, as far as Ireland is concerned, in a generation. We led there. And it did not stop there.

Two days later, when Bill Clinton arrived, we witnessed something very similar. Here was the leader of the most powerful nation in the world. He had worked harder than any of his predecessors to grasp the Irish nettle; to understand the bad side of Ireland, and seek to set it within the equation which so many earlier American presidents had simply buried in fine words and gluey sentiment. And with all his commitment, he stood equal beside the Taoiseach; and his wife, no mean politician herself, did the same beside Finola Bruton. We stood proud, and we stand proud.

There is, maybe, a danger: that we try to systemise, organise, fund and manage the national talent for success. There is a predisposition that way. Boards, authorities, Arts Councils, bodies, rise up to distribute homilies, and to give money away, generally to the wrong people, and for the wrong things. Most of the good that has been done in the twentieth century, in raising self-confidence, in winning on the running track, in the swimming pool, on the sports fields, has come from within the individual, not from the State. And while everyone wants funding, great talent, great ability, great achievement, are not easily bought with hard cash. It is the spirit and the inspiration which count.

I see it as a matter of some personal pride, vicarious, perhaps, but no less deeply felt, that part of the liberalisation may be laid at the door of a gnarled and ill-tempered Englishman. Jack Charlton was born some sixty years ago in a town a few miles north of Newcastle-upon-Tyne. He was marked for life with the accent of his own place, and he never dreamed that he would end up in a foreign country, making football in Ireland a symbol of greatness and freedom unsurpassed in a hundred years. He has put his mark on the country and its capacity for unprecedented achievement and brilliance. He has given us the Charlton Years.

Irish Independent, 16 December 1995

7

THE CLATTER OF THE SHOES
IN *RIVERDANCE*

It is a matter of debate, in millennium terms, whether Ireland ever existed. For its first 1,200 years it had no unity, no centre, no capital. After that it was Norman. That was an incomplete conquest succeeded by others, all of which might be described as "flawed", but all of which, from an administrative and military point of view, worked in the sense of depriving Ireland of separate independent identity, and therefore of becoming a threat. Reluctantly, the people on this island had to face the fact that they were "British", and serious efforts to think or do otherwise were stifled.

Only briefly, for less than five per cent of the last 2,000 years, an Irish State, legal, cultural, and more or less viable, has struggled with its identity, its economy and its moral isolation, in order to prove its existence. During this legal lifetime, the country has faced an uphill struggle, the reality in a sense much harder than the dreams and aspirations, the revolutions and uprisings, as well as banishment to the British colonies, combined with the voluntary emigrations caused by famine or poverty.

It was never easy from 1922 on, and it was so difficult at times — in the 1930s and in the period after the Second World War — that people did genuinely despair about the survival of such an awkward and unproductive commonwealth as the Irish one. The most creative commodity seemed to be words. The most productive national export was people, on the heads of whom dedicated and inspired education had been poured down by a largely selfless and ill-paid multitude of teachers.

It was hardly surprising, in the face of such an endemic crisis, that the population, in order to make sense out of this, expended huge energy in defining and redefining what it meant to be Irish. It became an obsession, and the residual hum of debate is with us today, unresolved, aggressive, perhaps increasingly pointless.

The job was done over and over again. It led to extravagant claims about a historical Ireland, a Celtic Ireland, a prehistoric Ireland, a linguistic Ireland, an Ireland of myth and legend, all with discernible identities. And it led also to claims about racial purity which are ridiculous, and about religious purity which have been seriously challenged in a number of ways. The cultural idea which links Celtic art to Irish art is an understandable but distorted one. The Celtic Movement was pan-European. The visual decorative images can be traced back to the Scythian culture of eastern Asia. This spread into various parts of Europe, eventually enjoying a flowering and richness in the island of Ireland, but without coming from that island people; in any case, we do not know where that island people came from. Nor do we know where the craftsmen who made that art originated.

Doubt has not impeded a relentless creative process in which there has been a forced marriage between qualitative inventiveness and the Irish identity. We have always needed the national thread cobbling up the centuries, not just throughout the Christian era, but during the previous millennium as well. And we confidently tell the Irish story — in culture, religion, myth and art — as though it holds together. If it does, then the hold is tenuous, the thread quite weak a lot of the time.

In the later years of the nineteenth century, the climate changed fundamentally, as the worldwide movement towards nationhood, and away from colonial and imperial dependency, inspired new thought and ideas. Figures like Douglas Hyde,

William Butler Yeats, John O'Leary, and a host of more directly political men and women, began the process of "creating" the tangible Ireland we have, with all its faults, today. And with it they created or invented, out of the past, a heritage of culture. They claimed, or tried to claim, everything in sight that might be considered "nationalist". And it was an approach that could not fail to work. The modern world is the product of that inspiration duplicated again and again, with varying degrees of validity. And it is therefore impossible to reconstruct any alternative to the Irish nation as represented predominantly by playwrights, poets, novelists, painters and musicians, with a few political giants like de Valera thrown in for good measure.

This invented past is of course in marked contrast with the true historical past. During this real, rather than invented time, writers as diverse as Jonathan Swift, George Bernard Shaw, Oscar Wilde, George Farquhar, Dion Boucicault and Charles Lever cherry-picked their way through their own definitions of Ireland and of its identity. They decided on their own definitions, confident in the confusion of a culture which had so many strands to it. They all had English lives, English publishers, English reputations. They viewed their Irishness — if they thought in terms which that word implies — with scepticism combined with inevitability. Where one is born is an inescapable fact and though an extreme view may be taken, as in the case of Arthur Wellesley, later Duke of Wellington, the more normal reaction is to heave a sigh of resignation and get on with life, ignoring the potential handicap of where one originates.

It was a geographical identification, not an emblem of nationhood. We like to pretend it bestowed "the gift of the gab", which is viewed as particularly Irish. But the Irish gob is no richer than the English one. A day or two spent in the Dáil shows how threadbare and barren our supposed wit is. Shaw's wit was a product of living on it. Oscar Wilde's was inspired by Mahaffy, developed at Oxford and polished in his clever observations of

English High Society, a conglomeration of the most artificial and absurd phenomena in the world. Shaw in a rather heavy-handed way, Wilde more lightly, traded on the dubious birthright of their Irishness, and found it mildly profitable. But both were shrewd enough to see it as a limited asset. And this has always been the cultural problem: how to be Irish enough, but not too Irish to preclude being English — or British — as well.

Joyce struck a perfect compromise, by making Dublin, the least Irish city on the island of Ireland, his subject matter, just as it had been his exclusive home. His knowledge and understanding of Dublin life and its people is seen as the quintessence of his Irishness. But it is really an illusion. He escaped Ireland, anyway, and his talent was enhanced by his exile. Other writers, like Frank O'Connor and Seán O'Faoláin, failed to make this break and in time came to live a divided life. Like Christian in the embrace of Apollyon, they wrestled with the "real" Ireland, with its purity smelling of incense, and its authority and narrow-minded bigotry. And it was a fight they lost.

The first generation, the one which "forged the conscience", had the advantage of pre-dating, often by many years, the coming into existence of the legal Ireland. They could look on with lofty disdain to see how the country might develop, but were ambivalent about whether or not to be wholly part of it. They preserved their independent choice of where they might place their allegiance.

Both Yeats brothers, George Moore, James Stephens, Edward Martyn, Augusta Gregory, Seán O'Casey, John Millington Synge, all transcended the burden of a birthright which might otherwise have dictated their effort, and dragged them down. They were free to walk away. They could express their disbelief in the very viability of Ireland — George Moore classically did just this, while William Orpen did it more emotionally — or simply depart from it, as Seán O'Casey did.

Probably the greatest of the writers of this group, in the coherence and completeness of his "Irishness", was John Millington Synge. He breathed in the pure air of an Ireland which, uniquely, he found in rural Wicklow, and in the West, notably during intense, brief visits to the Aran Islands. He did it from a lofty standpoint, in his birth, his background, his intellect, his moral and spiritual independence. He was the only Irish writer of that Protestant background who got close to the Irish peasant, just as O'Casey is that rare Irish writer, also a Protestant, able to penetrate the minds and hearts of the Dublin poor of his time.

In painting, Jack Yeats matched Synge, indeed paralleled him in an adventurous and stimulating way. The relentless desire was there, in the artist, to grapple with the whole tapestry of Irish life, in so far as it could be visualised, and to waste no time on any other subject matter. His commitment to this was lifelong, and it was total. And in painting the way he did, he created a set of cultural images with which the towns and the countryside could be peopled with greater authenticity than life itself was able to do. He is the quintessence of Irish creativity in the way that Dickens, or Cruikshank, or Fielding, or Austen, are of British life and character.

Why is Jack Yeats's subject matter, on the whole, so threadbare, and so marginal? A road across a bog. Two men meet. Under the stars or the flaming sun, they utter in the silence of the canvas cataclysmic messages, and then pass on. They adopt solitary poses. They perform. There is something isolated, desiccated, frantic about their fate. And in this Yeats has summarised the dilemma of being Irish, refined it, and handed it on to his disciple, Samuel Beckett.

Between these two men, painter and writer, we come close to the apogee of artistic and cultural statement. And if Synge is added, and W.B. Yeats as well, then it is easier to understand how Austin Clarke and Patrick Kavanagh emerged, the one an urban poet who came much closer than W.B. Yeats to real Irish life, the other a reliable poet of rural peasant life before and during the

Second World War. Seamus Heaney, as well as John Montague, came from similar roots, and made such an impact on the generation which grew up after that isolating and draining period of world conflict.

There was a haughty, Anglo-Irish generation of artists to start the century, succeeded by a diverse, more committed, but more bewildered group of writers, almost all of whom, for various reasons, left to make reputations abroad. Some came back. Some never really stopped travelling, depending for their livelihood on American universities and the BBC. They had reason to distrust an indifferent State which allowed so much of their freedom and outspokenness to be taken away by the Catholic Church. Writing, as a craft, was humbled and confined as a result of oppressiveness, and the deep suspicion that it was sexually subversive. Censorship reinforced this suspicion. Two generations suffered from that. And by the time the agony was over, Ireland was on the brink of becoming a member of the European Community.

There came then, in the early 1960s, a new wave of talent, in both writing and painting, which had experienced enough of foreign living to want to stay and confront their "Irishness" at home. They fought battles against censorship, and they won. But at the same time they were fighting a larger war, against the diminishing of Irish culture, its virtual annihilation through the blanket of international culture that swamps everything.

But before recording that dismal threat, which promises the annihilation of a national spirit in favour of an international one, puerile and boring, it has to be said that the State's role, during that period from independence up to the relatively recent past, has been profoundly, depressingly indifferent. Writers and artists have flourished despite the State's efforts to help rather than because of them. It has got marginally better in the last couple of decades, but only marginally.

Europe, which has damaged so much, and enriched so many, is in the process, hugely helped by television, of replacing the richness of Irish culture with material wealth and sophistication. For the first time, young people can be assured of jobs, and can therefore get homes and have families. Their standards are the universal, global ones of mass culture. They are shouting into their mobile phones a stream of clichés about business and pleasure, money and sex, then jumping into their cars and driving to security-protected houses lavishly funded by banks.

This is no climate for cultural excitement. We close the century and the millennium to the clatter of the shoes in *Riverdance* and the rock rhythms of *Messiah* at the RDS. Where is the culture in this? What world do we contemplate, looking forward into the new century? And what do we look back on as achievements in the century coming to an end?

Irish Independent, December 1999; review at the end of the millennium

8

WHO OWNS OUR CULTURE?

American culture is a branch of American imperialism. Like the dollar, its power is spread worldwide. It pumps itself relentlessly into the cultures of other countries, through music, film and television; and the freedom of modern communication systems aids the process. There is a motive of possession. There is a motive of control. There is a zeal on behalf of the American way of life. It needs to be spread and understood, embraced and admired. That is what empires are about. The crude, old-fashioned, military forms of conquest are, we hope, a thing of the past. A cleaner, cooler variety of control, carried out by multinationals, by banking, finance, debt and obligation, is now acceptable.

It is reinforced by culture. The link is forged between what might be called "original" countries, like Ireland, and the so-called "Irish" in America, who are the product of that export process. They represent a powerful section of the multiracial, multicultural roots of the American people. They lack the depth which the original countries have. Not only is time absent, the centuries of Irish history which are summarised and taken on in note-form, but there is another problem: the conflict between being "All-American" and being "Irish-American". There is a loyalty factor. And we see it in its more regrettable form, when Irish-Americans lend themselves to supporting violence in Northern

Ireland, for example, or providing funds for the purchase of arms and explosives by the Provisional IRA.

Fortunately, culture keeps its hands clear of this. And most people in Ireland, and probably most Irish-Americans, would like culture, rather than politics, to be at the heart of the entangled relationships between the two countries. Even then, there is a price to be paid. And the price is one of possession and takeover.

Joyce, Yeats, Synge, Beckett, seem more than half-owned intellectually by American universities, anatomised by American scholars, and rendered less usable, less approachable in the process. Is it deserved, this fate? In some cases it clearly is. James Joyce was not quite saved from oblivion by American literary scholarship. He was never in danger of being lost to us. But there was the shrewd gathering together of his manuscripts and papers, and it was backed by the necessary funds at a time when no one else had the cash. This was followed in the 1940s and early 1950s by the birth of a form of relentless scholarship which has raised him to a pre-eminent position among twentieth-century writers.

It is not necessarily as a writer that he occupies this position. Safely dead, endlessly edited, abridged, filmed, dramatised, Joyce has become subject matter for cultural investigation and exploration. He is the sum of uncountable numbers of academic theses. He is a factory template for the academic mind, there to be endlessly reproduced in different formats and disguises, all of them fulfilling Joyce's own expectation that he would confound posterity. And the posterity is largely governed from the United States.

We should not regret this. The deep dedication, the large expenditure, the numbers of teachers and students who have done all this to James Joyce, in the name of Irish literature and culture, compare favourably with the dusty treatment the writer got from his own country during his lifetime. The Irish pride themselves on not having banned *Ulysses*. It is a feeble flag to wave, in defence of cultural nationalism. While the armies of American academics tramp the world, seeking new angles on James Joyce, and producing further millions of words about him, what have we done? Well, we have progressed to putting down in our pavements brass signals, pointing the way to an unending James Joyce Soap Opera, which we reinforce, in mid-June each year, by dressing up in bowler hats and celebrating Bloomsday.

Anyone who attends the Yeats Summer School, in Sligo, will experience something of the same. The great embrace of American cultural imperialism is written in the titles of the lectures. It resonates in the dead weight of forced and complex phrases, in the embattled stares of men and women who are gaining credits, adding to their curriculum vitae, drawing down university grants for "further study", and guarding every syllable of supposed originality in what they have to say.

As with James Joyce, William Butler Yeats survives it all because his words transcend theirs. Unlike Joyce, he was in part responsible for creating his own cultural relationship with the United States, by visits and poetry readings, by lectures and interviews, establishing him and his work as icon-material within the great American-Irish cultural heritage.

All are vulnerable, the dead and the living, the small and the great. What worked for Joyce, providing material for one generation, was redirected towards Samuel Beckett, who for the last two decades has been responsible for a rival industry. He helped it on its way by being published in the United States, where for a time sympathy and support for his writing exceeded support elsewhere.

Empires are never exclusive. They bestow power and prestige, even on cultural possessions, perhaps most of all on culture. The reality for Ireland is to enjoy this patronage, but not to take it too seriously. Most of the writers, and other artists as well, demonstrated their real loyalties by living out their lives in cultures as old as our own, Beckett, Joyce and Yeats in France, Italy, Switzerland. In newer artistic forms of expression, like theatre and film, there is a shift. At the close of the twentieth century, the old process, of America absorbing greatness when it was fully established, has been replaced. We have moved on to the absorption of young writers, by giving them "in residence" positions, and embroiling them in the system in advance of their full achievement, and in anticipation that there will be a pay-off.

Meanwhile, at home, real culture and real creation try to live and survive, despite the imperial power, not because of it.

Irish Independent, May 1995

9

TELEVISION MAN

Television has had a huge impact on our lives. It has become the dominant collective source for information, entertainment, sports coverage, wildlife, humour, human tragedy, music, and above all for the chat show. We curse it, and we cannot do without it. It is intrusive and immensely powerful. And it has grown to be a worldwide monster, invading our homes and privacy, our minds and feelings, our beliefs and our ability to experience, and all this without our becoming involved. We simply sit and absorb as channel after channel pours forth an endless variety of choices over which we have less and less control.

For Ireland, its life spans the last four decades. And during that time, the most enduring figure of all has been that of Gay Byrne. He has been its conscience, internally. More than any other person appearing on Irish television during our lifetimes, Gay Byrne has been that essential icon of the late twentieth century, Television Man. Bland, easy to watch, uncontentious in himself, publicly uncomplicated, he has coaxed and encouraged, persuaded and ordered, monitoring a visual and verbal commentary on the country's life. And because of television's all-pervading power, this has made him the social conscience of the Irish people.

It has given him power as well, though this is less important than it might be, because Gay Byrne has no personal agenda intruding into the lifelong dedication to the task he set himself: to amuse and entertain. In this, the man's essential nature is close to the medium he uses. We think of television as "powerful", and this encourages us to invoke the term when we consider its major personalities. But television is really only powerful when it is in the hands of someone who has a clear and forceful agenda, and knows how to use it. Watching Gerry Adams on television, or Margaret Thatcher, it becomes easier to understand that the exercise of power, in the old-fashioned sense of our lives being threatened by the intention to change our way of thinking, is inescapably related to the personal agenda.

Television Man is concerned with performance. Gay Byrne has wanted, through all those years, a good show. And his audiences have wanted the same. Infinite variety has only been possible because the presenter is always the same; always open to new ideas, new directions, new points of view, new kinds of personality, but essentially himself unchanging. Like a sheet of blotting paper, or a sponge, he has soaked up the flow of social change for close on forty years, trusted by viewers to react to it, consistently, and on their behalf.

This suggests that Byrne is passive. It is more complicated than that. Professionally, he is a thinking man, with strategy in his performance, and a careful preparation for the kind of individual he is having to confront. He would not have lasted half a year, as a chat show host, if there had not been careful thought and research, careful choice and balance. He would not have sustained himself without a personality ideally suited, not just to the medium, but to the specifics of predominantly lightweight conversation designed to display the personality and ambition of one guest after another.

In this, Gay Byrne is, and has always been, admirably professional. He works within a clear sense of his own capabilities, and an equally clear recognition of his own character. There are times, of course, when it all goes wrong. But they are infrequent, and there is always the principle of *caveat emptor*: if you buy into the show by participating, on your own head be it.

Nevertheless, the idea of Gay Byrne as a comparatively passive recipient of other people's thoughts and feelings, unmotivated by any passionate interest in the subjects himself, is akin to the whole basis of television itself. The medium is, at heart, passive. We thought, all those years ago, when the Archbishop of Dublin, John Charles McQuaid, and President de Valera made their portentous speeches about what was in store for us, that some great force for good or evil was looming ahead.

Good and evil have certainly come out of it, but the high hopes, forty years ago, have not been realised. In fact, it has turned into an electronic version of the tabloid newspaper, and is fast being overtaken in its relevance to the individual living in a worldwide network of electronic communication and information, by other more immediate and more personally relevant channels.

It was meant to change society, spread culture, and under the prudent control mechanisms of benign Church authority and sensible political legislation, to be a moral and social asset. Believe it or not, that was the basic message which accompanied the launch of RTE.

And what happened? The Church lost its power, its moral authority, its dignity, even its ability to think straight. The politicians, unsurprisingly, treated it as a vehicle for themselves, tinkered with controls but gradually handed them over. And they were exposed. How mightily they were exposed! And then reduced in size to pygmy proportions. Good performers, with no special claim on our attention beyond the ability to contribute positively to the making of good television programmes, became central.

A good example of this is Ulick O'Connor. A frequent performer on Gay Byrne's *Late Late Show*, and deservedly so for the rasping, aggressive challenges which were his hallmark, he became the ideal pundit, with a view on everything. Sportsman, writer, wit, conversationalist, he was like a barrel full to the brim of beer. All Gay Byrne needed to do was to lean forward and turn the tap off. Gay Byrne was ideally conditioned to that task. He knew exactly the amount to let out, and exactly when to turn the tap off. And Ulick O'Connor was exactly right as the barrel. The laws of hydrodynamics and the force of social gravity released roughly the same mixture every time, either to the delight or the anger of studio audiences, and to the passing amusement of those watching their television sets.

Like a well-written and well-presented column in a mass-circulation tabloid newspaper, Gay Byrne undoubtedly made a major contribution to the moral and social change implicit in what television was doing overall. He first challenged the Church and particularly its bishops to admit, by coming on his shows, that they existed. Then he demonstrated that they were more or less human, like the rest of us. Then he showed us that they were fallible to the point of being in frequent breach of the moral code which it was their very existence to interpret and uphold. And in a sense the rest is history. Their copes and mitres, their grand cathedrals and weighty expositions on moral behaviour, were symbols of an undeserved power. Here was a façade, and there was very little behind it. The emblems of authority had no chance against the revelation that the bishops drank, slept with women, fathered illegitimate children, concealed sexual abuse within their dioceses. These wise guardians of the spirit were exposed by television as having allowed criminally cruel institutions to operate without the State's control. At heart, these princes of the Church had an amazingly limited understanding of the trials and tribulation of ordinary members of the Christian family, whose welfare they should also have been protecting.

Of course, Gay Byrne was only part of this moral and social revolution. But he was a considerable part, since these central issues — of where the Church stood in relation to the State, what each was doing about the other, and where the mass of the population fitted in — were meat and drink to Gay Byrne.

He was the people. That explained his existence, that gave drive to his own work, that justified the frequent *gobdaw* attitude he deliberately adopted, in order to get reaction out of the people he interviewed.

Professionally, he did develop, becoming more assured, more canny, more confident and therefore more powerful as a presenter. But he never lost the consistent simplicity of his own position. Even dealing with complex matters, even trampling over the feelings of individuals and groups, he got to the heart of issues, and managed often enough to turn them inside out, leaving us all altered by the experience.

The reverse happened to television itself. It started as a repository of high ideals and pretentious social and cultural aspirations. It was to change all our lives for the better. It was to educate, inform, excite, move, amuse and investigate. And though it has done all that, running through an endless programme of approaches, the fundamental objectives were not realised.

Today, it is somehow grubby and uncertain. The supply of films is running out. Film itself, as a medium, is failing to stand the test of time. Soap opera is part of the diet, hooking the most surprising people, but demonstrating that the real agenda is not cultural but financial. In other words, the whole of commercial television is geared to levels of viewing, and therefore to advertising.

For the chat show host to survive, he has to be exceptional to the point of outstanding. Gay Byrne has achieved that and has done it with a combination of common ordinariness and sprightly curiosity. The slab of airtime he confronts each Friday must look at first like a huge black hole, with each idea dropped into it disappearing from sight. As the week progresses, panic must often seize him and his staff. Each show has to be sensational. That is the nature of television. We want our senses to be excited. We are open to anything. But from the programmer's point of view, the essential question all the time must be: will it work?

Will the hyping up of P. Flynn work? Will the attempted anni-hilation of Annie Murphy go down with viewers? Will the bish-ops tolerate discussion of night attire, or will the flames of Heaven descend on Gay Byrne's head? Can we make the toys routine work again? And antiques? And show business personalities? And Ernest Hemingway's second wife? And Sinéad O'Connor? And Micheál Mac Liammóir?

Astonishingly, it *has* all worked. On the principle of the tabloid newspaper, it works even when it assaults our sensibilities, abuses our standards of decorum, enrages our moral code, insults those we admire, lays bare the pretensions and concealments of people in high office, and renders bishops and ministers of state vulner-able to the point of their humiliation.

And Gay Byrne *does* deserve the Freedom of the City of Dub-lin. Of the cities of Cork, Galway, Limerick and Waterford as well. What price such honours? What meaning have they? He has en-joyed great freedom for the past four decades, and it is our judgement on that which matters.

To have kept the ball rolling, over all those years, to have con-tinued to entertain and divert, inform and lay bare, and to do so in an even and consistent way, that has been major in its social contribution to the culture of the country.

We thought, forty years ago, that the culture was precious and somehow special. We thought that the Irish "way of life" was unique, and was there to be protected and enhanced by this new weapon of mass communication. We have discovered a different story. Few people have helped more towards that discovery than Gay Byrne. Should we praise him or blame him for it? Or have we become indifferent to the principle of cause and effect? Does it no longer matter? Or do we just go on soaking it all up, listening, looking, passive sponges in a world of unprecedented mass com-munication?

Irish Independent, May 1999

10

JOURNEY HOME

Some years ago, a much-respected matriarch of the Connors family, well-known to anyone with knowledge of the Travelling people, died in Peterborough, England. She had reached the advanced age, for a Travelling person, particularly a woman, of seventy. She was a mother and a grandmother. Quite how many offspring claimed descent is not recorded. However, when her funeral got under way, and set out upon the long journey back to New Ross, County Wexford, where she was to be buried, the close kin who gathered together for the journey filled no less than twenty cars.

The flower-decked hearse which led the procession was followed by two chauffeur-driven vehicles. It might have seemed normal, setting out for a graveyard down the road. But this intrepid band of Travellers were determined to live up to their generic name in terms which promised to be epic. Mrs Connors had made known to those gathered at her bedside, as she prepared to breathe her last, that it was her dying wish to have her body taken on an extended tour of her six favourite pubs.

History does not record them all in detail. But Mrs Connors was a true Traveller all her life. And being of a certain age, as they say, she had, along with a substantial number of her contemporaries, spent many years in England. It was not therefore surprising that the six pubs were spread across the parts of England and

Wales she had moved through during that long life. And a route was devised which led back to those wistfully remembered haunts of the past.

The pubs, not surprisingly, were also remembered by many of those occupying the twenty cars. And by the end of the journey all would remember them, deeply, and with feeling. Peterborough is on the east side of England, standing in what are known as the Bedford Levels, some way back from the Wash. The first objective was to cross the backbone of England, heading west, by way of Coventry, to the first pub on Mrs Connors's list, which was the Marlbrook, in Bromsgrove. Since my own ancestors come from Bromsgrove, I am pleased to be able to report that the unannounced arrival of this large cortege turned not a hair on the head of the publican, one John Taylor, who mildly observed that he thought the hearse might have broken down.

Women in black spilled out of the cavalcade of cars. Men with large thirsts on them ordered drink. The sum of £500 was spent on liquid refreshments during a two-hour celebration of the life and experiences of Mrs Connors, and her dying wish was deeply, richly respected. A mere £130 went on food.

At one point, according to the publican, one of Mrs Connors's sons went out to the hearse, opened up the back of it, climbed in and laid himself down on the coffin, to express his grief. "I think he had had a bit too much to drink" was the view of Mr John Taylor.

Refreshed, the mourners headed on westwards, into Wales. They stopped again, and then again. The itinerary had, as its last watering place, the Bull Inn in Haverfordwest, a remote bastion of hospitality on the long road from Peterborough. The publican, a Mr John, had to be reminded that Mrs Connors had once been a customer of his, during her travels around England and Wales. He surveyed the large crowds of men and women, some of them a little slow in their speech by now, and all of them slightly dishevelled from the long hours of travel, and he did the right thing by them. He started drawing pints.

He finished up all his stock of Guinness and then all his stock of lager as well. For the first time in his career as a publican, he found himself having to go to other hostelries in Haverfordwest to borrow liquid refreshment. In the meantime, the mourners went in search of food, and cleaned out the fish, sausages, chips and bacon in the local fish and chip shop, and the shop had to close down because it had nothing left to offer its regulars.

No dying wish has ever been more thoroughly honoured by so large a group of people acting with a unity of purpose which, had it been applied to Northern Ireland, might well have shortened the ravages of violence years ago. And, it must be said, no publicans in this country would have matched the Englishmen and the Welshmen who, whether or not they remembered previous visits from Mrs Connors and her large and growing brood, were models of their profession. They offered their all, and did so with a willingness that was exemplary.

This example of the culture of the Travelling people has about it an unquenchable character and determination which makes a nonsense of almost every solution ever put forward for solving something which is a problem, not for the Travellers, but for ourselves. One of the first stories I ever covered, for an English newspaper, as it happens, was the publication of the first Report on Itinerancy, as the problem was then called. I remember it with feeling, every time a new report, or a new analysis surfaces. They repeat the same platitudes. They achieve almost nothing.

We have changed the words, and the life itself has changed. The old sources of work, the earning from tinkering, casual labour on farms, diverse trading, have been undermined. The urbanisation of the Travellers has created a new set of problems.

The fundamental and more serious issues are still very much there. Life expectancy of Travelling women is seriously below that of the country's norm. This is in part because of the hard life, in part because of the large families — there is a price to be paid for being even one of Mrs Connors's brood — and the life expectancy of children, particularly in infancy, is a disgrace. So too are the educational facilities, and therefore the expectations.

But Ireland's capacity to report the state of things, to analyse it, and to do as little as possible, is as unquenchable as the thirst which drank dry the pubs of England and Wales, and created a legend still remembered and talked about on the road from Peterborough to Fishguard. Thus is culture honoured, both theirs, and our own.

Irish Independent, 1 April 1995

11

ORAL TESTIMONY

No institution in Irish life has contributed more to the sum of suffering and unhappiness than the pub. Countless families have been reduced to misery and starvation by the very existence of these dens of iniquity and vice. Drunkenness is the greatest evil facing the country, and addiction to the so-called "life" which is to be found in the pub is worse, in the sum-total of damage that it does, than drug addiction.

The pub itself is not responsible; as is always the case, people are. But if one wanted to find, concentrated in one place, the greatest quotient of despair, uncertainty, fear, inadequacy, together with false bonhomie, shallow friendships, betrayal of promises, dissipation of family resources, deliberate self-impoverishment, the equally deliberate path to ill-health, the neglect of wives and children, the undermining of trust, then the pub is the place to look.

I spent a great deal of my childhood doing just that — looking in at the vacant doors of pubs, waiting for my father to emerge in order that I might help him home, and preserve his life and what few coins might be left in his pockets. And I conceived then a deep dislike and distrust of everything to do with the pub. I visit them sparingly, and still find them threatening. Yet my feelings cannot come anywhere near the loathing which my mother must have felt, or the mothers of countless sons and daughters whose despair was lifelong.

The author of the first of these books, Kevin Kearns, gives us a hint of the reality, briefly, in the testimony of one woman, Máirín Johnston. "Men got their wages on a Saturday and they'd go off into the pubs and wouldn't come home with the wages." They were often paid there. If their wives went to tell them they needed money for housekeeping, they would be hit, or beaten. "I mean they would beat them something terrible . . . I mean, they would beat them when they were pregnant . . . and so many women miscarried as a result of the men's brutality." If there were fights involving husbands and wives, then the guards ignored them. "A man had a right to beat his wife." And he beat her black and blue, often breaking her arms, or disfiguring her permanently.

This true picture of misery and desolation is confined to a few pages, as part of the valuable if distorted oral testimony, offered mainly as a memorial to places which have now gone, or changed beyond recovery. It does not feature in the historical section, which is a celebration of the pub, and which lists such tedious information as the synonyms "for the state of being drunk".

Kearns's book has a serious purpose; his analysis of pubs and their history, traditions and habits, and their place in society, is reasonably comprehensive, and the oral testimony, while it is a laborious method of presenting evidence, leaves one with a sense of primary research work. Peter Costello's book is meant to be frivolous. The idea of visiting a succession of pubs, "in the footsteps of Brendan Behan, Patrick Kavanagh and the Ginger Man", is, to me anyway, deeply unattractive. And the quotations offered from the great drinkers of the past — Behan conspicuously present with several profoundly boring witticisms — offers a purgatorial odyssey worthy of Dante or Milton. Ugh!

Review of two books: *Dublin Pub Life and Lore: An Oral History*, by Kevin C. Kearns; *The Dublin Literary Pub Crawl*, by Peter Costello. *Irish Independent* Books Page, 26 October 1996.

12

THE RIGHTS OF THE BISHOPS

There are, of course, no special rights given to the Roman Catholic Hierarchy, nor to the bishops of that Church, under the Constitution. They are not keepers of public morality, or the conscience of the State, or, if they are, it is a self-appointed office. As individuals, whether they elect to speak "in their private capacity", as members of the Hierarchy, as bishops, as celibates, as theologians, or as human beings, the Constitution has them down as "human persons" [Article 40.1] and places them, in the same Article, as "equal before the law".

This personal right, or indeed set of rights — rights which concern the integrity of the individual — make bishops no taller than other men, save by virtue of their merit, their physical and moral capacity, and their social function. And the Article constitutes an extensive section in the Constitution. Running to six pages, it is among the longest. It is qualified, however, by the Article immediately following, on the Family. And here the social function of the bishops, either acting independently, or as a group, becomes significant.

With the individual human person, definition is not a major difficulty. It became so, in a very specific way, with the abortion row. The attempts then to define as "a human person" the foetus which, up to that controversy, had been treated with scant regard if it was stillborn, or naturally aborted, created huge problems which are still with us. But that apart, defining a human being or a human person in order to grant them the rights which the Constitution offers, was not a major difficulty.

With the family, however, we are in a quite different business of definition. And it is a business on which the Constitution has very little to offer, while the Churches have quite a lot. The Constitution sounds impressive. It speaks of the family as "the natural primary and fundamental unit group of Society", and it endows it as "a moral institution possessing inalienable and imprescriptible rights, antecedent and superior to all positive law".

But although it employs this solemn language, it does not actually define the Family. It does not say what it is, or what it is not. It does not, for example, encompass the one-parent family in its remit. If it did, then, straight away, we would have two "natural primary and fundamental" unit groups in society, one of them the family with a father, the other without. The one without a father must, by definition, have a child in it. But the one made up of a married couple does not necessarily have to have children to be a Family, under the Constitution. Having children clearly makes a huge difference, but does it change the definition? Are we looking at *three* different "unit groups"?

The unmarried mother, now very much a part of our social structure, recognised in law, helped financially by the State, and, according to recent statistics, responsible for a growing percentage of births, constitutes, with her child, "a family". Is she to be any less protected by the Constitution?

Take the argument just one small stage further. Suppose the missing father is already part of a "family", but one which he no longer feels much loyalty towards, and which indeed he may have separated from. In limbo presently, does he not straddle two families, both recognised by the State, both constitutionally defined, even if the definition including the unmarried mother as a "family" was not originally envisaged? And if he should move appreciably closer to the second of the two, and perhaps create another child, and decide to live with the second family, does he not become legitimately part of it? And does he leave a "family" behind him, whether or not his spouse has children?

Even without the existence of divorce, and within the framework of the solemn language of the Constitution, natural evolution has changed the meaning of the Family, and has forced that change upon us all. It takes no stretch of the imagination to fill in the remaining pieces of the jigsaw puzzle of modern family life in Ireland, with all the varieties of human cohabitation, perpetuation of the species, exercise of sexual, emotional, passionate and loving choice, as between human persons of the female sex, and those of the male, to arrive at a view of the family which is a long way from that which inspired the original constitutional thinkers.

Which brings one to Article 41.3.1, dealing with the State's pledge to guard the institution of marriage, and as part of that pledge also to block divorce. In many cases, to do so is to undermine the very idea of family which the Article, overall, was designed to protect. If the Constitution is a bit vague — as we have seen — about defining the family, it is positively ludicrous in the way it addresses the institution of marriage. The concept of marriage just pops up, a *fait accompli*, neither defined, nor given any rights, but presented as potentially under attack.

The relevant three sub-clauses of Article 41 are an accurate reflection of the extremely narrow concept of family and divorce as it was seen in the mid-1930s, both by society and by the churches, particularly the Roman Catholic Church, whose views on the indissolubility of marriage were, and are, so much narrower than those of other Christian churches. In the intervening decades, marriage has redefined itself the world over. So has the family.

We, however, in this country, have done so piecemeal, and in a timid and nerveless fashion, looking over our shoulders at the Church, and avoiding conflict or confrontation. It is preferable, seemingly, to perpetuate the agony of growing numbers of individuals, to promote a single definition of the family, and to impose moral constraints upon people who seek human solutions which fulfil aspirations to happiness.

Whose happiness, one might ask? Is divorce an agreed dissolution of a contract, or is it achieved through disagreement, argument, legal fighting, bitterness and pain. The State has made some attempt to provide exit routes from the contractual terms of marriage — and marriage is, at base, a contract. But unless there is a braver attempt to redefine the family, instead of letting it redefine itself — which it has been in the process of doing virtually since the State introduced the inadequate wording of Article 41 — we will have grief-laden months ahead of us.

Irish Independent, April 1994

13

THE DEATH OF JACK LYNCH

In the memorial service for Jack Lynch, at Mount Argus, we celebrated, in the words of Father Ralph Egan, "a great son of Ireland . . . who in so many ways served us so well". As he said the words, brief but moving, there was a faint upsurge of collective endorsement. The greatness was hard to quantify; the events in which he served his country diverse and subtle in their demands on him. But everyone there knew that this man, whose passing we mourned, belonged to a rare breed of heroes who reflected the best in the life of Ireland in so many different ways.

One of those ways was manifest in the simple form of service used, clearly chosen to reflect the ecumenism that was part of his complex and rich character. So we had a Quaker leading us in silent prayer, readings from a Presbyterian, a Methodist, and a member of the Church of Ireland, and the presence of a member of the Jewish community. And the Auxiliary Bishop of Dublin, Dr Fiachra Ó Ceallaigh, standing in for the Roman Catholic Primate, Archbishop Seán Brady and for Dr Desmond Connell, both in Rome, treated us to an enthusiastic recollection of Jack Lynch the sportsman, scoring a memorable goal in the All-Ireland of 1949.

The simplicity of the event was refreshing. It encouraged thoughtful deliberation, and was largely without pomp and circumstance. Indeed, after we had all come out of the Church there was a measure of confusion. Government ministers stood on one side, the clerics on the other, and the coffin bearers waited. One senior army officer announced to another a late change of plan, with the cortege starting and then stopping again, a short way down the road, to allow everyone get into their cars and join the procession. Eventually the line moved away and we were left to mill about and talk over a past when he had been in power, and which now seemed very remote. Again, it was in keeping with the character of the man. He disliked pomp and ceremony. Fittingly self-effacing, he had a well-developed capacity to slip away from the limelight. And I never knew a politician more jealous of his privacy, and more firmly resistant to virtually all applications for interviews. He kept no papers, wrote no diary, and what he remembered he rarely divulged.

He helped me sometimes with information, but sparingly, and always with the strict instruction that what he said was to be unacknowledged. I remember on one occasion, drinking whiskey in his house, with Máirín offering an extravagantly generous tea, and trying to persuade him that posterity needed to know more of what he had gone through. He was too polite to say, Posterity be damned! But he meant that in declining whatever offer was being made. He said jokingly on that same occasion that he was enjoying his retirement; he could listen to the radio without feeling it was his fault. He did not relish the added burden of reliving a career which was punctuated with challenges and difficulties. And this was the case even though he always seemed to handle political crisis with the same dexterity and skill he displayed on the sporting field.

I discussed with others, at one time, whether a "Life" might not be possible. The consensus was that to find a writer with the accomplishments to cover the sportsman, the Corkman and the politician would be a fruitless search. And a "Life" written by a committee of three would diminish rather than enhance a career which attracted widespread cross-party affection and esteem. Garret FitzGerald has correctly pointed out that, in attacking Jack

Lynch, the ever-present danger was that the attack would re-bound on the person making it, and would further enhance the respect in which Lynch was held.

I believe, and have always believed, that his apparent passivity was a form of quietism: in other words, a deliberate belief in letting matters run in order to test to their fullest length the extent and strength of the opposition within. And he faced a good deal of that from the time he became leader of Fianna Fáil and Taoiseach in 1966.

He has been faulted for this, not least during the gathering storm in Northern Ireland in 1969, the Arms Crisis and Arms Trials that followed, and the very difficult period up to the general election of 1973. Yet he cauterised effectively the deep and lasting wounds, self-inflicted by Fianna Fáil at that time, and he held the party together. He got rid of difficult men, who would not conform; yet out of a spirit of fairness could not confront and dismiss those who made a pretence of conforming, including, of course, Charles Haughey.

His most difficult period was in opposition, between 1973 and 1977, and particularly halfway through that term, when Michael O'Kennedy proposed a policy change for the party, demanding British withdrawal from Northern Ireland. The political cards were held by Liam Cosgrave and the Fine Gael–Labour Coalition he led with a remarkable deadpan aplomb which only became vulnerable at the end, with his "Blow-In" speech, and with Paddy Donegan's "thundering disgrace" outburst, and the resignation of Cearbhall Ó Dálaigh.

With hardly a journalist aware of it, and none prepared to give him a snowflake's chance in hell of winning the general election called in the summer of 1977, Jack Lynch demonstrated absolute skill and authority in recovering power with an unprecedented majority.

It was a high-point of achievement that he actively regretted. He saw the huge danger of such a large majority, the complacency it engendered, the back-biting and treachery which increasingly built up against him and the majority of the members of his government. It was a politically shameful period of which the full details have yet to be told. His downfall was coldly worked for, with different deputies recruited to embarrass him and work against him. And this they did, on the baseless offer that Charles Haughey could give them a better deal, a prospect of greater power, and the involvement of the riff-raff in Fianna Fáil who were disgruntled and peevish about being excluded from the party's achievements.

Jack Lynch told me at the time that the party needed to make up its mind. For better or worse, it had to choose its future way forward and live with the consequences. It was Brian Lenihan who told me, in advance of the event, that Jack was resigning. And we then went through the leadership struggle, curiously bleak and unhappy days in Leinster House which I shall never forget.

Then he slipped away and wasn't there anymore. The Fianna Fáil party expressed no regret. There was no presentation, no tribute, not a word, no line expressing gratitude. And yesterday afternoon one of those loyal ministers at the time came up to me to remind me of that fact, in words of deep regret and emotion. I did not need to be reminded. I wrote of it with astonishment and with foreboding. And then got on with the business of writing about the aftermath for Fianna Fáil which, as Conor Cruise O'Brien wrote so accurately on Thursday, was a tragedy with disastrous consequences.

Throughout Ireland today, as Jack Lynch is finally laid to rest, men and women will mourn him without understanding fully why they feel so personal a grief at his death. And the man himself would recognise the justice of that, for truly there were so many ways in which he served us so well.

Irish Independent, Saturday, 23 October 1999

PART 2

LITERATURE

14

THE ISOLATED SPIRIT

Personification, we were taught at school, was the investment of the non-human with human characteristics. "Life can play some nasty tricks" is an example, in which the abstract concept of "Life" is given the all-too-human ability to play tricks, pull strokes, trip us up. Robert Welch, the editor of the *Oxford Companion to Irish Literature*, does the same thing with Irish literature, no less. "Irish literature", he tells us, "is one of those literatures which changed its language, a circumstance of enormous difficulty, challenge and opportunity."

The idea is a nice one. There is Irish literature, clothed in Gaelic, writhing on the ground, changing its skin, like a snake, and emerging, after this enormously difficult and challenging moment in its destiny, clothed in the English language. This was then going to permit Jonathan Swift, Oscar Wilde and W.B. Yeats, to confound the known world. The view is, of course, untenable; put bluntly, the literature did not change its language. People, who make both history and literature, did that.

This personification is sustained, and carried to even more questionable assertions, in the Editor's Preface to this otherwise exceptionally well-written guide, or companion. Welch claims, for example, that "all the different territories and voices that comprise and animate Irish literary tradition go to make up one coherent but manifold cultural expression, something to be experienced and delighted in, not asserted". In other words, this inanimate force, Irish literature, produced the writers and the writing, and not the other way round. This in turn is extended to the idea that a sub-division of this, "Irish literature in English", produced that "clarion of brilliance and humanity", and, yes, all the usual suspects are lined up, from Swift to Heaney.

This is dangerous nonsense, and all too often academics get up to it. I don't mean the humble teachers of English, who often made the nightmare of our education bearable, and opened up for us the unforgettable magic of individual poems and stories, or of individual writers. If they were good, such teachers knew that writers mainly slaved in the wilderness and isolation of their solitary struggle for a place in the world, largely oblivious to the duty of being part of a 2000-year-old tradition.

I mean, rather, the lords of creation, occupying chairs in universities, and making fatuous reinventions and reconstructions of literature in order to leave indelible evidence of their interference. It comes *post hoc*, when a scheme or a design can be superimposed, turning human expression into a generic breed. It makes Irish literature sound a bit like claret — unique in location, of one colour, with outstanding chateaux, and vintages going back in time, which are to be savoured, both for their cohesive and for their manifold qualities.

This is the Aosdána approach to literature, an exclusive, nationalistic, insular and largely false representation of it as transcending the individuals who are responsible. Writing isn't like that, and has never been like that.

Luckily, the book itself doesn't fall into the pit dug for it by the Editor in his Preface. And this is because the Preface was written, mercifully, *after* the book, and therefore fails to do for the book what the Editor, also mercifully, fails to do for Irish literature, which is to put it inside a tidy definition. Instead, useful and thorough, indeed scholarly and well-written, articles provide us with an indexed history of enormous value.

Coole Park should have been there, as Garsington Manor is in the *Oxford Companion to English Literature*. John Quinn should undoubtedly have been there; he helped Irish writers, and without him Joyce's difficulties with *Ulysses* would have been much greater. William Congreve is another absentee. Madly, he was left out of the *Field Day Anthology*, which I criticised at the time, and he should have been with his school and college friend, Swift, in this guide.

But hunting for absentees is a game for the future. For the present, despite the marvellous celebratory speech with which Seamus Heaney greeted the patience and energy of the editor, Robert Welch, and the assistant editor, Bruce Stewart, the note of caution about the proper order in which we look at our heritage needs to be sounded. No writer worth his salt puts pen to paper as the servant of a tradition, or to fulfil cultural coherence. His supreme theme is within his own isolated spirit. It is the weak, not the strong, who believe otherwise. Ingrained within the hearts of the strong may be the geography and landscape of the country, or the infinite foibles of the people, but when we read Beckett, Joyce, Heaney, Synge, Wilde, and a host of others, we know they write only for themselves.

Review in the *Irish Independent*, March 1996, of *The Oxford Companion to Irish Literature*, Edited by Robert Welch, Assistant Editor Bruce Stewart, Oxford University Press.

15

BRENDAN KENNELLY

Richard Pine tells us, in his introduction to *Dark Fathers into Light*, that Brendan Kennelly's "express purpose" is "to define love". I put "express purpose" into inverted commas because I don't know what it means. "To define love" is already in inverted commas in Richard's essay but its source is not given. It is of course the greatest of all purposes in poetry, and if it is genuinely at the heart of a poet's work, then it will give life and energy and inspiration as an instinctive and glorious benefit.

Brendan Kennelly does that magnificently. He defines love for us in many different ways, and as well as doing it magnificently, he does it with energy and enthusiasm.

Love is indefinable. At the end of it all, at the heart of it all, it is part of everything we see and feel.

I was recently asked by my daughter, who is to be married, to help her in choosing poems to be read at the wedding, at the end of September in Sligo. She had an idea that W.B. Yeats would yield something and she had been given various Yeats poems that I read through and thought totally unfeeling. They were not about love, they did not express love, they were not the words of a man who had ever been in love. Was Yeats ever in love, except with himself?

I have been in trouble in Ireland for most of my life for the unfavourable things I have said and published about W.B. Yeats. At the heart of my judgement of him is the belief that in most things he is attitudinising and not being real. He is real in his criticism and often real in his poetry where it is about event as well as myth. But *love*? I wonder.

What appeals about Kennelly's writing is its robust strength of purpose. He *is* real. He *is* part of the landscape, as much part of the landscape as that looming Master Poet Patrick Kavanagh. And landscape is an important framework for what he writes.

That same driving force in the writing of poetry, which one finds, for example, in Kavanagh, in Dylan Thomas and in Louis MacNeice, is strongly present in Brendan's work.

In the end, when it came to responding to my daughter, I chose to offer to her for the wedding part of the fourth section of MacNeice's *Autumn Journal*. The actual lines I believe to be among the greatest expressions of love, defining it and making it live in a rare and wonderful way.

The secret of Louis MacNeice seems to me to be that, of all Irish poets, he achieved the virtually impossible break with the land, the people, the history and the identity of Ireland, and wrote matter that has about it a kind of Greek purity. The love is love of the heart, not love of the land, or love of the people and idea of Ireland.

Richard Pine also says, in an interesting piece of analysis, that "In the evolution of his poetry he [Kennelly] has moved beyond history into an engagement with the matter of Ireland."

What MacNeice escaped, Brendan Kennelly embraced. I hope, a little later on, to be able to give a philosophic and poetic dimension to what I say now in sober terms about the nature of his engagement.

He is my age. He was born in April 1936, I was born that September. We could not possibly have had more different upbringings. His was stable and settled. He lived in a village, belonged to a family, identified with a community, played sport and faced the challenges of education in a logical and essentially assured environment. I had an entirely different upbringing: never sure of my background, who was looking after me, nor of the make-up of my family. I discovered, at the age of ten, a step-brother and a step-sister, designating a new and previously obscured or hidden family. The family to which I did belong was broken up on my mother's death in my seventh year and never really came together again.

Yet when Brendan and I met first, 45 years ago, this disparity of experience and background was not the evidence that people saw with their eyes, heard with their ears, measured out in the strange artificial world of university.

Trinity College, when Brendan finally settled there — for he had a hard time coming to it — was dominated by people like me. We would have been hated if there had been enough Irish people from the west of Ireland, if you like, to express such hatred. They couldn't have come from Dublin because they weren't let. Such feelings were not, as I remember it, part of the agenda. But I am embarrassed, looking back, at the degree to which we set the tone, dominated writing, acting, music, everything. The games were those reviled by the GAA. The sporting occasions, like the social occasions and like the literary and artistic and cultural events, were Protestant and Anglo-Irish, or just plain English, with a good dose of colonial nepotism and ruling-class arrogance thrown in for good measure.

Yeats has been quoted, in extenuation of Brendan's capacities as a poet, in the phrase from *Anima Hominis*: "We make out of the quarrel with others, rhetoric, but of the quarrel with ourselves, poetry."

What was so enjoyable about going through four years of study in Trinity College, both literally and metaphorically, side by side with Brendan Kennelly, was the fact that there was no animus directed against the insufferable attitudes we, the majority at the time, struck in a college that had been denied an Irish leavening because of the absurd authority of John Charles McQuaid.

Brendan, of course, coming from another diocese led by an intelligent bishop, who, I understand, admired the footballing skills of the poet, was not inhibited. But I think for a time he was overwhelmed. One day, if he has not already done it, he will write in poetry about the tangled and extremely complex atmosphere of those days. But more of that anon.

I bought my first car from Brendan. He offered me an astonishing discount from his father's business in Ballylongford on a new Renault Dauphine in 1958, the year the car won the Monte Carlo Rally. I was enchanted with it and, getting married the year after, drove it all round Europe on a honeymoon lasting eight weeks. Brendan himself has never learnt to drive.

Augustine Martin has written of Brendan being "recklessly prolific" in the decade 1959 to 1970. I witnessed this phase at very close quarters. I owned Brendan's early books of poetry. I knew his close friend and associate Rudi Holzapfel well. I admired the books for their typography more than for their content. And I would have shared with Gus Martin the view that a reckless profusion of words was delivered when silence and infrequent pauses might have been better. Who is to judge?

We graduated at the same time. Brendan, shortly afterwards, went off to Leeds and did research work there for a time with Derry Jeffares. Derry had been our external examiner and has remained a good friend of mine ever since. We correspond and meet. I imagine the same is so for Brendan.

But he was not long away. I think he must have found the atmosphere of a provincial English university as rancid as I would have done, which was one of the reasons for my being at Trinity in the first place. He came back to what he loved, and to the emerging task of his "engagement with the matter of Ireland".

In due course, this led him towards an espousal of Charles Haughey as a politician who somehow favoured the artist in Irish society. God knows, Irish society needed such a figure. But Haughey was sulphurous in what he did, distorting the arts in many ways. The damage he has done will take many years before it is undone. Haughey's artistic taxation policy was and is almost certainly unconstitutional. It is on a par with the elitism of

Ansbacher. What he did, covertly, with Des Traynor and his close friends, which was to introduce them to an inside track financially, making them into an elite, he also did more publicly for artists. Not surprisingly, artists revered him for it. And luckily, though we find it easy to revile people who hid away large tranches of money from the Revenue Commissioners, we do not have the same attitude to artists. This is not because for them it was legal, but perhaps because life itself for the artist has always been unequal. We accept the compensation.

Brendan is not elitist. Haughey was elitist in the worst and most vulgar ways imaginable. I failed at the time to see why, in the face of this, Brendan was so enamoured of the man. It made no great difference between us, but it lay there like a beached whale, too slippery to climb over, too large to bother going round.

I was very much the journalist, Brendan very much the academic, in those early years after university. When he was Junior Dean in Trinity, I was able to help him over an embarrassment involving a Trinity publication, but on the whole I became increasingly distant and detached from the college and he became increasingly immured within in. Both aspects have changed since then, a very welcome development.

Brendan tightened the rigging and the set of his sails in the 1980s. *Cromwell, Judas*, his plays for women or about women brought judgement and maturity to his output. Gabriel Fitzmaurice has written about this, about how rooted the poet is in his place of origin as well as in Dublin, and how well qualified he is to write from the experience of a life lived in both rural and urban surroundings. I like this fellow poet's observation that "without words there is no Kennelly" because Brendan himself, by gesture, expression, warmth, greeting, belies such a view. Yet deep down he is exactly what Fitzmaurice says he is — nothing without the word. I know, because I am the same. To paraphrase Descartes — whom we both studied, perhaps excessively, in our second year under Professor Arnould — *scriptito, ergo sum*.

It is Gerald Dawe who spoke of Kennelly and the problem of audience, quoting Patrick Kavanagh, who said he needed "to build up a little audience for myself". But I think it was Dawe also who quoted Kennelly giving the other side of that desire: "I am terrified of self-importance and of the pomposity that is in all of us, because it is unintelligent."

Well, when you have a festival devoted to you by the love of a niece and other family members, perhaps you need to think again about that.

What I now have to say I did not send in advance to Brendan's niece, Mary. It is this: I brought with me a gift for the poet. It says things that would take a long time to tease out, but being modest work in the same vein that Brendan has spent a lifetime pursuing, certain corners are cut off.

Brendan

I knew him long ago.
He was the country boy.
Dimples in his cheeks, the bloom of youth
Shone on his brow and in his eyes.
He walked an alien territory
Determined to succeed.

The early autumn of that fated year, our first run
At the final trial for life that would then
Take us into life itself. University!
What a *trahison des clerc*! What a
Comfortable cushion against reality!

In the autumn days, peat smoke in the air,
As I might watch a rival, I watched him.
So sure he was, so different from myself.

Dressed in cavalry twill, a waistcoat, and
With a taste for bow ties, mannerisms,
I looked upon his shabby belted coat
In awe and secret envy and respect.

His walk was sure and proud, this country boy.
He had his secrets just the same as me.
He knew in one sharp lozenge of his mind
Where he was going, when he would arrive,
And told to none of us the plans he had.

We did different things. He never acted,
Never sang. Lived out of college; I know
He gave no parties; if he fell in love
He never told me.

We shared a love for Jeannie; prim she was
At College for the self-appointed task
Of getting a degree. Just that. No more.
While we were making up our universe
And filling it with heroes out of books
She held us with the simple smile of youth.
And only after many years, his eyes
Glinting with remembered admiration,
Was Jeannie mentioned in that special way.

Yes, we were friends. We moved together.
Our minds attentive to the common bond
Of writing. It wove its magic equally.
He came from Kerry, I from London town,
Yet Eliot and Joyce bound us together,
Chaucer was our companionship, and our
Handmaiden at our call Virginia Woolf.

We rode these fated messengers of art,
Learned from them, and in frantic essays, we
Delivered them again to those who taught.

Never reluctant, he forged through us all,
Forged through the terms of study, and the years,
The dimples set within his cheeks, his eyes
Bright as two cherries, dark and determined.

He carried always a case: square, battered;
And with his belted coat and rough black shoes
He seemed to tell us what we were was wrong.
And he was right. We were the past,
Residual monuments to some lost time
When Protestants believed they were in charge.
When British rule still held some sway on earth.
And this was where it rested, Trinity.

All wrong.
He held the power and knew the use of it.
And we within our puzzled ruling class
Espied the fateful writing on the wall
Tried to dismiss its message, and strode on.

We went to summer parties dressed in boaters,
Sang madrigals and puzzled over Beckett,
Drank beer, grew up, came to the end of things.

Our College days were over. Suddenly,
The country boy was ready to depart,
But now he was transformed, modest, assured,
The poet and the man stepped from us all
Away!
              Trailing remembered writers, all
Now the substance of a finished life
And packaged for the journey into Time,
He strode out from us, Irish colossus.

The substance of this essay was given as an address at the first Brendan
Kennelly Summer School, in Ballylongford, County Kerry, in July 2002.

16

SAMUEL BECKETT

I

"I must go on, I can't go on, I'll go on"

Samuel Beckett would have loved the competition. He was always a sportsman. To the end of his life he followed the Tour de France. He played cricket at Portora School, and went on to play in the Trinity College First XI when he was a student there. He might even have taken up sport as a profession. He did, after all, consider some pretty odd ideas, like being an airline pilot, and writing advertising copy. And he didn't really discover his true vocation as writer; like all true vocations, it discovered him. So there would have been a deep satisfaction, in this, the ninetieth year of his life and death, that he should be the subject, not of one mammoth Life, but of two mammoth Lifes, coming out at the same time, and both of them going for gold.

Instead of 700 pages of biography being hurled into the visage of posterity, no less than 1,400 pages will clash in cataclysmic disagreement over our heads in September. We have a Life from Bloomsbury, and we have a Life from HarperCollins. Nor is that all; for the royal and regal conflict is between England and Ireland, both countries laying claim to a writer who lived out his life in France, and wrote more than half his plays and books in

French, usually translating them himself into English at a later stage. Scholarship is set against imagination, the poet is fighting the professor, the world of academics is at odds with the world of writing and journalism.

In my left corner, Ladies and Gentlemen, stands Anthony Cronin, representing Ireland. Part of the ragged-trousered brigade, those writers who accompanied Behan and Kavanagh, drank with Peadar O'Donnell and John Ryan, listened to the philosophical niceties of John Jordan, and kept McDaid's in business. It has become, in retrospect, a golden age of the grubbier forms of literary passion, of pints and oaths, fights and barring orders, poverty and leaking shoes.

Cronin's book, *Samuel Beckett: The Last Modernist*, is to be published by HarperCollins. The book has already been claimed "the definitive biography" by Colm Tóibín. This Tóibín can't possibly know; the fact cannot be asserted, since nothing in the wide world is ever "definitive". And you would need to have read the other Life — indeed all the Lifes — before coming to judgement. Nevertheless, his additional claim on Cronin's behalf, that *Samuel Beckett: The Last Modernist* is "incredibly well-written and readable", has to be taken seriously. It is Cronin's biggest undertaking as a writer, a giant grasp at comprehension, and to some extent the vehicle by which he reclaims his position in Irish literature and letters.

Cronin has been through wilderness years. He would not see them like that, but many who have read and admired him as poet and as writer generally reckon that he wasted time and energy as cultural adviser and speech-writer for Charles Haughey between 1980 and 1992. They would see time wasted also in directing the affairs of Aosdána and acting as its chairman. It was only when he left the Taoiseach's office, in October 1992, and became "free" once more, that he was able to embark on the substantial undertaking of a modern Life of Samuel Beckett.

In my right corner, Ladies and Gentlemen, stands Jim Knowlson. He is as English as Cronin is Irish. He is the classic emblem of late twentieth-century biographical scholarship and diligence. His book, *Damned to Fame: The Life of Samuel Beckett*, which runs to a couple of hundred pages *more* than Anthony Cronin's, is authorised. Samuel Beckett asked him to write it, and gave him interviews during the summer and autumn of 1989. These are central to the book, as is exclusive use of family archive material. This book, perhaps with greater justification, is also looked on as definitive, but is different in content, style and approach from Cronin's.

It is obvious that the favours and the betting lie with Jim Knowlson. He has been a Professor of French at Reading University since 1981, and a teacher there since the end of the 1960s. An undoubted scholar in the field of Beckett studies, he had known the Irish writer for many years, and had visited him regularly in Paris, discussing his work, attending rehearsals of plays with him, corresponding, collecting from him manuscripts which are now in the superb Beckett archive at Reading. He would be seen internationally as a natural and obvious Beckett biographer.

Bloomsbury is the publisher of his book, and it has, to date, what might justifiably be claimed as "the inside track". Additionally, serial rights have been bought by *The Sunday Times*, and second serial rights are now being discussed in Ireland.

Jim Knowlson has a substantial academic record. He was editor of the four-volume *Theatrical Notebooks of Samuel Beckett*, and has written several other books on Beckett's writing, and many articles, establishing his claim within the world of Beckett scholarship.

Roll Up, now, Roll Up! This is a serious contest, with much more at stake than small points of academic fact or breezy speculation! This is a combat upon which the eyes of literature and the academic world will focus with great relish and anticipation. Beckett is big business. He is a cult figure in the world of writing, a craggy giant, filled with silence and patience. He has also spawned a steady flow of clotted, incoherent and obtuse rubbish which has already overlaid the austere purity of his poetic, dramatic and narrative art with a festering confusion of mumbo-jumbo. There is a simple economy in his writing, a magic and a sweetness to it; and this is matched by his life, which was kindly and generous and filled with more of nature than his critics like to permit.

Which of his biographers will best bring out the truth? Which of them will most compellingly tell us the better story? It is a finely balanced competition. And it has pretty weighty consequences for those who will buy one or other of the books, and, more importantly, for those who will read them.

Jim Knowlson doesn't make great claims about himself; he lets others do that for him. Anthony Cronin is equally modest and relaxed. Both are outwardly unmoved by the existence of "this other Life". One started as favourite; the other has come up on the rails, a rank outsider, carrying odds of twenty-to-one and bearing the slightly faded colours of the poet Anthony Cronin.

He is in no sense a scholar in the late twentieth-century sense of that word. Cronin carries a handicap. The late twentieth century favours academics increasingly, where biography is concerned, and is aggressively looking for credentials instead of writing talent. Machine-like polymaths, such as Jeffrey Meyers, who has driven like a steamroller through Ernest Hemingway, D.H. Lawrence, Joseph Conrad, Wyndham Lewis and Katherine Mansfield, or Matthew J. Bruccoli, who has given us, in extensive detail, yet perhaps without the necessary, subtle magic, Scott Fitzgerald.

Biographies of this kind are the required flavour and texture, even if the sense of ultimate "life" they produce often rests, as they do, like a row of weighty stones unread on bookshelves. The ragged-trousered thinking man, poet and critic, who carries his research on crumpled sheets of paper stuffed into baggy pockets of corduroy jackets, is an outmoded class of a person to be writing about so serious a possession of the academic fraternity as Samuel Beckett.

And that is where the battleground really lies. That is what the war is about. Who is it, at the end of this terrible century, who really possesses Irish writing and Irish writers? Is it the writers themselves, or the teachers? Cronin knew Beckett before Knowlson did, and knew him as a fellow writer. Indeed, Beckett sought him out, after Cronin had written about the novels in *The Times Literary Supplement* in the late 1950s. Those were the days when Cronin was experiencing that literary life which subsequently featured in *Dead as Doornails*, and is also touched on in *The Life of Riley*. It went back even further than that. When Cronin started as a poet, his first literary "friend", as one might say, was Thomas MacGreevy, and no one knew Beckett better, or earlier, than MacGreevy. It was MacGreevy who introduced Beckett to James Joyce, and then to Jack Yeats, and the younger man, then in a fog of bewilderment and uncertainty about his life, remained eternally grateful.

Cronin also knew at that time Patrick Magee and Jack MacGowran, the key actors who were presenting Beckett on stage. Today's actors and actresses, among them Billie Whitelaw and Barry McGovern, would perhaps be in the Knowlson camp, since Knowlson was always undoubtedly closer to Beckett, both personally and professionally.

A month ago, the question of book promotion was taken up, in the context of possible serial rights sale in Ireland, and Bloomsbury was considering the possibility of some kind of "confrontation" between the two writers. Michael Colgan, at the Gate Theatre, is said to have offered it as a venue on a Sunday night, and there was discussion as to who might chair such an event. The challenge — for such it would have been — was neither issued to Anthony Cronin, nor claimed by Jim Knowlson to have been a serious possibility, and the idea wavered and wobbled, and then eventually subsided.

In both camps there is nervous concern. The original publication date for Anthony Cronin's book was November. Then it was brought forward to the first week in October. Now it is being brought forward again, to coincide more exactly with Jim Knowlson's book, which was always scheduled for late September.

From both camps a convincing display of *sang froid* is to be detected. Jim Knowlson demonstrates the calm of intellectual comprehension. He has made many trips to Paris, has had meetings with his subject, towards the end of Beckett's life, and has brought back to Reading choice manuscripts and original Beckett material, enriching the library there to a truly remarkable extent. He has dug and delved, compared and checked, searched and re-searched, and the giant labour has at last come to rest.

Anthony Cronin has read and remembered, and has written his heart out. With fluent, liquid prose, with that characteristic emphasis he has, that mixture of bohemian perception with magisterial authority which makes his best book *Dead as Doornails* such fun to read, he has challenged what has become a citadel of academic exclusion.

The key to success, between the two biographers, will be hard to judge. In part, a writer of Beckett's complex make-up is approached through other Irish people who were close to him. Among these, certain names are critical, Thomas MacGreevy, obviously, and Jack Yeats; then there is Niall Montgomery and Owen Sheehy Skeffington. The first two are seriously important, the second two significant. The way all four are treated will be a measure of each biographer's penetration of subject, eagerly to be seized on when the books come to critical judgement. In the meantime, we speculate.

Beckett revered certain figures in his early years, and his writing skills and creative development owed an enormous debt, now easily overlooked, misunderstood, or reversed — so that it is Yeats, for example, who is seen in Beckett's debt, rather than the other way round.

Though Thomas MacGreevy is more dominant in a day-to-day sense than Yeats, Jack Yeats was a seminal force in Beckett's evolution as a writer. No one, in my judgement, understands the writer fully without a grasp of the painter, and of the relationship between the two men.

Niall Montgomery was close to both of them, and in his own right was an underrated figure in literary Dublin from the late 1930s on. And Owen Sheehy Skeffington was a friend to the writer for many years, and one whose own literary perceptions were finely tuned to the tradition from which Beckett drew so much strength.

Which way will it fall? To the English or the Irish? To the professor or the poet? Will the wayward writer be repulsed? Or will the academic be tumbled? Will it be research or writing, opinion or method, knowing people or judging books and plays, experience in the blood and heart, or experience in the brain?

And will we have a contest? Jim Knowlson is not sure about that. Nor is Anthony Cronin. In their very different ways, they are well-matched protagonists. They are totally different. And they are handling the hottest international literary property of the late twentieth century.

Irish Independent, 25 July 1996

ജ

II

Two Views of Samuel Beckett

James Knowlson clears up the question about the date of Samuel Beckett's birth on page one of his biography. The question is simple enough, though there has been much debate about it: Beckett's birth certificate shows the date as 13 May. Beckett claimed Good Friday, 13 April, throughout his life, though the birth was not registered until 14 June. But Knowlson has checked the Births and Deaths column in *The Irish Times*, where the birth, the previous Friday, was announced on Monday, 16 April.

Conclusive? Well, Anthony Cronin, in his biography, goes with the less checked version, correcting Beckett's own claim, and putting the birth still in May. It is a small difference, but indicative of the thoroughly researched and detailed approach of the "official" biographer, and the more factually haphazard one followed by Cronin. At this level — and it is only one level in biography, as will be shown below — Knowlson is comprehensive and detailed, pursuing many interesting new aspects, and cross-checking his findings, to produce, in the end, a powerfully complete structure for the writer's life.

The essentials are straightforward. Born in 1906 in Foxrock, in the family house, Cooldrinagh, the second son of a quantity surveyor who became a builder, Samuel Beckett grew up in the typical Protestant suburban environment of his class. He attended a local school, then travelled in on the Harcourt Street line to school in town, after which he went to Portora Royal School in Enniskillen. It was a predictable choice, in terms of class and religion, and Beckett worked well, and played sports with skill and talent. He then went on to Trinity College for an Arts degree, and for more sport, which, incidentally, gave him the distinction of being the only Nobel Prize-winner to appear in Wisden's Cricketers' Almanack, for his scores against Northamptonshire.

He went off to Paris, having had a chaste love affair with Ethna MacCarthy, and taught there in the École Normale, returning to lecture in Trinity for a time before abandoning the work, and settling in Paris more or less permanently. His intention, frowned on by his mother, was to be a writer, and his first books, *Whoroscope*, in 1930, and *Proust*, which appeared in 1931, were followed by a further couple of volumes of verse, short stories, some articles, and a novel, *Murphy*, which appeared just before the Second World War. There was another, unpublished novel, *Dream of Fair to Middling Women*; this eventually appeared posthumously.

As a writer, Beckett's start was indisputably shaky and uncertain. Posterity now causes universal reverence for everything he produced. But, apart from some good passages, virtually everything written up to and including the Second World War period is of limited merit, a fact which Cronin is less afraid to indicate than Knowlson. The same uncertainty is evident in his life and relationships.

Visits to Germany had demonstrated to Beckett some of the awfulness of Nazism, and he joined the French Resistance with his companion, Suzanne Deschevaux-Dusmenil, who had befriended him at the time of a stabbing attack by a pimp in the Paris streets. They both became involved in work against the German army of occupation. They escaped arrest after the betrayal of the group in which they operated; they then lived in the south of France. Beckett resumed his visits home to Dublin, and to his mother, after the war, when his circumstances as a writer gradually improved, notably with the success which *Waiting for Godot* achieved. Other plays, his earlier trilogy of novels, and an increasing flow of other writing, created a unique body of creative work which fully merited the Nobel Prize in 1969.

Knowlson's life adds substantially to our detailed knowledge. He deals with newly discovered diaries from the German period, he adds to our knowledge of Beckett's love affairs, he corrects and fills in innumerable facts and suggestions about how the writer's life relates to his writing. The book displays good, sound, authoritative scholarship. There has been unprecedented access to correspondence and documents, and a long period during which discussions with Beckett, in the full knowledge of Knowlson's potential role as "official" biographer, further enriched the details of his life. There are some excellent first-hand insights drawn from these many encounters he had with Samuel Beckett, and the book will undoubtedly remain a most reliable source for years to come.

Anthony Cronin's book is different. If Knowlson is the scrupulous academic, Cronin is the opinionated fellow-writer of Samuel Beckett, himself a more modest part of the story, familiar at first hand with Beckett's contemporaries and friends, as well as having had some contact with Beckett himself. Cronin is more judgemental. He is also more familiar with the ethos in which Beckett grew up. Where Knowlson reveres Beckett, seeming to suggest an unbroken drive of creativity shaping a haphazard set of experiences into a life of design and purpose, Cronin suggests quite the opposite: that Beckett's uncertainty and haphazard performance for at least forty of the eighty-three years of his life was exactly that.

The Cronin version, as an interpretation, is perhaps more truthful because less adulatory. Beckett has achieved the apotheosis of solitude in his art. He has done this but by way of many vicissitudes, which Cronin is more apt to point out, while Knowlson rationalises and excuses. Knowlson does so with the golden ideal of greatness — "Samuel Barclay Beckett, who was to become one of the major writers of the twentieth century . . ." is how the book opens — overshadowing everything. The definition "greatness" is inherently debilitating in biography.

Owen Sheehy Skeffington was a friend of Samuel Beckett for forty years. He was at school with Beckett's cousins, the children of "Boss" Sinclair. He recalls "Ruddy" [Rudmose] Brown saying of Beckett, "He may never do anything — but he's a genius!" He sent Beckett a telegram on the award of the Nobel Prize, saying, "Ruddy would be pleased." And when Skeffington stood for the Trinity College seat in the Senate, Beckett sent a telegram to him: "Dear Skinny, Count on me. Best, Sam." Skeff's is the best description of Beckett lecturing in 35 New Square, on Proust. None of this is in Knowlson, nor is Skeffington himself mentioned, a serious lapse.

There is too little derived from other people, including Niall Montgomery, a good friend of the writer, and Jack B. Yeats, substantially more influential on Samuel Beckett than either Knowlson or Cronin acknowledge. Cronin, on the whole, writes in a more rounded fashion about Irish friends and acquaintances of Beckett, and, as one would expect, shows a decidedly more instinctive grasp of the Dublin scene.

Knowlson is too shrewd an academic to go over the top in his assessment of Beckett, as a writer, or to gloss over the awkwardness of the man; and this ensures the avoidance of bland hagiography. But it is probably beneficial that two Lifes have appeared at the same time, Cronin's offering, from a rather different standpoint, an anchor against excess. Given the growing tide of nonsense being written elsewhere about Beckett, these two books will become central to study of him and his work. Taken together, or indeed read separately, they provide a splendidly rich account of a key literary figure of this century.

Review for the *Irish Independent*, September 1996: *Damned to Fame: The Life of Samuel Beckett* by James Knowlson, Bloomsbury; *Samuel Beckett: The Last Modernist* by Anthony Cronin, HarperCollins.

୫୦

III

When Beckett was First in Love

She lay stretched out on the floorboards with her hands under her head and her eyes closed. Sun blazing down, bit of a breeze, water nice and lively. I noticed a scratch on her thigh and asked her how she came by it. Picking gooseberries, she said. I said again I thought it was hopeless and no good going on and she agreed, without opening her eyes. I asked her to look at me and after a few moments — after a few moments she did, but the eyes just slits, because of the glare. I bent over her to get them in the shadow and they opened. Let me in. We drifted in among the flags and stuck. The way they went down, sighing, before the stem! I lay down across her with my face in her breasts and my hand on her. We lay there without moving. But under us all moved, and moved us, gently, up and down, and from side to side.

As an example of erotic writing, this is hard to beat. There is the idea of it being "hopeless and no good going on", and then the going on. There is the man's head in the young woman's breasts, and his hand on her, as the water gently rocks the punt in which they are lying. And then there is the bright sun beating down on them, the hesitation, the desire, the glare, the shadow, and the movement, "gently, up and down, and from side to side".

The passage forms the climax to *Krapp's Last Tape*, and has a magical intensity in the play, since it seems to emerge from the ragged indifference of the old man, playing his past life out again on spool after spool of recorded memory. This particular tape he seeks out, plays, discards; he eats a banana, records his dismissal of "that stupid bastard I took myself for thirty years ago", and finally goes back and plays the tape again. But this time he goes on, beyond the boat moving up and down. His youthful self tells him: "Past midnight. Never knew such silence. The earth might be uninhabited."

There has been much speculation as to the girl's identity. In another brief line in the play, Krapp refers to "The eyes she had!" And this would suggest that the model for the unnamed young woman was Ethna MacCarthy, who was Samuel Beckett's first love, and who was almost certainly the inspiration for the writing of *Krapp's Last Tape*. But Beckett himself, though he adored Ethna, never had a sexual relationship with her, and the words do suggest that they made love. This make Peggy Sinclair a more likely candidate for that sexual part of the composite portrait, such as it is, which constitutes the climax of the short play. Peggy Sinclair is also more centrally identified through references to a novel by Theodor Fontane which both Peggy and Beckett himself liked. And on visits to her and her family, notably in the summer of 1929, they spent time on the Baltic sea, and boated there, something not recorded with Ethna.

In other words, we have writer's licence here. But in a much deeper sense we are looking at a tribute which actually does stretch across the thirty years between his innocent love affair with Ethna MacCarthy, and his composition of the play, which happened in February 1958. Beckett had heard in December 1957 from Con Leventhal, who had married Ethna, that she was suffering from cancer of the throat, and that it was terminal. He visited her in Dublin, and then wrote to her from France, descending into a mood of considerable depression. He put into the play his curiously complicated presentation of happiness recalled over a gap of thirty years, just as he also put in the despair and anger of old age, and the might-have-beens of Krapp's long life.

Ethna MacCarthy was the first of Samuel Beckett's women. She was a fellow-student at Trinity, and was strikingly beautiful, with black hair and black eyes which Beckett's great friend Georges Pelorson described as penetrating and sagacious. She was predatory, "a kind of panther", and was adored by many men, including Denis Johnston, who took her out when he was a Trinity student, at the time of the Black-and-Tan curfews, and certainly got further with her than Samuel Beckett, both hiding behind walls from military patrols, and lying in each others' arms on the ground.

But in fact Ethna MacCarthy, while she attracted many younger men, and had them as admirers, also had an older lover, a married man and Trinity professor, and maintained the younger men in platonic relationships. This did not reduce the intensity of Beckett's love for her, and it survived for many years, through other affairs which were sexual, and in effect up to the time of her death. Whatever other inspiration he drew on for *Krapp's Last Tape*, it is towards a memory of Ethna that he directed the emotional force of the play, its hauntingly lyrical search for the recovery of past happiness, yet couched in circumstances which avoid sentimentality.

Again and again, in Beckett's work, his experiences, as a child, as a young man, with people in authority, and with women, inspire his writing. And in general the view of women is far less lyrical than this particular episode in the punt. The happy life, between men and women, could be sensibly equated, in the Beckettian view, with the relationship between the two characters in *Happy Days*, where we can't be entirely sure that Willie, at the end, isn't intent on blowing Winnie's brains out with the revolver she has taken from her handbag.

There are several ludicrous sexual encounters humiliating to the central figure in Beckett's works, and emphasising inadequacies, both physical and emotional. Whether it is legitimate at all to trace these to actual women or to events is questionable, but it would seem that Beckett loved women, suffered from them, was intimidated by them, and sought out strong and determined women as partners, whether distant or close, long-term or for short relationships.

This may reflect the profound influence of his mother. She was a severe person, from a Quaker background, with an education in a Moravian school. She ran the Beckett household at Cooldrinagh, in Foxrock, with a hand of iron, and her stern regime affected her husband, the children, the maids, the gardener, and even the animals. She was loving and kindly as well; her niece, who used to stay with her when her own parents went away, says that she always had outings and interesting things arranged. These included trips in the donkey cart, and it was in character for her to reserve most of her overt sympathy for the donkeys which she rescued from cruel situations. This, incidentally, was one of the bonding forces in Mrs Beckett's friendship with Jack Yeats, who was also a keen defender of the donkey, and on the lookout for allies in this perilous work of rescue and recovery.

The next important love interest in Samuel Beckett's life, after Ethna MacCarthy, was Peggy Sinclair, the daughter of "Boss" Sinclair and "Cissie", Beckett's aunt. Cissie was his father's sister. She had married the Jewish art and antiques dealer who later took a celebrated libel action against Oliver St John Gogarty in which Beckett appeared as a wretchedly uncomfortable witness, with echoes throughout his later writing. The Sinclair house was bohemian, and the attractive seventeen-year-old girl with her green eyes attracted Beckett. The family had moved to Kassel in Germany, and the first encounters were when Peggy was on holiday in Dublin. But Beckett, by then heading towards his first academic job in Paris, began to learn German, intending to visit Peggy, which he did, both there, on the Baltic, and in Austria, where she went to study music and dance.

The romance between them was frowned on, not surprisingly, since they were first cousins. Peggy wanted to take it further than Beckett, and was more physical, but in the end it broke up, with tears. Peggy died of tuberculosis in 1933, and Beckett was much affected. He was put off by the physical aspects of love, and wrote quite savagely about women's bodies, notably in his *Dream of Fair to Middling Women*, which was written during the summer of 1932, though not published until 1992. And it seems that in his mind love and sex were separated. This view, reinforced by the obvious implication in his writing of not infrequent encounters with prostitutes and visits to brothels, was clearly resolved in the late 1930s, when he had a big affair with Peggy Guggenheim.

They met in James Joyce's company, and Peggy Guggenheim is among those responsible for exaggerating and distorting the stories about Samuel Beckett and Lucia, suggesting that Beckett had been engaged to her. After a dinner in Joyce's company at Fouquet's, on the Champs Elysées, Beckett and Peggy went back to her apartment where first he persuaded her to lie with him on the sofa, and then "we soon found ourselves in bed, where we remained until the next evening at dinner time". Their love affair was passionate but in the main unhappy. Peggy was in love with him, as she was — or claimed to be — with many men; his own feelings for her are not so easily defined. There was obviously a great initial attraction, but not one that lasted, though the affair certainly went on, according to her, for more than a year. The best time was a twelve-day episode when they lived in the house of Mary Reynolds, a friend of the writer Djuna Barnes.

At this time he met Suzanne Deschevaux-Dumesnil, the woman who later became his wife, arguably fulfilled the role of mother as well, and was his companion from the late 1930s on. Indeed, Peggy Guggenheim made jokes about Suzanne's practical abilities, set against her own erotic skills. Suzanne was several years older than

Beckett, and seems to have been accomplished and talented in so many different ways as to qualify for the perfect writer's or artist's wife. For the rest of his days, it could be said that she gave him the happiness and contentment which he needed in order to combat the often inexpressible anguish of creation.

They had an open "marriage" without the marriage, a firm relationship which was based on shared interests, friends, taste and affection. She admired his work enormously, worked for him herself often enough in dealing with publishers and theatre managements, and seems to have accepted his other liaisons with women, which went on during the next two decades.

But in all essentials, between his mother, his early love affairs, his tempestuous time with Peggy Guggenheim, his consorting with prostitutes and his transient later liaisons, with Suzanne as the later cornerstone in his life, Beckett had run the race common to most men and to most artists. The darker side of sexuality, the distressing views given of women in some of his works, have to be set against the loveliness of other episodes, including the haunting swish of the boat as it moved in over the flags, the eyes, which were slits, opening to look into his, and then his head buried in her breasts. "We lay there without moving. But under us all moved, and moved us, gently, up and down, and from side to side."

Irish Independent, September 1996

17

SEAMUS HEANEY

I

Seamus Heaney, Irish Laureate

Of the four Irish Nobel Prize-winners of the twentieth century, Seamus Heaney is the closest to the Irish earth. He expresses better the native spirit of place, the language and feeling of ordinary people, the tug and tension of a profoundly mixed society which, throughout its history, has been at war with itself. He recognised this war in his own make-up as a poet. He recognised it in the society which surrounded him while he was growing up. And he sought through words and feelings to express it and resolve it.

Almost twenty-five years ago, trying to explain what it meant to be an Irish poet, he confronted this issue. Little did he know then, in the traumatic spring of 1972, that the greater part of his life as a poet would be lived against the background of conflict and division. He plucked from Shakespeare, on that occasion, a phrase describing the act of writing: "Our poesy is as a gum which oozes from whence tis nourished." And he went on to say that poetry, which is secret and natural, has to make its way "in a world that is public and brutal. Here the explosions literally rattle your windows day and night, lives are shattered blandly or terribly, innocent men have been officially beaten and humiliated in internment camps — destructive elements of all kinds, which are even perhaps deeply exhilarating, are in the air."

For Heaney the poet, the difficulty was not one of confronting that "public and brutal" world which surrounded him, for that would have signalled a descent into rhetoric. It was to confront the quarrels, the differences, the conflicts within himself. It was this private battle he described then. And it is that same battle which we have read in the earthy simplicity, the simple rugged words, the thud of meaning in the clatter of hoofs, the ripple of water, the feel of barley in a coat pocket.

Seamus Heaney always realised that at the very heart of his imagination were two forces that tugged both together and apart. He had, as it were, an English literary father, an Irish literary mother. The feminine force was the ground he stood on; the masculine force was the language he used to describe it. "I speak and write in English, but do not altogether share the preoccupations and perspectives of an Englishman. . . . I live off another hump as well."

He was challenged for this. People thought him not Celtic enough, not Irish enough. And there were good examples behind the criticism, men such as Austin Clarke, who managed to transmute the metrical idiom of Celtic verse while sticking with the language spoken around him by the majority. Heaney had a different agenda. He saw things more simply, more directly, and he saw them from experiences and tensions which were growing for him, while they had been declining for Clarke.

The truth is, Seamus Heaney had been educated in a mixed, not an Irish society. He expresses in one of his essays his admiration for Philip Hobsbaum, who taught him at Queen's University, and who brought, as it were, London to Belfast in order to feed the hungry appetites of his students, Heaney among them. Out of this derived dutiful and invaluable respect for many great English poets. Take Wordsworth, for example, a poet who so often comes

to mind as one reads Heaney. We think less of the Wordsworth of
the lyrics. Heaney reminds us of the deep, wide-ranging, magical
poet of *The Prelude,* who explores the universe in the faint glint of
a star on a frosty night, or measures his youthful vigour in the
sibilant hiss of a skate across the frozen surface of a lake. Heaney
would not have existed in the form in which we have him had he
been educated in the Republic instead of Northern Ireland. And
he recognises and praises this divine accident.

He speaks of the formidable inspirational impact of discover-
ing himself and his roots through the exercise of language upon
experience, and anyone reading his verse becomes swiftly aware
of this delight in discovery. The examples are so many, and so
wonderful. In "The Wife's Tale", in the sudden silence after the
threshing machine has stopped, we are made to hear the crunch of
boots in stubble, and to feel the bread:

> He winked, then watched me as I poured a cup
> And buttered the thick slices that he likes.

And in that same collection, the poem "The Forge", from the first
line of which he took the book's title:

> All I know is a door into the dark.
> Outside, old axles and iron hoops rusting;
> Inside, the hammered anvil's short-pitched ring,
> The unpredictable fantail of sparks
> Or hiss when a new shoe toughens in water.

He took the evolution of his own talent at his own pace. He
never pushed it too hard or too fast, graduating geographically
and emotionally, from Derry to Belfast, from Northern Ireland to
the South, to his Wicklow cottage, to his Dublin home, and increasingly to the platforms and lecture rooms of the world. When that
intruded, his life was already firmly his own, so that he remained
in control, and continued to fulfil a calm and measured destiny
which has led him to this well-deserved international recognition.

He quotes somewhere Patrick Kavanagh saying that "a man dabbles in verses and finds they are his life". It is a wonderful vision of accidental inspiration and its realisation in forms which work, and which will survive.

Seamus Heaney has always been generously accessible, both in his capacities as teacher and critic, but even more so in his personal relationships which have an even-tempered aspect to them, a kindliness which I think Beckett had, and which Jack Yeats certainly had, though perhaps not his brother, Willie.

I share with the English poet Anthony Thwaite the view that Seamus Heaney was perhaps overpraised to begin with, and would add that the Irish predilection for heroes has produced some silliness and lack of balance in dealing with his reputation. Then there was a reaction. Now there is likely to be a flood of literary hysteria. But it is a mark of Heaney's own sound judgement of himself that these evolutionary developments never disturbed him, never unbalanced him, never really affected him at all. Nor will they in the future.

Irish Independent, 6 October 1995

ॐ

II

Seamus Heaney at Sixty

It is almost five years since Seamus Heaney won the Nobel Prize for Literature. In that time he has enriched us with further collections of poetry, further examples of his tact and judgement in the world of literature and literary criticism, and further expressions of his essential warmth and humanity.

He is a kindly and gregarious man. I have never witnessed, nor heard of, cross words or the disparagement of other writers. In the Irish context this is remarkable, even more so in the context of the period through which he has lived his life as a poet. Literature in Ireland is now well emerged from a long era of paucity and difficulty, of limited publishing opportunities, of even more limited funding for the pursuit of the literary life. But for Heaney's generation, the memory of hard times is always there. And this did produce a measure of jealousy and in-fighting, which ironically had its own appeal.

Seamus Heaney's success in side-stepping that derives from an innate generosity of spirit combined with a personal policy of containment. In his life and his art he has followed a carefully plotted and gradualist path through the history of his own cultural territory, mixing sympathies and understanding of contemporary and remote events.

One of his most supportive commentators, Helen Vendler, writes in respect of Heaney's use of the image of ancient victims of ritual sacrifice in the bogs of Ireland that there is "a generalised cultural approval of violence dating back many centuries". If there is, then Heaney side-steps the analogy, and lets the message rest unexplored.

This is both wise and characteristic. In his poetry he places small segments of observation, intuition, feeling, perception, side by side, making up a complex and fragmented philosophy of life. This reflects both his own background, and the age through which he has lived. It has been an age totally different from that experienced by W.B. Yeats's generation, which was formative of the Irish character, or the succeeding generation, which had to cope with despair and setbacks of an impoverished and isolated period in history.

For Heaney, the anguish has been quite different. Close on thirty of the sixty years of his life have embraced the Troubles in his own part of Ireland. Instead of working in the gloom of post-war Dublin, in the poverty of post-war Irish literature generally, he has had to confront the permanent curiosity of the whole world at the phenomenon of Ireland grappling with huge political upheaval. And this in turn has forced him and other artists to embrace in their work the rediscovery of historical and symbolic meaning.

It is a truism that at sixty we begin to develop a new view of ourselves and our relationship to the world in which we operate. It is a time for reassessment. It is, ironically, a time when many people withdraw themselves from circumstances in which the pace is set by others, and establish a more measured movement in their work.

This is both easier and more difficult in the case of a writer of stature who has been rewarded with great prizes and extensive publicity. Heaney is emblematic, whether he likes it or not, of his period and his people. He speaks for a complex set of beliefs and an even more complex set of experiences. And for many years to come, the people of this country will be looking to him for guidance. This will not be in the form of advice, but in the form of a spiritual shape for their lives, a set of expressions and perceptions which nourish and confirm them in the hazards of daily living.

Jonathan Swift would have approved of the line in one of Heaney's poems: "Between my finger and thumb / The squat pen rests; snug as a gun."

Irish Independent, 9 April 1999

18

THE NIGHTMARE OF HISTORY

We want our writers to speak to us now. If art is real, then it should last, not as a memento of the past but as a message for the present. It should reach forward, and become a metaphor for living, and go on re-presenting itself for the new generations which discover it.

Michael Ignatieff was a timely choice for the 1995 Bailey's James Joyce Lecture. Experienced in current affairs, a television commentator and presenter, with interests in politics and social change, he confronted the age-old challenge of literature's relevance, not just to life in the general sense, but to public life and political affairs.

The case for the first kind of relevance is really the case for immortality in literature. This is the meaning of John Millington Synge, that what he wrote, almost a century ago, should have direct value for us, now. This is the meaning of Jonathan Swift. Their voices are not part of history, nor are they lodged in the artistic expression of their own time. They are ours, to reinterpret for the present. And it is the quality of this which divides Synge, for example, from O'Casey, a playwright who has weathered less well.

Synge is among the most modern of all our writers. He liberated himself and his art in his own time with an ease and directness which is breathtaking. Swift did the same, though it was never easy for him. He left us wit and satire; but he also left us a strangely dense mixture of scorn and compassion eminently suited to our own times.

James Joyce made the going, both for himself and for us, more difficult. He lodged himself in the past, reaching out to posterity more through his language than through his ideas. He chose frozen moments, and then brought them back to life in spectral radiance, which dazzles us through words rather than through perceptions. The inspiration is musical and linguistic, to a point at times when tedium enters in.

His history was past history in his own time, and his exile fixed it even more firmly in the past. He dug around in the entrails of Time. He thumbed the pages of newspapers, often at one remove, seeking gossip, detail, and a curiously exact but suspect verisimilitude. He never really knew twentieth-century Ireland, except at second-hand. He understood it from afar. But he located himself, in every possible way, within a timewarp which is Proustian. His own life, his wife, his remembered friends, his father, his teachers, became symbols for the wider storm cloud of history, which in *Ulysses* he described as "the nightmare from which we are trying to wake".

Michael Ignatieff in his lecture took this as a text, and used it in order to rescue us from the past. It was a brave attempt. And it was entertaining to be reminded of the more telling moments in Stephen Dedalus's lesson to his pupils about the stranglehold with which history stifles hope. Yet is it true? Is it a nightmare? Do we feel clammy, enclosed, trapped, when we think of history? Is it something from which to be liberated?

Or is it ourselves? Ignatieff, whose writing and broadcasting straddles fiction and current affairs, argues in favour of James Joyce as an exemplar for those entrapped by history. Until 1993 he saw the inhabitants of this island in that light, needing rescue as the Bosnians need it. And he was able to create relationships between Ireland's conflict and ethnic strife around the world, in Canada, Kurdistan, Ukraine, Yugoslavia.

History is race, history is ethnic difference, history is vengeance and confrontation. Then came the Peace Process. "How wrong I was," Ignatieff claimed, in his lecture. "The post-1989 period offers extraordinary examples of peoples managing to escape the compulsion to repeat their history."

To make Joyce part of this modern world-shift in attitudes is tempting. It conforms to the idea that a writer can speak to the present from the past in which he delivered his words and images. It further modernises him. And it is offered in order to give to Joyce the kind of eternal appeal that Synge has; or Swift.

Yet it needs more than the Stephen Dedalus episode from the beginning of *Ulysses*. It is a far better use for the writer than the tourist purposes to which he, above all other Irish artists of any kind, has been so seriously subjected. In this context, Joyce is a set of tawdry images, of the clip-clop of the cabby's horse, the roguish moustache of Boylan, the bowler hat of Bloom, and the lean, youthful longings of Stephen. It has become the Bloomsday diet of gizzards, kidney and stout, presided over by a riff-raff of publicity-seekers and self-promoters.

He deserves better by far. But he did ask for this parody. Our celebration of him conforms to the thread of pastiche, the multiplicity of voices, and the sense of a fixed period. Joyce saw history with the jaundiced eyes of his youthful alter ego, Dedalus, when he observed that Ireland was under the twin masters of the Imperial British State and the Roman Catholic Church. The Englishman to whom he addressed this view was Haines, never a very sympathetic character, who then observed that an Irishman would have to think like that. "We feel in England that we have treated you rather unfairly. It seems history is to blame."

Ignatieff offers an uncertain approval of this view. Yet, almost a century later, with the Imperial British State a thing of the past, and the Roman Catholic Church losing power and respect by the minute, the nightmare of history is there. It has become one in which Haines would certainly say that it is the Irish who have treated the English unfairly for the past eighty or so years, and not the other way around. The maintenance of history, as a clammy, enclosed, trapped atmosphere is supremely an Irish disposition, not an English one. The Irish trade in the past; the English deal with the present. And history is no longer to blame. That might make a lecture for 1996.

Written for Bloomsday and published in the *Irish Independent*, 17 June 1995

19

"IT SEEMS HISTORY IS TO BLAME"

This lecture came about through a modest *jeu d'esprit*, an attempt to defend the character and role of Haines in the opening chapter of *Ulysses*. It was intended as a provocation, no more. And it was rooted in the largely unexpressed idea that Joyce in fact owed much more to England than to Ireland, in material terms, and also in terms of the recognition he received as an artist.

No one, of course, can take from Joyce the elemental structure for all his books, the deep and abiding sense of Dublin which pervades each of them, and runs on, in a sequential presentation of his hero's life, in different degrees autobiographical, as almost all fiction, in one sense or another, must finally be. But that process was carried out on foreign soil. Joyce became an expatriate long before Ireland became independent. He pursued a life which had a dual focus: Dublin gave him birth and experience, London gave him financial security. It did so by providing him with his crucial patron, Harriet Weaver. London also offered him the critical framework of support and judgement so vital for his evolution, and honoured him with a Civil List pension, with biographers and commentators, and with a reading public. It gave him literature and language. Whether it is William Blake's buttocks, self-identification in *Hamlet*, or the image of Shakespeare's wife, Anne, putting pennies on the dead bard's eyes, the burden of past literature for Joyce is the literature largely known to the world as English.

I made a joke about Haines last summer. On further study, the joke is on me, and with me. Joyce liked the English. He couldn't stand them, but he liked them. His greatest friend, in his life, was an Englishwoman, Harriet Shaw Weaver. Searchingly, Joyce asked her is she had not a little Irish blood. "I am afraid I am hopelessly English," she said. And continued to give him huge sums of money, which he spent in a prodigal, irresponsible and selfish way.

It is not my purpose to engage in an examination of Harriet Shaw Weaver, and her place in Joyce's life. Nor is it within the scope of this lecture to explore other aspects of Joyce's debt to England. One enjoys his receipt, for example, of a Civil List pension, his solid treatment by English critics, the support he got from the literary establishment, the fact that he was published, read, understood and discussed. And Dublin? I think the right words are those that Richard Ellmann applied, as you will hear, to the central figure in this paper. Dublin, in its view of Joyce, throughout the greater part of his lifetime, was neurotically insufferable.

Dublin gave him a hard time. Ireland did, as a whole. Virtually throughout his lifetime he was treated by the majority of Irish men and women as somehow "disgraceful". It is not my purpose to excoriate the Irish for what they failed to do, in the way of help for James Joyce, or what they did in such abundance in making his life difficult, in humiliating his work, his morals, his ideas and his talent. Nor is it my purpose to over-praise my countrymen for the calm, balanced judgements they made about James Joyce, and for the discrimination, favourable and unfavourable, in their early criticisms of his work. The record I set before you is of a different order, and in the first place is personal.

I have always had a sneaking regard for poor old Haines, the third character to make an appearance in James Joyce's *Ulysses*. He is, briefly, an inhabitant of the Martello Tower in Sandycove. He doesn't have the gross intrusiveness of Buck Mulligan, nor that man's vulgarity, his boldness, his badness. He doesn't have the deviousness of Dedalus, the inner secrets of that interior monologue, the private divagations in the territories of death and guilt. He is just polite, logical, intelligent. He's a good, well-constructed, well-realised Englishman.

He worries about their breakfast. He ushers in the milk lady. He cooks the rashers. He is apologetic because he woke up both Mulligan and Dedalus the night before, coming home late. He seems prudent with his money, and, until Mulligan is told by Dedalus that today is pay day, it is the thought of the medical student that Haines might well be touched for a quid, even a guinea. Greedy, Mulligan, greedy! The extra shilling, which on top of the pound turned it into a guinea, would, in those days, have bought six pints of porter.

Haines thinks that Mulligan's tea is rather strong. "By Jove, it is tea." And, yes, we have to get through that bit about not making water in the same teapot, a further example of Buck Mulligan's awful vulgarity. "I'm giving you two lumps each," Haines tells the other two, in a classic minor example of the obviousness of the English. They are so predictable. One knows what they will say before they say it. And one thinks one knows what they mean. How mistaken this is. No one ever quite knows what an Englishman means by what he says. "I'm giving you two lumps each" carries with it something of the threat of poison.

Yet despite this and other banalities, Haines is revealed to us as a writer, and a scholar, sensitive about Irish life and letters, proud of the strange route he is in the process of taking through Dublin, indeed Irish, cultural life. When he speaks, he is misunderstood by the milk lady. She doesn't speak Irish. He does, of course. Even so, he manages to appear ridiculous. But he pops his hat on his head, ties a scarf round his neck, threatens to make a collection of Stephen's sayings, and at all material points is made to appear the most foolish of the three of them.

Yet again, his heart is warm and generous. For all the ribbing, Stephen sees that there is kindly feeling in the man. But Haines is cautious; unlike the bold Buck Mulligan, whose stomach is fashioned like that of a gannet, Haines doesn't swim immediately after breakfast, for fear he might get into trouble in the water. He says: "We feel in England that we have treated you rather unfairly." And he even goes on to say: "It seems history is to blame."

You all know the detail, of Haines, in that first chapter of *Ulysses*. Indeed, many readers of Joyce — possibly nine out of ten — see Haines only in his first presentation, since they start out on the book with good intentions which are not always fulfilled. And even among those who have examined the issue in the greatest detail, not excluding Richard Ellmann, Joyce's biographer, there is a shortage of sympathy and a shortage of fact. Where we have a vast literature on Oliver St John Gogarty, *alias* Buck Mulligan, and his part in the life and work of the artist, we have virtually nothing on Haines. And in part what I give you now is a remedy for that imbalance. I believe that almost every serious commentator about this man has got him and his purpose in the book hopelessly wrong. First, however, let us see it from Haines's point of view.

In Chapter One of *Ulysses*, James Joyce presents, through Haines, an important range of subjects which will be key in the whole story of the book. Buck Mulligan is roaring and confronting, raging about everyone and everything. Stephen is cogitating the nature of his own life, his love for his mother, his feelings for his father, and his relationship with Ireland. Meanwhile, this "ponderous Saxon", "bursting with money and indigestion", is actually the mainspring of the story. And in the course of this vital, key chapter in the book, it is Haines who lays before us several of the most critical, most pivotal, most essential arguments of the book.

When I first addressed the actual performance or contribution of Haines in Chapter One, I had the distinct impression that he was like the figure of Jean Santeuil, Proust's early fictional hero. Santeuil is a prototype, living through many of the episodes which were later to be featured in *À la Recherche du Temps Perdu*. They were at one remove from the novel which Proust was preparing to write. In certain ways, I argued originally, Haines offers up the ingredients of *Ulysses*, in summary form, in that chapter, and then, his purpose fulfilled, decamps, never properly to be seen again.

Haines has eighteen separate episodes where he is the "voice" or motivator of a passage. There are eighteen chapters in the book. Could we be looking at some relationship between each of those eighteen focuses in the part he plays in the first chapter, and the eighteen actual chapters in the work?

Well, the answer is no. But the question began to develop a life of its own about Haines and what he really stands for. And I will now develop that life.

The first mentions of Haines come before he appears in the story at all. He is the subject of discussion between Buck Mulligan and Stephen Dedalus at the end of the first, introductory phase to the book. We have had the *Introibo ad altare Dei*, and the presentation, by Mulligan, both of himself and Dedalus. Then their voices sink, and Stephen asks quietly, "How long is Haines going to stay in this tower?" In that one sentence we have, in metaphor, a central theme of the book: in other words, How long are the English [Haines is their representative] going to stay in Ireland [our home, the Tower, the place where we live]? It is one of the central themes in all Joyce's writing. It is present in *A Portrait*. It is part of the climax to that novel. It is a principal reason Dedalus leaves Ireland. It is the reason Joyce writes *Ulysses*. In *Ulysses* itself it is the theme for much of the action. An important example would be the Wandering Rocks episode, which is loosely strung together by the movement of the Lord Lieutenant and Lady Dudley from the Vice-Regal Lodge in the Phoenix Park to the Mirus Bazaar, where money will be raised for Mercer's Hospital.

There is no implication, in Stephen's question, of Haines being "neurotically insufferable". But in Buck Mulligan's answer to it, there is every sense possible of outrage and dismissal:

> —God, isn't he dreadful? A ponderous Saxon. He thinks you're not a gentleman. God, these bloody English! Bursting with money and indigestion. Because he comes from Oxford.

> You know, Dedalus, you have the real Oxford manner. He
> can't make you out.

To this first clear presentation of the age-old antagonism and rivalry between the English and the Irish are now added other important themes. One is that of the black panther, which remains significant right through *Ulysses*. Another is the concept, again coming from Mulligan and to be repeated later in dramatic terms, that Haines is mad; "a woful lunatic", is the phrase used.

The second presentation of Haines — he has still not appeared on stage, as it were — concerns another source of envy, that of money. And again the bad-mouthing comes entirely from Buck Mulligan. "He's stinking with money and thinks you're not a gentleman." Moreover, all this money has been made "by selling jalap to Zulus or some bloody swindle or other". There are no grounds for this allegation about Haines's wealth. But Mulligan has touched on a critical theme — shortage of cash — which is a *leitmotif* in Joyce, within his fiction and outside it. Meanness, the ability to buy a drink, the closed fist, these are thematically Irish, and Dublin, and Haines is labelled as essentially free of them. Not bad for Haines, you might think. But think again.

We may pause and ask what Joyce has done here. In terms of fiction he has demonised Haines through Buck Mulligan. The burden of turning this somewhat obvious Englishman into a threat, even a sinister figure, who has nightmares and looses off a gun at an imaginary black panther in the middle of the night, is placed firmly on Mulligan's shoulders. And Mulligan is demeaned by it, possibly as Joyce intended. Quite clearly, Richard Ellmann translates this fiction into reality, missing the point of Mulligan being the target, and inventing the idea of Haines being "neurotically insufferable" on the basis of Mulligan's evidence, of which there is very little. Yet if we consider reality, the originals for these two characters, Mulligan and Haines, lived together quite happily in the Tower, much longer without the real source for Stephen, in other words James Joyce, than with him.

Take three real people, place them together for a few nights in a Martello Tower. And if one of them is a writer, and uses the experience as brilliantly as Joyce does, the results will inevitably be a distortion of the real event. If all three of them are writers, as in this case they were, how much more complicated will the story become, as we shall see, both as story and as biography.

Let us pass on to the third episode. Haines makes his first appearance off-stage. He calls out: "Are you up there, Mulligan?" And what does Mulligan say to Stephen? "The Sassenach wants his morning rashers." Food again. Indigestion. But not just food again. Food is an important event, or theme, in the book, a defining commodity of Jew and Gentile. This is in contrast, if you like, with Leopold Bloom's own breakfast. This is to feature shortly in the novel, and is to be drawn from a rich repertory of dishes loved by the wandering Jew — "thick giblet soup, nutty gizzards, a stuffed roast heart, liverslices fried with crustcrumbs, fried hencods' roes. Most of all he liked grilled mutton kidneys which gave to his palate a fine tang of faintly scented urine" — but though the summary is of the inner organs of beasts and fowls, there is no mention of the pig. Rashers are not part of Bloom's orthodox kosher diet.

Mulligan joins Haines. Stephen is left up on the parapet of the Tower. The call is now for him to come down. "Haines is apologising for waking us last night," says Mulligan.

Both here and later, Haines is invoking images from *Hamlet*, another of the great themes of *Ulysses*, and important for this first chapter, the main symbol of which is the "heir". All three men, for want of contradiction, are first-born sons. They are the inheritors of their father's wealth, their mother's love. And the use of the battlements of the Tower remind us of the opening scene of *Hamlet*, as do the references to the black panther, and bad dreams. What is the first line in *Hamlet*? It is a line seeking identity. "Who's there?" asks Horatio. And we take the whole of the play finding out the answer.

We pass to the fifth episode. Haines is at last on stage. The tall Englishman rises from his hammock and opens the door. Light and bright air enter. And Haines stands in the doorway. Mulligan indulges in gross vulgarity about the candle, and we extend the exploration of food and drink to milk and honey.

Sixth point: "I'm giving you two lumps each. But I say, Mulligan, you do make strong tea, don't you."

Seventh point is Mulligan talking about prepuces.

Eighth point: Haines speaking Irish. This is authentic, and a close reference to this remarkable Englishman's capacity to out-learn his Irish friends in command of their "native" language, which neither Dedalus nor Mulligan possess in the way Haines does. And of course the lady bringing the milk to the Tower thinks he is speaking French.

Even this is turned sour by Mulligan, who proclaims that "He's English, and he thinks we ought to speak Irish in Ireland."

Ninth point is in Haines's favour: he seeks to pay the lady bringing them milk. "We had better pay her, Mulligan, hadn't we?" Stephen studiously busies himself with filling out their three cups and says nothing. "Pay and look pleasant," Haines tells Mulligan. And Mulligan manages to pay the main part of her modest bill, twopence short of the total.

Tenth point offers another direction in the story, where Haines indicates the way towards the National Library. Ponderously, "I have to visit your national library today." And then, knotting easily a loose scarf around the collar of his tennis shirt, he adds: "I intend to make a collection of your sayings if you will let me." Then he says: "That one about the cracked lookingglass of a servant being the symbol of Irish art is deuced good." Stephen's interest is in whether or not this will make him any money. Our view, I suggest, of these three interjections is the predictable one: that they endorse the image of the "fearful Sassanach". Everything that Buck Mulligan has said, or implied, about Haines is fulfilled out of his own mouth. Yet it is more subtle than that. Joyce the writer is making us believe in Haines, not in order for us to hate him, but in order for him to be carried into the story, which requires that we believe in Buck Mulligan and Stephen as well. And we do.

The eleventh point is Haines taking the initiative again. It is he who invites them: "Are you coming, you fellows?" And so they leave.

The twelfth exchange — if my analogy between Haines and the Tower and the British and Ireland is accepted — is then ironic. Haines, almost with distaste, turns to look at the Tower and asks Mulligan and Dedalus if they pay rent. When they agree that this is the case, and tell him it is paid to the Secretary of War, Haines comments, laconically, "Rather bleak in wintertime, I should say. Martello you call it?" I think Haines would almost certainly have known more about Martello Towers than either Buck Mulligan or Stephen. Also, he, by whom I now mean the original, and not the fictional figure, and Gogarty, were the real tenants; Joyce was a brief visitor, who left shortly after the events told of in the first chapter. But Joyce turns it all around, so that the "Irish" — himself and Gogarty — are represented as the true tenants, and Haines as their temporary guest, going slightly mad, thus reinforcing the idea of an analogy with nations.

The next, the thirteenth exchange, which follows immediately after the thoughts about the Tower, and also reinforces the second idea, that the Martello Tower has some association with *Hamlet*, and the spirited opening of that play, lies in a single question: "What is your idea of *Hamlet*?"

At one and the same time, the inimitable Haines manages to raise a central theme in *Ulysses*, and also to botch it. And once again it is the mocking Buck Mulligan who pours scorn on the idea of being able to discuss *Hamlet* so early in the morning, just after breakfast, and before the day has properly begun. Nevertheless, they respond; and Mulligan gives to Haines a brief summary of Stephen's supposed theory of *Hamlet*: "He proves by algebra that Hamlet's grandson is Shakespeare's grandfather and that he himself is the ghost of his own father." Quite straight-faced, Haines points at Stephen: "What? He himself?"

It is at that point that Joyce introduces a new note in the story, and it comes from Stephen — an unexpected streak of kindness towards Haines. Resisting Mulligan's irrepressible desire to tease, Stephen says, "We're always tired in the morning. And it is rather long to tell." In a subtle way, Joyce is beginning an important shift in emphasis. So far, through the story, the apparently close companions have been Dedalus and Mulligan; now this alters, and it is Stephen and Haines who develop a closeness, while Mulligan capers down towards the Forty Foot, to have a bathe. Haines almost wrecks this, presumably by looking up towards Dalkey quarry, since there are no cliffs beside the Tower, and seeing a likeness to Elsinore.

We have reached the fourteenth exchange. It leads to yet another crucial theme in the book, or possibly two, both of them introduced by Haines. The first is the father–son relationship: "The Son trying to be atoned with the Father"; the second, the theme of faith. Haines suggests blasphemy in Mulligan's comments, and in particular his reference to "Joseph the Joiner". "We oughtn't to laugh, I suppose. He's rather blasphemous. I'm not a believer myself, that is to say. Still his gaiety takes the harm out of it somehow, doesn't it?"

Stephen, of course, has heard this and related blasphemy "three times a day after meals" from Mulligan, and is unmoved. But Haines then conducts a catechism, and not only does it embrace a key theme in *Ulysses*; it actually invokes for us all over again the theme of *A Portrait of the Artist as a Young Man*, and the liberation of its hero from the very thing which Haines is asking. "You're not a believer, are you? I mean, a believer in the narrow sense of the word. Creation from nothing and miracles and a personal God." "There's only one sense of the word," Stephen replies. And Haines says: "Either you believe or you don't, isn't it? Personally I couldn't stomach that idea of a personal God. You don't stand for that, I suppose?" And Stephen grandly concludes this profound and essential exchange: "You behold in me a horrible example of free thought."

Haines has by no means elicited from Stephen the full range and shape of his personality. But we have made important advances: we have come closer, and are now approaching major characteristics in Stephen Dedalus. There now follows, in the fifteenth exchange involving Haines, Stephen's identification of two burdens which Stephen seeks to set down. "I am," he says, "the servant of two masters, an English and an Italian." The first is the British Empire; the second the Holy Roman Catholic and Apostolic Church. Have we come here to the heart of Stephen? I was struck by what Father Bruce Bradley had to say to us, in his own lecture in the series, on the question of the survival of Joyce's faith. We want to know for how long, and in what ways. I was also struck by Ken Monaghan, in his brief addendum to that lecture and then again in his own lecture, also on the question of Joyce's faith, and whether or not, on his deathbed, Joyce accepted the last rites. Both these men, and many other commentators, have failed to answer this question, though it has not shortened the range of their examination. How strange then that the other "master" to whom Joyce refers, the British Empire, is given so little attention. How he felt about it, and about its inhabitants, has inspired remarkably little critical literature.

I think in the same comment, provoked by Haines, responded to by Haines, brings us also to the heart of the Englishman. He says to Stephen: "I can quite understand that. An Irishman must think like that, I daresay. We feel in England that we have treated you rather unfairly. It seems history is to blame." Do we hate those we have wronged? Hardly, if Haines is an example to go by. Yet the exchange, as I hope to show in due course, brings Haines and Stephen close together in what I might describe as mirror-dance — remember the cracked lookingglass? — a mirror-dance in which each person is contemplating the territory occupied by the other. Haines has left England, and come to Ireland; Stephen will leave Ireland and go to Europe.

Sixteenth exchange, and we have another profound and central theme of the book, given, it must be said, by Haines at his most awkward: "Of course I'm a Britisher and I feel as one. I don't want to see my country fall into the hands of German jews either. That's our national problem, I'm afraid, just now." Bloom, of course, has not yet made his entry. But for the book on which we are embarking, this is quite an attitude to stomach. It is now generally offered — and I think mistakenly — as evidence of anti-semitism in Haines.

The final two episodes, the seventeenth and eighteenth, are trifling. As Buck Mulligan prepares to plunge into the sea, Haines, sitting smoking on a rock, makes reference to the risk of swimming too soon after breakfast — the old British indigestion rearing its head.

And the final episode? Mulligan dives and Haines turns away. "We'll see you again," he says.

There you have it. Haines has invoked, or provoked, touched on, examined, hinted at, a large number of the key themes in *Ulysses*, and has done so in terms which Joyce makes subtle and amusing. Ostensibly, he has served a purpose. It is questionable whether Joyce needs him any more; or at least so I thought, writing my short piece on the subject, last summer. Irreverently, I speculated on the possibility that the poor fellow would disappear, after the indignities heaped on him, principally by Mulligan. One might expect him to escape out of the pages of *Ulysses* for ever. If Joyce had tried putting me in his book, that would have been the way I'd have felt. Get out of it. At the first opportunity. Have nothing whatsoever to do with it. And isn't it a puzzle anyway, having Haines there? What purpose does he serve? Joyce surely has no place for him after those fatuous early remarks.

Unfortunately though, Haines is there as a character, and characters in fiction are not easily killed off once they have established themselves. Haines has rights in *Ulysses*. He occupies both a personal and a symbolic role. And Joyce certainly has a place for him later in the story. And he does keep him. Before coming to that, however, I want to identify Haines and clothe him, as literary history and critical analysis have clothed Buck Mulligan.

Haines was modelled on Samuel Chenevix Trench (1881–1909). The negative view of Trench, *alias* Haines, may be traced in biographical terms directly to Richard Ellmann, who introduces him as "insufferable" in his biography of the writer. In the final revised edition of his Life of James Joyce, this is either modified or developed — depending on the reader's point of view — to "neurotically insufferable". This is a surmise, on both occasions, and on both counts.

There is some justification for using the term neurotic about Trench, since he did commit suicide five years after the Sandycove episode; but it is highly tenuous. We do not know the details. Suicide is not the product of neurosis. But beyond that, the prejudice against him seems to have derived from a jaundiced reading of James Joyce's *Ulysses*, not from any knowledge about Trench. Indeed, Ellmann's ignorance about Trench is only adequately concealed by the tiny amount of attention he gives to him in the course of his biography. What Ellmann states as fact is either wrong or unsustainable. The same may be said for Ulick O'Connor, who, in his biography of Gogarty, gets Trench's parentage wrong, by a generation. As I have indicated, Ellmann has no reason for saying that Trench was insufferable. Even in the guise of Haines he is more than tolerated, Stephen in particular responding in a way that is more mannerly than Buck Mulligan's rudeness.

On the question of his name, Ellmann tells us that Trench changed it from Samuel to Diarmuid, or Dermot (he uses both versions). Trench did not *change* his name at all. What he did was to add the name Dermot by deed poll to his other names, keeping the name Samuel, and the further names he had, Richard and Chenevix. He did this quite publicly, notice of it appearing on the front page of *The Irish Times* for 15 March 1905, a detail unchecked by biographers, and first published in a wonderful scholarly account of Samuel Chenevix Trench by his third cousin once removed, Chalmers, or Terry Trench, whose friendship and scholarship I greatly value, and whose wife was a niece of William Orpen, the portrait painter.

Incidentally, Terry Trench's father was W.F. Trench, Professor H.O. White's predecessor as Professor of English at Trinity College, and before that Professor of English in the Queen's College, Galway. Here there was a more direct connection, and one worth pursuing by some research scholar, but at present beyond my time and capacity. As an examiner for the Royal University of Ireland, W.F. Trench was one of Joyce's examiners in 1902, and is named at the head of the second paper for the B.A. degree examination that year. The Galway connection is not directly relevant, but of course Joyce had two connections of his own, through his family, and through Nora Barnacle's.

More, now, about the Trench family, before giving further consideration to the man whom Joyce, in Ellmann's rather coy phrase, "allowed [to be] his principal model for Haines". The man who could be described as "the father of all the Chenevix Trenches" though not of all the Trenches, was Richard Chenevix Trench (1807–86), author, scholar, poet, philologist, and Archbishop of Dublin from 1864 to 1884. Another of his descendants, Charles Chenevix Trench, when I told him my mission, said that this was difficult. That the Archbishop had no less than fourteen children, each of whom had eight children. And he advised me to consult another member of the Trench family. So I did, and so it turned out. There are a lot of Trenches. But the count was wrong. Of the Archbishop's children, of whom indeed there were fourteen, seven had no children, and only one son had the eight so broadly imagined.

Joyce had every reason to be interested in "the father of all the Chenevix Trenches". Richard Chenevix Trench was the son of

Melesina Trench (1768–1827), whose maiden name was Chenevix (pronounced with the ending soft and silent). She was a poet, and no doubt from her there derived a good deal of the literary talent, including that of Samuel, later to be also Dermot, the model for Haines. The Chenevix family was of Huguenot extraction. Melesina's grandfather was bishop, first of Killaloe, then of Waterford and Lismore. This grandfather predeceased his son, her father, and was responsible for Melesina's upbringing, at least in her early childhood. And it may be that it was her brother, also Richard Chenevix, who was both a chemist and a writer of plays and poetry, and who lived in Paris; but no records, not even those which exist in Melesina's book of selected memoirs, letters and other papers, and called *The Remains of Mrs Trench*, confirm this relationship. The book, incidentally, was edited by her son, the Dean of Westminster, later to become Archbishop of Dublin. To him we shall shortly turn.

Samuel's father was Melesina's grandson, one of the fourteen children of the archbishop, and was called Frederick Chenevix Trench (1837–94). He had another son in addition to Samuel, Julius, and three daughters. But before coming to him, let me attempt to justify my argument that the Archbishop would have been of more than passing interest to James Joyce; but this time in his own right. One is tempted to spell the word "w-r-i-t-e", since Archbishop Trench, long before he became the leading Irish cleric of his day, was deeply, even profoundly involved with words, language, philology, linguistics. Trench was the initial inspiration for the New English Dictionary. He was associated with the Philological Society, one of whose beliefs was that the universal dissemination of the English language would have a two-fold purpose: the extension of literature, and the healing of the 300-year split between Rome and Canterbury. Trench was forcefully committed to Church reorganisation, in the sense of bringing about reconciliation with Rome, but strenuously opposed to Gladstone's campaign for the disestablishment of the Irish Church. When

Gladstone accomplished this, Trench worked with the new set of dispensations, as one would expect. But he saw the road to reconciliation differently, and may well have been right.

However, it was as a philologist that he is likely to have made an impact on Joyce, and this is not idle speculation. Before and after Joyce's birth, Trench's name was almost a household word among anyone interested in the English language. He lectured students on "Language as an Instrument of Knowledge", wrote his first book, *On the Study of Words*, published in 1851, and followed it with *English Past and Present*, which was published in 1855. The books were hugely popular; the first went into nineteen editions by 1886, the second book was in its fourteenth edition in 1889. Thus, when Joyce was born in 1882, Trench, on the subject of words, was a household name and remained so for Joyce's childhood and youth, arguably until Joyce set out for Europe. When he was two years old, in 1884, the first instalment of the New English Dictionary, the first fascicle, appeared. Its continued evolution, under various editors, was to span almost the whole of Joyce's life. We have no record of his knowledge of it, no certainty that it was ever part of his library, and no certainty either than Trench's books were known to Joyce. Yet, as a matter of opinion, I think it inconceivable, working backwards from Joyce's knowledge of words, that any other dictionary would have come near rivalling the New English Dictionary as a fundamental and regularly employed source for the essential knowledge about words which shines out of almost everything Joyce wrote.

The Trench books were seen as promoting language study as a source of, or a route towards, religious knowledge. And the popularising of the subject was in a sense a preamble to the preparation of the New English Dictionary. Trench addressed the Philological Society in two papers entitled "On Some Deficiencies in our English Dictionaries", and these were later described as "if not a lexicographical Bill of Rights, it was at least a manifesto for dictionary-makers". In due course, Trench relinquished to Herbert

Coleridge his leading role in work leading towards the Dictionary. But his impact was enormous, and is so close to so much that
we subsequently find in Joyce's interest in, and use of, the language, as to be uncanny.

At the risk of delaying my persistent and dedicated progress
towards the rescue of this maligned Englishman Haines, I will
give you the central thesis upon which Trench approached the
idea of a dictionary. He broke down into seven the essential cate-
gories required in a dictionary: obsolete words, word "families",
first uses of words, alternative uses, synonyms, the literary "log-
ging" of usage, date and etymology (formation, derivation), and
the exclusion of "non-standard" English. Trench saw dictionaries
as inventories of the language, and he saw words as neutral, neither "good" nor "bad". The dictionary-maker is a historian, not a
critic. He would not have been in favour of Krapp picking on
"spool" . . . sp-o-o-l! Nor would he have been in favour of any ex-
clusions, on moral or other grounds. He was no Bowdler. A man,
you might say, after Joyce's heart when it was neither profitable
nor judicious so to be.

He perhaps comes closest to Joyce when he writes:

> For myself I will only say that I cannot understand how any
> writer with the smallest confidence in himself, the least meas-
> ure of vigour and vitality which would justify himself in ad-
> dressing his countrymen in written or spoken discourse at all,
> should consent in this matter to let one self-made dictator, or
> forty [he means Samuel Johnson or the Académie Française]
> determine for him what words he should use and what he
> should forebear from using.

Trench was a liberal; he had a broadly catholic disposition, and no
words were to be excluded on any grounds, least of all moralistic
niceties. It was all for him, not a selection, as with Dr Johnson, and
not on the basis of authoritarian discrimination, as with the
Académie.

It is a pleasure to be able to quote the following, from a letter sent to me by one of the Trenches:

> The single most valued item on my bookshelves [writes Terry Trench] is the Archbishop's (if I may so call it) New English Dictionary, subscribed to by my grandfather (his first cousin once removed) in 1899, by which time the first 3 vols. had appeared. My father [this was W.F. Trench, professor of English in Trinity College] must have taken it over in the 1920s, I suppose, until it was completed in 1933, and I was happy to continue the tradition with the four supplementary volumes in 1972–86.

I often wonder, as they made their night-flits from lodging to lodging, did the Joyce family scramble to load up those three volumes as well as the other works on language by Archbishop Trench? Was the New English Dictionary the source for James Joyce's ever-deepening investigation into the Milky Way of words?

Now we skip a generation, as far as language is concerned. Frederick Chenevix Trench, father of the incumbent of the Sandycove Tower, was a soldier, and had a not inconsiderable military talent. Almost all the recorded Trenches wrote; even this military man published several studies of warfare, and his son, the model for Haines, wrote a pamphlet, *What is the Use of Reviving Irish?*

At the time of the birth of Samuel Chenevix Trench — "Samuel" is the chosen name — the father was serving as military attaché in the imperial city of St Petersburg. He was then a colonel in the 20th Huzzars. He retired with the rank of Major General six years later, and was made a Companion of the Order of St Michael and St George. There is some discrepancy about his progeny, between the Dictionary of National Biography and the Trench family records, but it seems he had two sons and three daughters. Neither of the sons married, and Samuel committed suicide at the age of twenty-seven. His father also committed suicide, a fact recorded in early editions of the Dictionary of National Biography, but later suppressed, with the detail changed to "died" (August 1894).

At the time of this tragedy, Samuel was twelve years old. It is difficult to imagine the effect of such a death on a boy of that age. Perhaps in the event were sown the seeds of his own early death. It does not excite either pity or terror in Ellmann. All he has to say is that "Five years later Trench was to blow his brains out, perhaps with the very weapon with which he and Gogarty had so nearly blown out Joyce's." Once again, a misconstruction of the facts, and an unsympathetic one at that.

Richard Samuel Chenevix Trench, to give his full name before the addition of Dermot, went to Eton and then to Balliol. He was a year older than Joyce, three years younger than Gogarty. It was at Oxford that he met Gogarty, at meetings of the Oxford Gaelic Society, and they became friends. I suspect that they were friends in the genuine sense, liking each other's company, respecting each other, and pursuing enthusiasms together. In other words, not in the least like the characters presented by Joyce in Chapter One of *Ulysses*. All later interpretations have to be taken with a great deal of suspicion, since any incorporation in Joyce's work or life, and indeed any involvement with Gogarty, led inevitably to later distortions. And we do have to be careful about that. But Gogarty learned the little Irish he had in Trench's company. And clearly liked him enough to share the Sandycove Tower with him for a number of weeks, indeed for far longer than he shared it with Joyce.

Richard Samuel Chenevix Trench was genuine in his love of the Irish language, and, being English, thorough in realising and perfecting it. It would be wrong to assume from the title of his pamphlet, *What is the Use of Reviving Irish?*, that Trench was unsympathetic towards the language. He asks the question both in a mood of inquiry and of irony. He was a supporter of the language, and of the Gaelic League. He believed in the collective inspiration of language and culture, and in it giving to Ireland independent self-confidence. As well as writing the pamphlet, he wrote letters to the *Freeman's Journal* taking issue with the antagonisms towards Irish of the Provost of Trinity College, Dr Traill.

Gogarty sneered at much of this, as is evident both within *Ulysses* and outside it. W.F. Trench, a cousin, and then professor in Galway, as has already been explained, wrote to Samuel while he was at Oxford, sharing enthusiastically, we may infer (since the letter is lost), his love of Irish. And Samuel replied to him with details of an Aran Island holiday. (This is only four years after Synge's first visit, therefore placing Chenevix Trench in the vanguard of those who took practical action about Irish culture and language.)

He writes:

> Every Irishman in my opinion should speak his own language & I follow with the greatest interest the splendid attempt which is being made by the Gaelic League to rectify the saddest mistake Ireland ever made, the throwing away of her native civilisation. . . . It is very interesting to find someone of my own name who shares, as I infer from your letter, my enthusiasm for Irish.

(Such was this enthusiasm, in fact, that when Chenevix Trench adopted the additional name, Dermot, he did so using the English form of the name, well knowing, as a Gaelic scholar, that, in Irish, a different form, "Diarmuid", would be used. It is an example of the ponderous, correct, Anglo-Saxon mind.)

Gogarty invited Chenevix Trench to the Sandycove Tower. He arrived there on 9 or 10 September 1904. He stayed until mid-October. Joyce stayed from 9 September to 14 or 15 September. It appears that Gogarty got rid of Joyce, for reasons not known, and then subsequently sought to spread about the idea that it was Chenevix Trench's eccentric behaviour that had driven Joyce out. This places in jeopardy any full reliance on Gogarty's recollections, including his statement that "He upset Joyce literally and metaphorically." And Gogarty's claim that "All went well for some weeks, for we were using the Tower only to sleep in, except on weekends" is clearly wrong in respect of Joyce, though not of Chenevix Trench. Others who knew Trench well at this time were C.P. Curran and Padraic Colum. Curran was emphatic in saying

that Trench was *not* Haines nor the model for him, either in part
or in whole. Colum accepted that he was, but wanted a more
sympathetic portrait, "to distinguish him from the Haines of *Ulysses*". Colum's tribute, as quoted by Terry Trench in the *James Joyce
Quarterly* article, is generous as to his character, describing this
"engaging young man" as "sympathetic and cultivated". "As I
knew him and as my friends of the time knew him, he was help-
ful, disinterested, visionary."

The power of fiction is such that it can readily and easily dis-
tort fact, and this must be borne in mind in respect of the analysis
above, of the events in Chapter One, and in what now follows.
The first chapter of *Ulysses* appears to make Haines the outsider.
Buck Mulligan and Stephen Dedalus are connivers in his distress
and isolation. Mulligan is portrayed as the lead figure, whereas
Dedalus plays the more ambivalent, more conciliatory, role. What
were the facts?

Well, for a start, it was James Joyce who departed, as I have already made clear; Trench who stayed. Joyce was replaced by
James Starkey (alias "Seumas O'Sullivan"), to whom Joyce wrote
his intemperate note demanding the packing up and dispatch of
his trunk from the Tower. Others came: Padraic Colum, Arthur
Griffith, Dermot Freyer and Joseph Hone. It was a regular literary
meeting-place. Thoughts were thought, lines rehearsed.

This was so in the specific sense of real theatre, in which these
young men were much more directly engaged than Joyce.
Chenevix Trench himself was a gifted actor. He played the part of
Hanrahan the poet in Douglas Hyde's *The Twisting of the Rope*, and
Colum's recollection of the performance is worth quoting:

> I remember having seen three or four actors play this role, but
> I do not recall any one of them's [*sic*] having impressed me so
> much as he did. Exuberance is the characteristic of Hanrahan,
> the poet, and Dermott [*sic*] Trench went the limit in
> exuberance. By a stroke of genius he garbed himself in a cast-
> off hunting jacket of scarlet [*we would say, pink*], thus making

us visualize the vagabondage of the poet, dependent on hand-me-downs, and the arrogance that claimed a cavalier's accoutrement.

And Joyce was entirely absent from all this. These are the facts. The fiction suggests that Haines was the outsider, and that Stephen was present before Haines came. For fiction, this is entirely legitimate; fiction is about the imagination, and it suited Joyce to present a sharp triangulation of forces, supposedly British, Protestant Irish, Catholic Irish.

Both Trench and Gogarty were from the same broad, Anglo-Irish roots. The branch of the Chenevix Trench family from which Samuel is descended, while it does have family associations with Ireland, is less Anglo-Irish than might appear from the earlier details. Though the founding figure, the Archbishop who had fourteen children, carries weight and purpose in ecclesiastical circles in Ireland in the mid-nineteenth century, he in fact came from a profoundly "English" background, and always regarded himself as English. I am tempted to put the word into inverted commas, at this particular point in the lecture, since regarding oneself as [quote] English [unquote] is part of the impossible territory of self-identification with which the Anglo-Irish have always been faced. Despite everything to the contrary, the Archbishop, it must be remembered, was Dublin-born.

They, the Anglo-Irish, are such a varied crew. Men like William Wilde — indeed women like his wife Jane — William Morgan Jellett, father of the painter and a Unionist MP for Dublin University, would have thought of themselves as Irish. Richer landed gentry, with possessions in England, or houses in London, might well have had a different view. Quite where Gogarty stood, as early as 1904, when the only realistic prospect of Ireland having greater identity was through Home Rule, is itself a question worthy of a lecture. And of course James Joyce himself remained, technically, British until his death.

It is Joyce's skill as a writer to turn Trench and Gogarty, as Haines and Buck Mulligan, into virtual opposites, leaving Stephen Dedalus as a middle ground figure, ameliorative, in the centre, indulging in that strange and appealing distancing of himself through the device of the interior monologue.

Modern interpretation allows us to characterise Trench as "English", despite the fact that he came from that Irish "aristocracy" deriving from the Huguenot connection. He had plenty of Irish ancestry, but just happens to have been born in either England or St Petersburg, and not in Meath or Connemara. Gogarty has a cultural claim on "Irish" origin, by virtue of his Dublin birth, notwithstanding his schooling at Stoneyhurst; it is related essentially to his period as a Trinity student. Joyce is base Dublin, though with Galway, Cork and other connections, so movingly outlined in Ken Monaghan's lecture last month.

So we have a fictional distortion, entirely legitimate, but nevertheless no basis for biographical certitude. And the result has been a heavily weighted prejudice against Haines, and consequently against the original, the "neurotically insufferable" Richard Samuel Dermot Chenevix Trench.

Yet here we have to ask another question. Just how much of a distortion is it? Is Haines all that marginal? Does he have a trivial role in the novel? Or is there more to his contribution? When he leaves the Tower, has he performed more than a function of exciting mockery, mainly against the English? As he plants his hat on his head, and tosses the end of his scarf over his shoulder, setting out to buy some real Irish poetry, can he be said to have performed any purpose in Joyce's large scheme of things?

The Englishman, like all his tribe, is dogged. He is not to be so lightly dismissed. He turns up again in the Scylla and Charybdis episode, this time on his way back to the National Library from Gill's, where he has been to buy a copy of Douglas Hyde's *Love Songs of Connacht*. Well, in fact, he does not turn up. The chapter completes its brilliant and complex examination, in the director's

office, of Shakespeare's play *Hamlet*, with Stephen Dedalus growing steadily more dismissive of the debate. The absent Haines is
only referred to. "I couldn't bring him in to hear the discussion,"
the librarian, Best, says. And then adds those lines: "Bound thee
forth, my booklet, quick/To greet the callous public,/Writ, I ween,
'twas not my wish/In lean unlovely English." And John Eglington
(the essayist, William K. Magee, for the characters, at this point,
are real people, undisguised) rounds off Best's remarks with a
touch so close, it brings a blush to my cheeks as I remember the
effect from early days in Dublin, early visits to Sligo and Donegal.
John Eglington says: "The peatsmoke is going to his head."

Then it is Stephen's turn. He has a brief, mildly conscience-
stricken thought about Haines, a quote from Chapter One, a con-
fessional reference to himself as a thief, and the apostrophising of
Haines as precious, by which I mean valuable, but lost. "We feel
in England. Penitent thief. Gone. I smoked his baccy. Green
twinkling stone. An emerald set in the ring of the sea."

Harry Blamires, a scholar who has analysed *Ulysses* chapter by
chapter — clearly a tedious fellow, one of that familiar band we
call critics — suggests that Stephen, in the reference here to England, and the direct quote from Haines of "We feel in England" is
rejecting Haines's sentimental interest in the emerald isle. It may
be so; the words do no more than refer to it, identifying Haines. I
am not sure rejection is present. (I am equally unsure, in respect of
another of Blamires's speculations, that Haines was ever seen by
Joyce as a "property-owning usurper".) But what is here is the
skilful identification of something quite different: the appalling
tendency of the English towards generalisation — "We feel in
England" — how does Haines know this sweeping stuff about all
the English and most of the Irish?

But something even more important in respect of Haines
emerges at this point in the novel. It is the heart of his presence, it
is the vortex of his purpose in the book. He has been peripheral,
off-stage, the butt of critical and sardonic comment, and the

character who attracts a form of Irish racism — dismissal or hatred of the English oppressor — so common as to be casual and
off-hand, and excusable. Stephen rises and decides to depart, not
just from the National Library, but from its voluble, opinionated,
fluent, superficial and trivial inhabitants, with their endless discussion of *Hamlet*, Shakespeare, the English language, and themselves. We have reached the pivotal point in *Ulysses*: the first half
is over; the second, more experimental, more inventive half is
about to begin. And Stephen is going to change gear, alter the
pace of his progress, define himself, become more isolated, and
turn towards some undefined "home" again. "Life is many days,"
he thought. "This will end." And then: "One day in the national
library we had a discussion." And he goes out of the vaulted cell,
into a shattering daylight of no thought. And he asks himself:
"What have I learned? Of them? Of me? Walk like Haines now."

"Walk like Haines now"? Is this a piece of self-instruction, a tab-
let of personal law, an edict, a moment of truth? It is, most certainly, a moment of decision, in favour of the solitary isolation
which has singled out Haines from the book's beginning, and will
now define Stephen through to the book's ending. Haines, the Englishman, is a pariah in Ireland, an object of mockery, the vulgar victim of Buck Mulligan's ferocious insensitivity. We see him wandering back to the National Library, where he is the subject of a milder
thread of mockery. We see him on his way to his *mélange* with Mulligan in the D.B.C., and carrying in his hand, reading it no doubt,
Douglas Hyde's *Love Songs of Connacht*. Haines is chosen by
Stephen for a very special purpose. The hero of the book wants a
final guide to his own style and attitude, and he finds it in Haines.
"Walk like Haines now." The decision remains with the created
character through the book; it remains with the creator himself
through the rest of his life. Joyce did walk like Haines from then on.

The last but one appearance of Haines in *Ulysses* need detain us
only briefly. Haines appears again, having coffee with Buck Mulligan in the D.B.C. in Grafton Street. The meeting is of relatively

small account, but does include Mulligan pointing out to Haines the seated figure in the corner, of Parnell's brother, John Howard Parnell, city marshal. Then Mulligan tells Haines what he has missed, the debate on Shakespeare. "I'm sorry," Haines replies. "Shakespeare is the happy huntingground of all minds that have lost their balance." The conversation between the two men is about Stephen, what he will make of himself, whether or not he will write, if he can be a poet. Mulligan dwells on this, and on the dangers of madness, a preoccupation anyway of the medical student. But Haines remarks, somewhat pompously, on the fact that "I tackled him this morning on belief." Mulligan persists about writing, giving as his opinion that Stephen "is going to write something in ten years". This is accurate enough, since 1914 was the year *Dubliners* appeared, and the year *A Portrait of the Artist as a Young Man* was finished. And we are in 1904. "Seems a long way off," Haines says. "Still, I shouldn't wonder if he did it after all."

The two men finish their *mélanges*, munch the soft pieces, plaster butter on their scones, and Haines himself slips two sugarlumps, lengthways, into his coffee through the whipped cream. "This is real Irish cream I take it," he demands. "I don't want to be imposed on."

We meet Haines finally, this time in more ghoulish circumstances, in Oxen of the Sun. By this stage, both Bloom and Stephen have become isolated figures. Both, in their fashion, follow the lead given by Haines, who is isolated from the very beginning to the end of his minor role in this great epic. Here, it is clear, Haines has gone mad. The chapter is of pastiches, and the mode in the one dealing with Haines is the gothic novel. "The secret panel beside the chimney slid back, and in the recess appeared — Haines!" In hallucinatory state, he is presented with a portfolio of Celtic literature in one hand, and a phial of poison in the other. He stares out with a ghostly grin, and offers his valediction: "I anticipated some such reception, for which, it seems, history is to blame." And with an "eldritch" laugh (weird, unnatural, hideous) he prepares to depart for ever. He confesses to the murder of Samuel Childs. (You will recall that Joyce attended the trial of this tailor, charged with the murder of his brother, and took from it several interesting ideas for *Ulysses*.) And now Haines is confessing.

> And how I am punished! The inferno has no terrors for me. This is the appearance is on me. Tare and ages, what way would I be resting at all, he muttered thickly, and I tramping Dublin this while back with my share of songs and himself after me the like of a soulth or a bullawurrus? My hell, and Ireland's, is in this life. It is what I tried to obliterate my crime. Distractions, rookshootings, the Erse language (he recited some), laudanum (he raised the phial to his lips), camping out. In vain! His spectre stalks me. Dope is my only hope . . . Ah! Destruction! The black panther! With a cry he suddenly vanished and the panel slid back. An instant later his head appeared in the door opposite and said: Meet me at Westland Row station at half past eleven. He was gone.

That is the end of the story of Haines. Numerically, we are halfway through *Ulysses*; structurally, we are well into the second half. All the defining, by Haines, of Stephen's way forward has been completed, and his role is over. The Englishman may depart. He does so in a flurry of violent gothic language which hints at the possible madness which engulfed the real Haines in suicide, less than five years after these events. Joyce is too sensible as a person, too skilful as a novelist, to do anything as gross as hinting at the fate which the real Haines faced.

In his passing, both as character and as man, Haines, or Trench, or both of them — since in art they become inseparable — left a stain on Joyce's work far deeper, far more permanent, than has ever yet been suggested. And I hope this apotheosis, both of the man and of the character, will be remembered as the tribute I intend it to be.

Lecture given on the occasion of Bloomsday 2000, at the James Joyce Centre, North Great George's Street, Dublin

20

JAMES JOYCE AND TRIESTE

James Joyce arrived in Trieste on 20 October 1904, accompanied by Nora Barnacle. They had run away together, on borrowed money. Lady Gregory gave five pounds, George Russell ten shillings and James's younger brother, Stanislaus, the biggest investor, claimed later that he had provided seven pounds. The couple had a bad first night, Joyce getting himself arrested, with Nora left sitting in a public park for many hours unaware of what had happened. She was used to sitting in parks; Joyce left her in one in London, on their way to Europe, when he went to seek help from Arthur Symons, and he did the same in Paris when he left her waiting in order to scrounge for cash.

James and Nora were to stay in Trieste until the First World War, and then return again for nine months after it. Their circumstances remained fairly desperate until the last three years, 1912 to 1915, which saw *Dubliners* published, his play *Exiles* written, and good progress on *A Portrait*, and with the early parts of *Ulysses*. They were both entirely irresponsible about money, begging and borrowing it with no intention of repaying, and frequently being put out on the street by landlords. In a kind and friendly way characteristic of the city, Trieste has littered its buildings with signs indicating when and where this famous cuckoo in the nest settled. Within a month Nora got pregnant, having her two children, Giorgio and Lucia, in quick succession. Joyce wrote and drank, much of the time in the company of Stanislaus.

The story of this period in Joyce's life is told in detail in Richard Ellmann's biography, which raises the central question as to why a very detailed retelling of the story might be necessary. It is so for three important reasons. Firstly, John McCourt brings to *The Years of Bloom: James Joyce in Trieste 1904–1920* a great deal of fresh material. He has lived and worked in the city for the past ten years. His researches into its life, the politics of the intensely interesting period when it was the major Austro-Hungarian seaport in the Mediterranean, have yielded a rich and well-told narrative.

Secondly, and of far greater importance, he creates for the reader the close parallels between Trieste and Dublin. Joyce brought his own city with him, in his mind, and laid it like a palimpsest over his new home. The docks and quays of Trieste were a close reminder of the Dublin quays. And the brothels, filled at home with soldiers and sailors, were very like those around the Piazza Cavana. Joyce modelled the Nighttown brothels in *Ulysses* on these. We know this from the language, which John McCourt dwells on and explains. He shows how the rich and fertile argot of the streets and bordellos of Trieste was transformed into the vivid and imaginative language for the sexual drama which takes place in Mrs Cohen's with Florrie, Bello, Kitty and Zoë.

The third area of revelation in this book is more sombre, but is overdue in Joyce studies. If *The Years of Bloom* has a hero, it is Stanislaus. He came to Trieste at Joyce's request, cared for the family, taught in Joyce's place when he was too drunk or ill to teach himself, minded the children, lent the parents money, which he rarely got back, and sacrificed everything in the interest of James's undoubted genius. As the story unfolds, one comes to despise James Joyce, whatever one's feelings may be about his rich and fertile writing. "Don't let my debts trouble you," he reassures his brother, who was unsuccessfully trying to stop eviction. He was particularly cruel when he had received from his English benefactor, Harriet Shaw Weaver, the huge sum of two thousand pounds, and in a letter told this to Stanislaus, who at the time was hard up. Joyce's younger brother reminded him of an outstanding debt of ten pounds, and said it would be a help to have the money. Joyce did not reply.

During the First World War the Joyce family became refugees in Zurich, where the greater part of *Ulysses* was written, returning to Trieste, which they regarded as their natural home, in September 1919. But Joyce's friends, his brother Stanislaus, who for a time had been interned, and his sister Eileen, who had also helped the family, were no longer prepared to tolerate his selfishness. The city itself, now part of Italy, was changed. The permanent exile needed to move on. He stayed in Trieste less than a year. The move to Paris, in July 1920, placed him at what was to become the international centre for art and writing over the next two decades. Joyce, neither a nostalgic nor a sentimental man, did not look back. But during the rest of their lives, the family continued to speak the Italian of Trieste in their home, and Joyce himself to immortalise so much of it under the guise of the Dublin of *Ulysses*.

Review for *Daily Telegraph* of *The Years of Bloom: James Joyce in Trieste 1904–1920* by John McCourt, Lilliput Press

21

MY BROTHER'S RIB

Patrick Kavanagh went through many difficult times in his life. You could say he was born to trouble as the sparks fly upwards. But in a life of many dark episodes, few times were as grim as the first half of the 1950s. He enlivened them for himself during a period of a few months by producing his own magazine, *Kavanagh's Weekly*. This appeared first in mid-April 1952, and it shattered the quiet and suppressed cultural and political life of the city with its outspoken attacks on hypocrisy and lies. In a remarkably short period of time Kavanagh made a prodigious number of enemies. He did this without making any money or establishing the weekly. At the end of June, on the front page, he announced that the next and thirteenth issue would be the last, and would be sold for one pound instead of the usual sixpence. The inflated price included the twelve previous issues as well, and the whole is now a book collector's dream.

It was not the case then, however. Kavanagh did announce that the magazine would go on if some benefactor gave it £1,000 or more. But nothing came in, and it closed, the final number being a single essay entitled "The Story of an Editor who was Corrupted by Love". In it he confessed that he had worked under the delusion that he had a large body of friends. He described them as being friends "of his genius". In reality he had none at all.

Worse was to follow. An article appeared in *The Leader* attacking Kavanagh, and inspired, Kavanagh thought, by the bitterness his own *Weekly* had generated among artists and writers. Kavanagh believed he would win the libel action he then took against the newspaper. But his so-called friends advised him badly. In the event he lost on the weakness of his own testimony. He was an appalling plaintiff. Not only did the defence not call any witnesses. It did not even have to reveal who had written the article!

The case was later appealed to the Supreme Court, and there the lower court judgement was set aside and a new trial ordered. But it did not take place. The symbolic victories and defeats had been registered, and it was enough. In any case, there was insufficient money to pay any of the lawyers.

Kavanagh was already sick. And some time later succumbed to cancer of the lung. He went into the Rialto Hospital where, surprisingly, he was visited by Archbishop McQuaid, who had helped him on several occasions. The surgeon was Keith Shaw, who died in February this year at the age of eighty-one.

The surgery necessitated the removal of one of Kavanagh's ribs, but was otherwise successful, and the poet was well-treated. He regarded the event as benign, but in time got to thinking about the missing rib, and eventually approached Keith Shaw to find out what had happened to it.

Shaw replied that he had it. Kavanagh expressed the view that the rib was in fact his, and might he have it back? Keith Shaw reluctantly agreed, but on the condition that Kavanagh give him an inscribed and autographed copy of *Tarry Flynn*. The meeting for the purpose of handing over the rib took place in Mooney's on Baggot Street Bridge, and the inscription read: "To Keith Shaw, MD, FRCSI, this simple pastoral as a token of remembrance: of the curious happiness I knew when in the Rialto Hospital. Patrick Kavanagh." He added, more as an afterthought: "As promised in exchange for a rib — my own rib."

When the surgeon, Keith Shaw, died last month it reminded me of the rib. And when I met Peter Kavanagh, the brother, whose latest book, *Patrick Kavanagh: A Life Chronicle*, has been published in circumstances which provoke a longer, less benign and more tangled story, I asked him about the rib.

"The fuckers stole it!" was the prompt answer. Peter Kavanagh, who has devoted his life to being his brother's keeper, went on to catalogue other posthumous disasters. His lifelong concern, reflected not just in this latest book, but in others that have preceded it, is with the memory of the man the younger Kavanagh described as "Ireland's greatest Catholic poet". And that, provocatively enough, is another story.

Irish Independent, March 2001

22

DIARIES OF A LADY

Augusta Gregory was widowed in 1892, at the age of thirty-nine, and obliged to reconstruct her life, which she did to telling effect. Sir William Gregory, who had been almost as old as her mother when they married in 1880, had rescued her from despised status within her own family, the Persses, and had then given her a highly entertaining social life in London which had obscured the mounting debts which her husband's gambling had incurred. Emotionally the marriage had not been entirely satisfactory, Lady Gregory having an affair with Wilfrid Blunt early on, but one child, Robert, was born.

The subsequent reconstruction of her life is really the subject-matter of these diaries, which portray an energetic, increasingly independent and assured woman transforming herself from the natural sympathies of her class, which were imperialist and unionist, to become a key shaper of Irish nationalism and cultural independence.

The editor, James Pethica, is an English professor at the University of Richmond in Virginia, and is currently working on the relationship and collaboration between Lady Gregory and William Butler Yeats, so that his introduction gives perhaps too much emphasis to this, and too little to the other friendships of the period. Lady Gregory had a gift for friendly encouragement, particularly of artists. She was better with men than with women. She was decisive in her views and actions, and every indication is that she was a supremely good hostess, putting her guests at ease, but making them work for their hospitality.

It could be inferred from the entries in her diaries for these ten years that she never really understood William Butler Yeats. But she gave selflessly to his interests as a writer, and worked more consistently for him than for the others involved in the same literary struggle. Socially, she seems to have understood George Moore better than Yeats, and emotionally to have been closer to Jack Yeats and to George Russell. They did not test her loyalty or her intellect in quite the way the poet did.

The diaries tell only part of the story. They are breathless in style, filled with dashes instead of full stops, and crowded with incident. It is entirely remarkable the amount she did, the people she saw, and the way she showered generous acts of kindness and concern like confetti in her regal wake. She gives a wonderful picture of contemporary life, dashing over from Coole to Killeenan to Raftery's grave in the little churchyard there, and explaining to the villagers, who thought the name "Raftery" on the stone was not quite enough, that it put him with Homer, who, she told them, was also known by just that single name.

The pace of life does not allow her to examine in sufficient detail the changing beliefs she had about Ireland. These she expressed elsewhere, often to telling effect. Nor does she go into the perplexing issues surrounding Yeats's poetry and plays. But the pace itself, which saw her at Coole, in Dublin, and in London, promoting, helping and defending the work of all her friends, makes a wonderful narrative. Posterity has been given a slightly dusty picture of Augusta Gregory, midwife to the works of others. These diaries hiss and vibrate with her powerful movement through the pages of Irish literary and artistic history. We witness her mind and emotions in vigorous activity. We see clearly her regal figure, and bow to her passionate energy and her uncompromising dedication. It is a rich experience.

Review for the *Irish Independent*, May 1996, of *Lady Gregory's Diaries, 1892–1902*, edited by James Pethica, Colin Smythe

23

THE IDENTITY OF JONATHAN SWIFT

A ll the biographies of Jonathan Swift, which begin with the *Remarks* of Lord Orrery, published in 1752, fail to give a coherent picture of the man. Their authors, and there have been very many, grapple as though in combat with the nature and substance of Swift's mind and heart. And they come off second-best. This happens invariably. Swift defeats them in their attempts to "discover" him. He blocks, he evades, he lays false trails. He is deliberately misleading. He does not want the full story of his life to be known, and he goes to extraordinary lengths to create uncertainty and doubt. It was not just in his lifetime that he did this; it is for posterity. The trail of false clues is persistent and comprehensive.

He begins to lay his trail of deception, unusually, over details of what happened *before* his own birth. It is Swift who tells us that his father died several months before he was born. He gives us also, though indirectly, the cause of death, an attack of the "Itch" after being on circuit as steward of the judges. (The "Itch" was a subcutaneous infection, virulently contagious, and caught from a mite found in contaminated bed-straw.)

There could be no clearer indication of a question mark over his parentage. Though Swift is also reported as saying that his own birth "came time enough to save his Mother's Credit", there was no need to say anything at all. And by saying what he did, he created a doubt which has persisted ever since.

The idea of Swift's illegitimacy is presented to us in the first biography, and has been with us ever since. Orrery, the author of that work, which sold widely, and went into many editions, raises the possibility of Sir William Temple being Swift's father, and this was clearly the gossip during the Dean's lifetime. But Orrery then dismisses it as rumour, which of course it was. Nothing could be more compelling than the raising of a rumour, only to scotch it. Temple's name remained associated with Swift from then on.

Sir William Temple could not have been Swift's father, since he was living at the time in the Netherlands. But William Temple's own father, Sir John Temple, Master of the Rolls in Ireland, could have been Swift's father, and was certainly associated over many years with the Swift family. He was also responsible for the employment of Jonathan Swift the Elder at the King's Inns in Dublin, the job that took Swift senior on circuit and led to his early death.

After more than half a century, a portrait of the young Jonathan Swift was, in the summer of 1999, rediscovered and brought to Dublin for exhibition in the National Library of Ireland. It adds substantially to our knowledge. Like almost everything connected with Swift, its authenticity has been challenged, and Swift scholars have rejected it, saying it is not a portrait of the writer. But it is almost certainly the work of Thomas Pooley, Irish portrait painter of the late seventeenth century, one of the few artists known to Swift. It belonged to an early Swift enthusiast, Thomas Percy, Bishop of Dromore. And it is inscribed "Jonathan Swift when a student in Dublin College". He wears the gown of a Bachelor of Arts from Dublin University.

Leaving aside the arguments based on circumstantial evidence, the iconographic argument is compelling. When set beside the best-known portrait of Swift in his maturity, painted by Charles Jervas and engraved many times with Swift's approval, all the physical evidence strongly supports the attribution. The same nose is a strong feature. The eyes, direct and uncompromising, are structured and set in the face in exactly the same way. Even the eyebrows are identically long and full, and, as we know from other portraits, in later life they became a thick and bushy feature of Swift's old age. The mouth, full and sensuous in both cases, has the identical dimpling at the corners, and there is also the identical dimple in the chin. The high forehead, for which Swift is renowned, and which is evident in his skull, a plaster copy of which is preserved in Marsh's Library, is to be seen in remarkable fullness in the youthful portrait.

Many of these arguments, about the physical similarities between the youthful Jonathan Swift and the mature writer in London in 1710, may be applied to the supposed father, Sir John Temple, and the half-brother, with whom Swift lived for ten years, Sir William Temple. Once again, we find close physical resemblances. The same eyes, mouth and nose are clear in the case both of Sir John Temple and Sir William Temple. The portrait of Sir John Temple is particularly interesting, in that it was painted quite early in his life, bringing it close to the youthful portrait of Jonathan Swift. It almost certainly dates from before 1630. Sir John Temple was born in 1600, so we are probably looking at a man in his twenties. In the case of Swift, he has probably just turned twenty.

If we then turn to the portrait of Sir William Temple, it relates to the mature Swift portrait, based on the Jervas painting. The facial characteristics are comparable, though the eyes differ slightly, Swift's being more prominent. The style of wig is wholly different, almost half a century dividing the portraits.

If we rely on this exercise of facial similarities, then we have an alternative version for Swift. The question then arises: does it help or hinder us in the understanding of his life? Does it stand up to examination in the context of events? Where does it leave us?

Jonathan Swift was certainly born in Dublin, and his mother was certainly the widow of Jonathan Swift the elder. If the real father was Sir John Temple, Master of the Rolls in Ireland, then we can explain the mysterious journey to Whitehaven, in Cumberland.

Rather than being "spirited away", he was sent there to live with a nurse for a time, possibly for as long as three years, to keep him out of the way. Swift himself concocted what is clearly a spurious explanation for this departure from his mother, based on the idea that the nurse kidnapped him, and was then told not to bring him back for fear of death on the high seas. When he returned, his mother left for Leicester where she had originally come from, and resettled there. At this time, 1677, his supposed father, Sir John Temple, died. Swift's mother remained in Leicester until her death in 1710. After returning to Dublin, Swift went to school in Kilkenny, where William Congreve, the playwright, was also a pupil. He went on to be a student in Trinity College, and came to know the city when it was still largely medieval in its buildings and streets.

These were troubled times. The restoration of Charles II, seven years before Swift's birth, had ended the Cromwellian interregnum, but established an uncertain Protestant succession. When Charles II died, his brother and heir, James II, began dismantling what had been achieved since the Restoration, seeking to reintroduce the Roman Catholic faith. Protestant fear of this led to the invitation to William of Orange to "invade", which he did, in November 1688. "The Glorious Revolution" brought William III to the throne with Queen Mary, Protestant sister to both Charles II and James II. King James, who had fled England in ignominious circumstances, was anxious nevertheless to regain the throne, and he moved his campaign to Ireland. In the troubles that ensued, many Protestants fled the country, Swift among them. His loyalties became divided, between England and Ireland, and much of his writing thereafter reflects these troubled experiences. The sense of belonging to both these parts of the realm, and of facing conflict in both parts, had a lasting effect on much of his life.

Jonathan Swift spent ten years in the household of his supposed half-brother, Sir William Temple, diplomat, scholar, statesman and gifted writer. No other man had so great an influence on the growth and development of Swift's mind, and on his abilities as a writer. Temple taught him how to deal with great men, and how to manage state affairs. He gave him an understanding of the subtleties of politics, and introduced him to political society at the highest level. It is difficult to see how any of this could have happened at all, unless Swift had considerable appeal, legal or by virtue of a blood relationship. Sir William Temple gave him many tasks. He recommended him as a secretary to Sir Robert Southwell, who was Secretary of State to William III, and accompanied the King on the campaign in Ireland which culminated in the defeat of James II at the Boyne. Whether Swift in fact took up that appointment, and what then happened, has never been adequately explained.

Swift returned to Moor Hall, and remained a member of the household. At the same time, he was pursuing his career in Holy Orders, occupying a living in the northern part of Ireland, in the parish of Kilroot — which he hated — but which also led to his first serious interest in a woman together with the possibility of marriage. He then made further advances as prebend of St Patrick's Cathedral and rector of Laracor, County Meath, a part of Ireland he grew to love.

At Moor Park, Jonathan Swift met Hester Johnson, later named in his writing as Stella. She had an ambiguous position in Sir William Temple's family, and it has always been widely believed that she was the illegitimate daughter, either of Sir William Temple, or of his younger brother, Henry. If it were possible to prove this, and indeed to prove the rumour about Swift being the illegitimate son of Sir John Temple, then he and Stella would be closely related, offering a sensible explanation of their lifelong friendship. On Temple's death, Swift became his literary executor. Hester Johnson was treated with special favour by Sir William Temple, who left her a substantial sum of money on his death, further evidence of family ties.

Jonathan Swift made his way in the world, both as an Irish prelate and as a man of affairs, involved in politics. He acquired a position that was tantamount to that of guardian to both Stella and her companion, Rebecca Dingley. He encouraged them to move to Ireland, and helped to establish them in Dublin, where they spent the rest of their lives, making one protracted visit to London during this first decade of the eighteenth century.

Swift was busy to begin with in completing the publication of Sir William Temple's works. Earlier, living at Moor Park, he had written much poetry, first in the style of Abraham Cowley, in particular modelling his work on the Pindaric Ode, but later using the octosyllabic line in rhyming couplets, a form of verse which became peculiarly his own.

He wrote also the early draft of *A Tale of a Tub*, his first great satire, as well as *The Battle of the Books*, and these were first published in 1704, together with another work. There is much dispute about whether or not they had Swift's blessing, or were pirated.

He dedicated *A Tale of a Tub* to John Somers, a member of the ruling Whigs, and for a time Lord Chancellor. Swift was seen as a Whig, partly a legacy of the political loyalty of his former patron, Sir William Temple, partly because of his association with other Whig writers of the period, among them Joseph Addison and Richard Steele.

There was a further reason: the Church in Ireland rated Swift's negotiating powers highly, and used him in the Church's interest to obtain the remission of parish taxes known as First Parts and Twentieth Fruits. At the time, churches were in disrepair, and sometimes derelict as a result of the religious strife of the seventeenth century, and the uncertainty in Ireland both before and after the Battle of the Boyne. Once again we have the image of him as influential and well-connected.

Late in 1707, Jonathan Swift met and fell in love with a much younger woman, Esther Van Homrigh, the daughter of a Dutch merchant who had settled in Dublin and had been very successful. After his death, his widow and four children moved to

London in that year, and Swift became a friend of the family and especially of Esther, to whom he gave the name Vanessa.

The true period of Jonathan Swift's greatness as a pamphleteer and journalist lasted from 1710 until the death of Queen Anne in 1714. Queen Anne's succession to the throne of England, on the death of William III in 1702, had resulted in a number of changes which to some extent helped in the process by which Swift moved from being a Whig to his later espousal of the Tory interest. She was a staunch defender of the Protestant succession and of the established Church. Though initially she favoured the Duke of Marlborough in his campaigns in Europe, and had as her own favourite his wife, Sarah, Duchess of Marlborough, by 1710, when the Tories won a significant electoral victory, she had turned against both.

Swift arrived in London in the autumn of 1710, again charged with working for the Church in Ireland, and seeking remission of dues from the new administration. He approached members of the Cabinet and was soon taken up by Robert Harley, Lord Treasurer, who led the Tory administration, and recognised Swift's potential value as a brilliantly gifted writer.

The two men became close friends, with the additional friendship of Henry St John, the gifted leader of the Tories in the House of Commons. Harley's task was to bring peace, and end the expensive war. He achieved this with Swift's help, and the Duke of Marlborough was discredited and went into exile with his duchess.

Swift recorded the whole period in a series of letters sent from London to Stella and Rebecca Dingley in Dublin. Known later as *Journal to Stella*, the account is intimate, witty, full of gossip and information about affairs of state, and threaded through with Swift's deep affection for these two women, who constituted the only real family he had. The letters tell us much about the warmhearted and funny side of Swift, his affection for his friends in London, his relationships with great men in public life, and his involvement in the literary and social life of the city.

What he did not record in *Journal to Stella* was the developing relationship with Vanessa. Letters show that this also flourished, and many encounters and events, together with his poem about love, *Cadenus and Vanessa*, point to a rich and passionate experience enjoyed by them both.

Swift enjoyed a uniquely powerful and privileged position. But this depended, as did the power of Robert Harley, who had become the Earl of Oxford, on the survival of the increasingly sickly Queen Anne. When she died in 1714, the Tory administration fell, the Hanoverians came to the throne, in the person of George I, and Swift was probably fortunate to have been made Dean of St Patrick's Cathedral, in Dublin, to which he returned in sorrow and with foreboding about his own future.

Esther Van Homrigh followed Swift back to Dublin. Clearly, from their correspondence, they loved each other. But it did not suit Swift to have her living at Celbridge, close enough to the city, which she visited quite frequently. Swift was widely known, and so was his well-established relationship with Stella and Rebecca Dingley. There were even rumours of a secret marriage with Stella. He felt compromised and threatened, and the letters during this Dublin period are haunted by his anxiety and Vanessa's dissatisfaction.

There was no easy explanation Swift could give of his filial duties to his two supposed relations, and his more passionate exchanges with Vanessa, recorded in many letters sent between them. Of those that have survived, Swift's outnumber Vanessa's roughly two-to-one.

The turbulent private life was matched by difficulties Swift had as Dean in the early years of his incumbency. His known Tory loyalties were at odds with the power of the Whig administration, eventually led by Robert Walpole. And it was not until the *Drapier's Letters*, in which Swift defended Irish commerce from Wood's Halfpence — a debased coinage designed for imposition in Ireland under the control and promotion of an ambitious entrepreneur — that he reversed with great success his unpopularity, becoming a hero in Ireland of unprecedented popularity.

He wrote other pamphlets that defended the Irish. *A Modest Proposal*, which deals in stark terms with the poverty in the country, and ironically suggests the remedy of people breeding their children to be sold as food, is perhaps the most famous of these.

Swift became that dangerous thing in Ireland — a folk hero. He went through the anguish of Vanessa's death, in 1723, from consumption. In 1728 his beloved Stella — who had been like a daughter to him — also died. He travelled the country, met with friends, wrote poetry and prose. He published in 1727 his great masterpiece, *Gulliver's Travels*. And reluctantly, painfully, grew old and crotchety.

The characterisation of Swift as a misogynist and misanthrope, bitter and angry at life's tragedies, grew to surround his memory, and to blot out the blessings of love and friendship with which the greater part of his life had been crowned. Though star-crossed in many of the events, his was a hugely fruitful and vigorous life, and his legacy of brilliant poetry and prose, invention and wit, is indestructibly at the heart of the literature of Ireland, an emotional and stylistic goldmine which all writers have since acknowledged. Of his life, probably the greatest shadow of all concerned his identity. Was he in fact Swift at all? Or was he a member of the Temple family? No final answer can ever be found.

Written for the occasion of the Swift exhibition in the National Library of Ireland, Dublin, July 1999

24

THE DEAR LITTLE BOOK

I listened with my customary admiration as my friend Helen Lucy Burke savaged the latest group of "Little Books", on Mike Murphy's Arts Programme. The books in question come from the giant Orion Group, and are published under what was once a distinguished imprint, that of Phoenix, which brought out a famous series in the 1920s. The present offering, valiantly defended by that great leveller in our culture, Mike Murphy, are sound-bites: the first five chapters of "The Voyage to Lilliput", from *Gulliver's Travels*; two chapters from *The Jungle Book*; a Keats selection, called, perhaps misleadingly, since it might frighten people with the length of the poem, *The Eve of St Agnes*; and a host more.

Helen Lucy Burke's principal criticism was subjective: that the books were not her cup of tea, and were not really books. She made other points as well, about the egregious pornography of that very boring French writer Alina Reyes, and the absurdity of extracting love poems out of Francis Turner Palgrave. But her general approach was a characteristically vigorous dismissal of a form of trivialising. Mike Murphy, by contrast, saw point in sound-bite writing. (He would, wouldn't he? Or so you might say.) It gives readers the chance to extend, by a little tiny bit, the cliché of their lives, to touch base with Catullus, dip into Friedrich Nietzsche, leapfrog through one-third of Shakespeare's Sonnets, which have been renamed *Love Sonnets*, and dabble in an abridged and edited *Guide to Happiness* from Epicurus.

Are we then to have a Swiftian *Battle of the Books*, late-twentieth-century style? We already have it, in commercial terms. Penguin have their 60s Classics, a cheap celebration, at 60p, of their sixty years of existence, and offering the same sound-bite approach to literature. Moreover, and absurdly, they have claimed, at that lower-than-newspaper price, "best-seller" status for the series, which unsurprisingly has outsold more convention-ally priced paperbacks. Doubtless, similar claims will be made for the Orion series.

The idea is not new. There have always been small books; there have always been cheap editions. And alongside both Pen-guin and Orion one must place the longer-running — and gener-ally far better value — of the Dover Thrift Editions, which are priced at 95p, and are "complete and unabridged" versions of the great classics — plays, novellas, and philosophical texts.

The small books have uses. I have seen them as place-settings at the dinner table. A ninety-year-old-friend in a nursing home finds them easy to lift up, and short enough to represent not too great a challenge. They seem more fitting to the end of life than they do to its beginning, when we really lifted the whole job in our youthful hands, and believed, with Milton, that "a good book is the precious life-blood of a master spirit, embalmed and treas-ured up on purpose to a life beyond life". One wonders if pub-lishers, at the end of the millennium, see books in that light at all?

Irish Independent, January 1996

25

GREAT IRISH WRITERS

When we say "That's Great!" do we mean what we say? Do we know what we mean? When someone asks the question: "Have you seen the latest James Bond film?" And then adds: "I thought it was great!" Do we take this to mean, "of the very highest quality", "outstanding", "the best in its class"? Or does it just mean "great crack", great entertainment, great for its effects, or "great" in a kind of misgiving way? And if one-in-ten of the Irish people think that Maeve Binchy is "the greatest Irish writer", bar none, and with no conditional clauses, what do we do? Do we blame the Irish people? Do we blame Maeve Binchy? Or do we look a bit more carefully at the words we use?

"Great", among other things, means "having a high position in a scale of measurement". Maeve Binchy, who is one percentage point greater than James Joyce, has probably sold more copies of her books than any of the other nine listed authors sold when they were alive. And anyone who has had difficulty reading James Joyce will grit their teeth and say savagely about Maeve Binchy's popularity "That's great!" They mean that the prodigious success of this most accessible of authors is somehow a victory for the common man and the defeat of intellectual complexity, academic arrogance and a whole range of pretensions about art and culture.

Roddy Doyle, who has been writing for a rather shorter period than Maeve Binchy, but has sold large numbers of his books, is regarded as "the greatest Irish writer" by eight percent of the population. If we add Roddy Doyle to Maeve Binchy, that is twenty per cent of the Irish population collectively regarding them as "the greatest". It takes Oscar Wilde, George Bernard Shaw and Seamus Heaney, added together, to equal Maeve Binchy and Roddy Doyle.

Brendan Behan, who in his lifetime was "great" in a rebellious and tempestuous way, is reduced in public esteem to a modest five per cent. The man whose funeral rivalled that of Daniel O'Connell for attendance figures, is shrunk in his immortal fame to the lowest share of all in the "greatness stakes", with Sean O'Casey beating him by one point.

By contrast, Patrick Kavanagh, twenty years Behan's senior, and greatly overshadowed during his lifetime by Behan, has outstripped him to find a place equal with Roddy Doyle, and only four places behind the leader.

William Butler Yeats deserves the lead he has over the rest. Not alone great in his writing, and great in his sense of national purpose and destiny, he was the leading figure of Ireland's greatest family. His is a triple-star achievement.

Begrudgery has taught us to have doubts about accolades, hero-worship and praise. We are suspicious even of the idea of "great" families, and of greatness itself, unless we can inject a measure of scepticism into the judgement.

But when "great" means friendly, accessible, readable, easy, simple, enjoyable and familiar, which has been Maeve Binchy's outstanding achievement for huge numbers of readers, it explains the votes of twelve per cent of the Irish people.

For the *Irish Independent*, on the popularity of writers

26

WILLIAM BUTLER YEATS

Yeats looks just what I expected. A cross between a Dominie
Sampson and a starved R.C. curate — in seedy black clothes —
with a large black bow at the root of his long naked throat. He
is egregiously the poet — mutters ends of verse to himself with
a wild eye, bows over your hand in dark silence — but poet he
is — and very interesting indeed — and somehow sympathetic
to talk to — I liked him — in spite of various things — and I
got on well with him . . . It is strange to talk of deep subjects of
life and death without any self-consciousness, and I must say
he induces that, and does it himself. . . . Today Augusta made
me add my initials to a tree. . . . It was most touching. WBY did
the carving, I smoked, and high literary conversation raged
and the cigarette went out and I couldn't make the matches
light, and he held the little dingy lappets of his coat out and I
lighted the match in his bosom. No one was there, and I trust
no one saw, as it must have looked very funny.

Violet Martin, joint author, with her friend, Edith Somerville, of
The Real Charlotte and *Some Experiences of an Irish R.M.*, is writing
to Edith in the summer of 1901 from Coole Park, where she is a
guest along with Douglas Hyde, John M. Synge and others "of the
literary crowd". She was never really part of it, and, like George
Moore, observed from the outside its mixture of high seriousness
and absurdity. She did this with considerable wit; and when Roy
Foster uses the quotation — almost exactly midway through the
first volume of his splendid life of W.B. Yeats — he does so to

telling effect, capturing both the appeal and the uncertainty which were so persistently and pervasively at the centre of the poet's character.

Yeats was always, more or less, in crisis. Born in virtual poverty, educated in different schools and different parts of London and Dublin, William Butler Yeats became a writer through tears and sweat, his meagre earnings swallowed up by a struggling family over which there presided that inept genius, John Butler Yeats. His eldest son was saved from domestic obliteration by being Irish, and by living mostly in London. He forged there, in the British empire's capital, both his Irish nationalism, and the main strands of the Irish literary revival which he led and dominated. He then brought them back to Dublin with undoubtedly very mixed results, not just in the 1890s, but really to the end of the period covered by this first volume, which takes us up to 1914.

The London theories, about how to give life to Irish writing, and how to create a national theatre, ran into the ground in the treacherous sands of Dublin's cultural and religious antagonisms. "What did we Irish do," Frank Fay pleaded, in respect of Yeats and the Abbey Theatre, "that the gods put so much bitterness & jealousy into our hearts?"

Yeats was torn apart by women; if it wasn't Augusta Gregory fighting with Maud Gonne for his artistic or revolutionary soul, then it was Florence Farr fighting with Annie Horniman for his playwright's skills or to rectify his obvious lack of judgement as theatre manager. He was torn apart by loyalties. He kept through these years as "apprentice mage" one foot in London, one in Dublin. He was committed to Irish nationalism, but he wanted to be part of the Rhymers' Club circle in London.

I take issue, incidentally, with the use of the archaic word "mage", and also with Roy Foster's reference throughout to Yeats as "WBY". His name was Willie, and even if he disliked it, the family did use it. The initials are very cold. And though he was a "magician" as poet, the idea of wisdom and learning, which the word also carries, is not really consistent with the man who emerges from these pages.

He dissipated prodigious amounts of energy, yet found time for the inspirational silence which brought forth his magical poems. He was autocrat, snob, quite a schemer, on occasions a figure of pathos, like his father. And yet the sense of humour was there, the human appeal, the likeability. One comes away from Violet Martin's poet, thinking of her head bowed between the lappets of his seedy black coat, and believing in him and his coherence as an artist.

There are many such images drawn together in this authoritative biography. George Moore, after falling out with the poet, wrote with brilliant lack of sympathy about him, but truthfully as well. There is something apposite in the description of Yeats back from America, "with a paunch, a huge stride, and an immense fur overcoat", deriding the middle classes, from which the poet did himself come, for their lack of financial support for Hugh Lane and his proposed Dublin modern art gallery. George Russell, who also broke with Yeats, wrote to Augusta Gregory, telling her to pack Yeats off to America or London, and prevent him wrecking the Abbey Theatre. "Every time I meet WBY I feel inclined to throw him out of the window. He has no talent for anything but writing and literature or literary discussions. Outside that he should be fined every time he opens his mouth."

These quotations, the views of his contemporaries, are of immense importance in Foster's Life, since he relies on them and on Yeats himself, through his letters, for the commentary and criticism in the book. Like the good historian he is, Foster frequently remains on the sideline himself about broad interpretation and human judgement. Indeed, there are times when the torrents of fact and quotation stand in the way of that biographical creativity which should bring them all together and transmute them into the rounded personality of man and poet, as Violet Martin manages in her brief pen-portrait. If the book has a fault, then this is it: we see William Butler Yeats from innumerable perspectives which derive from documented sources, and not from any totally assured judgement by Roy Foster himself. He is outstanding in his portrayal of Augusta Gregory, and her crucial role in Yeats's life. He handles very skilfully the complex history of the Irish national theatre. John M. Synge seems, in the end, to elude the author, both in his own character, and in his powerful but controversial relationship with Yeats. And I remain confused about Maud Gonne and the destructive love she and Yeats shared.

The narrative depicts a life far more painful than any previous biography has come even near to suggesting. Yeats really had no childhood, and what he had was confused, difficult and clearly embarrassing in terms of the poverty and condescension. Years later he imagined a quite different childhood, and recorded it with the benefit of hindsight, in *Reveries over Childhood and Youth*, and Foster leans heavily on this to describe the experiences. But Yeats undoubtedly fed on his family's memories more than his own, and gave to Sligo a relevance which it had only in his imagination and his poetry. Moreover, as Foster makes clear, once Lady Gregory comes on the scene, she, Coole Park and the countryside around Gort "provide an Irish base to replace Sligo". If it is as callous as that, then Sligo, as a place rather than poetic territory, mattered no more, really, than Dublin and London.

His becoming a writer was a period of terrible struggle and privation, both physical and emotional. Maud Gonne erupted into his life, creating turmoil, but inspiring him as well. And here again Foster gives us the fullest possible treatment of the story. By 1895 Yeats is an established poet, and the Irish literary revival is already the subject of a secondary literature recording the phenomenon. He dominates it all. He needed, it seems, to be in charge, and a lot of what he touched turned sour as a result, so that his falling out with George Russell is a really bitter event, and his estrangement from George Moore, while it does provoke sympathy with the wounded poet, also raises questions about how difficult Yeats at his worst could be. This seems to be territory that Foster does not seek to investigate.

Nevertheless, this is a wonderful work of scholarship. It turns Yeats around, making us see his poems from within his life, and helps us to experience them in a way that is both revealing and intensely moving. Time and again, as I read, I found myself taking down the *Collected Poems*, the *Plays*, *Autobiographies*, and feeding on them with new insights and with enormously enriched pleasure. The often quite grim youthful experiences, the yearnings, the search for love, the magical evocations of place and time, which we have all known for so long, take on a new and deeper intensity as we explore with Foster their background and their inspiration. This is a great story of Ireland's greatest poet, and it is superbly told.

Review published 20 April 1997 in *Washington Times* of *W.B. Yeats, A Life. Part 1: The Apprentice Mage* by Roy Foster, Oxford University Press.

PART 3

ART

27

JACK YEATS, WILLIAM ORPEN, MAINIE JELLETT

In January 1912, the Russian dancer Anna Pavlova visited Dublin. Her worldwide fame carried no great weight in the city, and she received an indifferent critical response to her dancing. William Orpen was a personal friend and a great admirer, who painted two portraits of her. Recalling from memory the visit, he associates with it an occasion when W.B. Yeats "gave a discourse on dancing, rhythm, Pavlova's good points and bad, etc."[1] He objected to what he thought was "terrible rubbish" in the poet's remarks, made a few derisive comments himself, and left the hall. It was, as he realised later, a terrible blunder to insult Ireland's greatest living poet. As for Pavlova, she was in the city for a week and then gone, and her feelings — which Orpen respected — were of less account than the collective susceptibilities of Ireland's "intellectuals", gathered to debate her merits over glasses of ginger beer and sandwiches. But Orpen chose the event, twelve years later, to demonstrate how much had changed in the intervening years. Such amateurism, he implied, would no longer be expressed in the new Ireland that had come after independence. "A new era has come to the land," he wrote in 1924. "No longer is the shamrock put to shame. . . . Ireland is face to face now with the

---

[1] William Orpen, *Stories of Old Ireland and Myself*, London, 1924, p. 93.

working out of her own destiny, and all little jealousies and trifles are being washed out. There is work for all, and no time for idle criticism."[2]

Orpen's words were mocking and ironic. He did not believe, either in 1912, or in 1924, or indeed at any time in his life, in a separate Ireland from the cultural or artistic viewpoint. He mocked the idea of it, and in *Stories of Old Ireland and Myself* made light-hearted fun of individual episodes where supposedly the cultural life of the country was evolving. He did not accept the myth and symbol of Yeats's poetry, which was clearly an important part of this process, and clearly had little time for the man. He thought that George Russell painting fairies was slightly less ridiculous than George Russell under the influence of French Impressionism. And he believed that Dermod O'Brien would never be other than a second-rate painter. He believed in the act of painting, not in its cultural impact. He taught the practicalities — of how to draw, of how to mix colour, of what made a good composition. And he practised it.[3]

Orpen knew that he had come out of a British tradition in art, that of the South Kensington art schools, topped up by the abilities and talents of great teachers at the Slade School. He knew this worked. The Kensington system, when he was a student, could stand comparison with art schools anywhere in the world. And the collective effect of his training was to undermine any belief in a separate, nationalist art collectively expressive of Ireland. If painters painted Irish landscape, or Irish genre scenes, or portraits, or events out of history, then by definition these were "Irish". But they were no more and no less Irish than the paintings which had been painted by Daniel Maclise and William Mulready

---

[2] Ibid.

[3] See Bruce Arnold, *Orpen: Mirror to an Age*, London, 1981. Fuller details are in the correspondence, part of which is lodged in the Orpen Archive, in the National Gallery of Ireland.

in the nineteenth century, or by James Barry and George Barret in the eighteenth century, or by Thomas Cooley and James Gandy in the seventeenth century. They were Irish by location; it was an issue of geography, not one for cultural celebration.

It was a perfectly legitimate attitude to adopt, and was shared by other Irish writers and artists, men and women, some of whom, like George Moore, became tired of the whole "movement", and of the emergence of the Irish "nation" with its separate "culture". He deserted it. Others, like Susan Mitchell, at first sceptical, eventually joined it and enriched it.[4]

This division of attitude in Ireland was reasonably clear-cut. In normal circumstances it would not count for anything substantial in a survey of Irish art in the twentieth century but for two significant facts. The first is that William Orpen, after establishing himself in London with early, brilliant works which he showed at the New English Art Club and elsewhere, returned to Ireland in order to teach. In doing so, he became a significant force culturally and in his influence on younger painters. He did so during the crucial period 1900–14, and taught with such success that his stamp as a figure in Irish art is overwhelmingly strong. He set the tone and style in painting for his students and their generation; they in turn became the teachers and passed the same tradition on to a second, and even a third generation of artists in ways that have no comparison. No other major Irish painter in the twentieth century had a comparable impact.

The second significant fact lay in the painting rather than the teaching; Orpen was a twentieth-century "Master" in any accepted meaning of the phrase, and good as his teaching was, his painting was even better. He left an array of jewel-like canvases, some of

---

[4] See Susan Mitchell, *George Moore*, Dublin and London, 1916, for a lively and penetrating picture of Moore's negative attitudes about Ireland and Irish cultural nationalism. George Moore references are too numerous to mention, but the best general account of himself and the period is to be found in *Hail and Farewell*, London 1911–1914.

them Irish in theme, but the majority transcending any nationality or regional identity. *A Woman,* for example, is one of the great nudes of the twentieth century. In the sense that it was painted by an Irishman, in Dublin, in 1906, it is "Irish". It was, unsurprisingly, the subject of much comment at the time. Yet even a century later the work is difficult to place within any specifically Irish visual context. Similarly, another early masterpiece, *The Mirror,* does not fit in to the cultural ethos from whence its creator came. It belongs indubitably to the New English Art Club tradition; it is a "London" painting; the model, Emily Scobel, part of the Fitzroy Street set in which Orpen moved at the beginning of the century, in his post-Slade school days.

The point needs no further emphasis. What Orpen witnessed, at first hand, during the early years of the twentieth century, was the careful crafting of an Irish identity, in social, political and cultural terms. He treated it light-heartedly, as did most of those who came from the same tradition. Success in London allowed him to distance himself, from the professional point of view, and Dublin increasingly became a playground. Both as painter and in his ordinary life Orpen was a pragmatist; he believed in the reality of what is, and not in some imagined perfection. And this view, which included a powerful sense of his own worth and physical presence, exemplified in the extraordinary number of self-portraits — for example, *Ready to Start* — governed his development, distancing him increasingly from the country of his birth.

His London success did exactly the same to George Moore. He abhorred the second-rate. The way in which Orpen dealt with the combination of background and experience provides a distinctive concept of national art in Ireland in the modern period which has to be accommodated. It is one thing to recognise the heavily orchestrated creation of an Irish national identity in the early years of the twentieth century, even to admire it. But as the century draws to its close, scholarship needs to be more objective in its acceptance of awkward strands of creative excellence which were not relentlessly tied to the evocation of a harmonious Irish world narrowly conforming to norms.

Orpen became quite shrewd about not speaking his mind on the national question. Words were dangerous. Yet he taught a series of visual lessons about the pre-eminence of the work over the place in which it is done, or the cultural demand it is meant to satisfy. He clearly detected, in the Ireland around him during the first two decades of the twentieth century, and emanating from numerous pundits whose names are by-words in the pantheon of the so-called "Irish Revival", a set of artistic and cultural guidelines about what being Irish meant. And he saw the fruits of this process in innumerable paintings, plays, poems and other literary efforts falsely raised above the second-rate position they should have occupied by their deliberate support of a nationalist point of view.

He had scant regard for this. The *faux monnayeurs* were there, in his view, to be mocked, laughed at, even if the price paid for this attitude was heavy. And in his letters, and in his own writing, particularly *Stories of Old Ireland and Myself*, there is a constant theme of mockery about Irish self-deception, alleviated only by his disarming trick of belittling himself as much, if not more, than those whose acts he criticises. But though he lived this life of humorous doubt and indulgence towards the country of his birth, in his paintings, and in his teaching, there was quite another story being enacted. This was rigorous, professional adherence to the very best that could be done in pencil, chalk, crayon, watercolours and oils.

Not only did he perform exceptionally, as painter of portraits, genre scenes, historical events, and perhaps most famously in his massive study and indictment of war as recorded in his book, *An Onlooker in France*; but he was enormously successful at it as well. This habitually acts upon the Irish as a kind of cultural aphrodisiac. They fall about in amazed admiration when one of their number achieves success on the world stage, as Orpen did in his lifetime. And the conventional response is to take pride in the success, and accept that a little of it resulted from birth and upbringing. Orpen rarely played the Irish card, except to make fun of those who treated it seriously. There was a departure from this frivolous attitude of mind in the period leading up to the First World War, when Orpen painted several deliberately "Irish" canvases, *Sowing New Seed*, *The Western Wedding* and *The Holy Well*. The first is a deliberate allegory; all three are comments upon Irish life, but all are marred by the deployment of caricature, and this in the end is an accurate reflection of Orpen's own judgement about his country. At the peak of his success, in *Stories of Old Ireland and Myself*, he defines the position, drawing a clear line between himself and his country, and littering the pages with dismissive asides against a movement he had never believed in, and also against its principal practitioners.

It was an act of supreme irony. He had taught Irish painters. The best of them, when the State came into being in 1921, were his pupils. And his name was to remain central in Irish art well after his death in 1931. There was further irony in the fact that at least two of those students, Patrick Tuohy and Seán Keating, were strongly nationalist. This was not expressed as strongly in Tuohy's painting as it was in Keating's, or at least not in any obvious way. Tuohy's wonderful painting *A Mayo Peasant Boy*, in the best Orpen tradition, transcends all obvious symbols relating it to the west of Ireland. It is a uniquely powerful example of an international genre, that of the direct and innocent portrayal of youth.[5] *The Model*, which Tuohy regarded as his masterwork, is faithful to the principles taught by Orpen and is technically brilliant. For Ireland it is a disturbing image, that of the adolescent girl posing in the nude against the kind of flamboyant draperies recommended and used by Orpen in his portraiture. And it is a mark of Tuohy's

---

[5] *A Mayo Peasant Boy*, Hugh Lane Municipal Gallery of Modern Art. The painting was owned by the architect Joseph Holloway, who was a friend of Jack Yeats and keenly interested in the theatre. He presented the work in 1934.

courage as an artist that he carried off the complex challenges presented by the subject. It is hard to imagine any other Orpen pupil
painting a similar work as early as 1914, certainly not Keating.
Keating was more overtly engaged in the business of creating
paintings that were intended as historical icons, and these are
found in public collections in Ireland, where they conform to a
nationalist ideal in visual art. But Keating had a natural and warm
sense of domestic life, and his studies of Irish peasant interiors are
often finer works than his flying columns or civil war heroes. In
these and related works we see Keating's instinctive response to
the west of Ireland, to Irish peasants in domestic settings, to the
romantic vision exemplified in Synge's writing, all of which
Keating continued to paint throughout his life, despite the passing
of much of the custom and dress. In the end, the relationship between Orpen and Keating pivoted on their conflicting views.
Keating wanted Orpen to give up his life to Ireland; Orpen,
wisely, saw his future in England.

This disdain, as it were, was offensive to nationalists. One of
the more voluble of them was a fellow-painter, John Butler Yeats,
more than forty years Orpen's senior, who nevertheless saw himself in rivalry with the younger man. So powerful was Orpen's
position, as early as 1906, that Yeats told his son, William Butler:
"At present my object is to paint better than Orpen — that is the
only path to salvation."[6] And he made the point that Orpen was
the only Irish artist making a living out of his painting. But the old
man never succeeded. He knew himself to be "imprisoned in an
imperfect technique", and said as much. And he remained a cap-
tive until his death sixteen years later in New York.

---

[6] Undated letter, probably 1906, from Gurteen Dhas, Dundrum, published in *J.B.
Yeats: Letters to his son W.B. Yeats and Others, 1869–1922*, London, 1944, p. 89. The
age gap between the two men was forty years. The letters from John Butler Yeats
contain many references to Orpen's ability and his focus on success.

It was different for those whom Orpen taught. They knew the technique. What Orpen could not do was to transfer the spirit and cohesion of his own artistic inspiration to his students and followers. An impressive number of painters in Ireland during the first half of the twentieth century drew and painted so very well, and seemed naturally in command of the requirements of form and composition. And, to a degree, they owed this to Orpen's teaching and the powerful shadow of his greatness as a painter. But flatness intruded with the passage of time, and a pedestrian dependence on solid, safe teaching and conventional performance created an academic self-satisfaction that was increasingly mocked. The academic approach was presided over by Dermod O'Brien, President of the Royal Hibernian Academy from 1910 until his death in 1945. O'Brien, in the Nathaniel Hone tradition as a painter, was an agreeable and kindly man, who helped younger artists by buying their works, and trudged around different parts of Ireland painting generally indifferent landscapes when he wasn't painting portraits. In Orpen's absence — he never returned to Ireland after the First World War — the idea and the practice of academic painting settled around Dermod O'Brien. He and the main body of RHA painters became loosely, in some cases reluctantly, committed to the new nation in their involvement with country life, urban scenes, political events, the painting of the Shannon Scheme (by Keating), and other expressions of patriotic art. And their output was generally worthy, solidly executed, conventional, but on the whole uninspired.

ℰ

What had been originally inspired by Orpen's own mockery of the fervent revivalist thinking at the beginning of the century became in its turn all too open to mockery and more pungent criticism at the hands of modernist painters. At about the time when Orpen was metaphorically washing his hands of Ireland's cultural and nationalist pretensions, the life and vigour in art was passing to a different group. And in the chronology of events it would be natural to turn to them in order to pick up the new strands in Irish painting during the period immediately after the First World War. But something far more magical had already taken place in the life of quite another artist. One now emerges almost from the shadow of Orpen's overwhelming presence at the beginning of the century, yet fully armed to take over the unfulfilled role of shaping a national ethos in terms of visual image and metaphor.

The figure in question is Jack Yeats. Yeats never had pupils. It is questionable if he ever had teachers who made any impact on him, other than by example. He went through no rigorous art school training comparable to Orpen's studies under Henry Tonks and Philip Wilson Steer. He never taught art, and throughout his life had very little to say about it, though the argument that he never talked about art at all is an exaggerated one. He never wrote about art, still less did he make any comments on fellow artists. He was a mute, silent observer. For so powerful a painter, and a hugely respected presence on the artistic landscape, it is odd that Jack Yeats never had followers, either. There are no painters in Ireland who relate to Yeats in a way comparable to the relation-ship with Orpen, Keating or Tuohy, or indeed a score of other painters whose style and technique can be directly traced to Or-pen's teaching. Yeats, by comparison, stands alone.[7]

But he does so more by accident than by design, more by the lateness of his development, and its uncertainty, than by virtue of qualities which can be seen as unique. Though seven years older than Orpen, Yeats did not impinge in any comparable way as a painter until well into the 1920s. He had no serious reputation in England until after Orpen's death. And he struggled in his own

---

[7] There is a substantial literature, including Hilary Pyle, *Jack B. Yeats, Catalogue Raisonné*, in three volumes, London, 1992; *Jack B. Yeats, a Biography*, London, 1971, by the same author; and her catalogues of watercolours and drawings. The author of this essay published a Life of the artist, authorised by the family, in 1998.

country for many years against indifference and mockery. But he had a singleness of purpose from the outset that came to be allied with the evolution of Ireland in the twentieth century in a remarkable way. He was valued by a relatively small though influential group for his capacity to represent faithfully Irish people and the life of the nation.

Almost from the outset of his career as an Irish artist, Jack Yeats had the support of Lady Gregory. He also had the backing of his father and sisters, perhaps less so of his brother. And he enjoyed the friendship and encouragement of Synge, George Moore, Seumas O'Sullivan, James Stephens, and others. They formed a nucleus for nationalism in art, and they also had the support of politicians such as Eamon de Valera.

Though he was almost thirty before he embarked on his career as an Irish artist, he did so in such an original and appealing way that it stamped his name and his work indelibly on their imaginations, and they occupied a key role in the development of the fledgling nation. He did it by setting out to portray Irish life in everything he drew and painted in a way that was new, refreshing and truthful. He sought to penetrate the national character, to understand it, to reveal it, to give it dignity, to raise it to self-respect and even to greatness. It seems an obvious task for an Irish artist to impose on himself. And yet Irish art, and indeed British art, had created a conventional view of Ireland that was at best sentimental and at worst gross caricature. Peasants were the peasants of Erskine Nichol or of *Punch*. Provincial life was the life of Dion Boucicault or Charles Lever. The majority accepted this. Even after the Revival, the caricature view lingered on. It needed the deadly purpose of John M. Synge's genius, or indeed that of Jack Yeats, who became the writer's friend and working colleague, to demonstrate that self-respect and truth required something different.

Having demonstrated, during his early years as an illustrator and cartoonist, as well as in his first serious paintings for exhibition in 1897, his capacity for action, character and drama in art,

Yeats turned his attention to Ireland. He held first one and then a succession of exhibitions broadly entitled "Life in the West of Ireland". They were essentially modest in scope, made up of line drawings, wash drawings, watercolours and prints. He exhibited in places like the Engineers' Hall in Dublin, and his canvases sold modestly. He held exhibitions in England with the same title. He also made prints for his two sisters' Cuala Press, and these were more widely bought and served as new and acceptable images of Irish life — truthful, full of energy, inspiring.

For much of the period during which he was laying down, as it were, his artistic credentials as a recorder of Irish life and character, he was living in Devon with his English wife, Cottie. Each summer they travelled to Ireland for periodic working holidays, and to keep up friendships with those who were at the centre of the literary revival, his brother W.B. Yeats, Lady Gregory, Synge, and the American promoter of Irish painting and writing, John Quinn. In retrospect, his associations with the Irish Revival, and notably with Synge during their time in Connemara and Mayo, and with Lady Gregory, have been exaggerated. In reality, Jack Yeats was a minor figure, unsure of whether or not to live in Ireland, and lacking in confidence about his work to the point where he had a nervous breakdown in 1915 almost certainly caused by a sense of non-fulfilment as a painter. But he continued to range the West of Ireland, from Kerry to Donegal, drawing and painting people, events and places, and putting an increasingly distinctive stamp upon the representation of a national identity.

His powerful early masterpiece, *The Circus Dwarf*, predates the breakdown, and follows his arrival in Ireland by only two years. It was rejected by the Royal Hibernian Academy in 1912, the year it was painted, but then exhibited in the Armory show after its exhibition in London, the previous year. It attracted early critical attention. There was perceptive identification of an important Jack Yeats characteristic: "The people Mr Yeats is interested in are a rough, hard-bitten, unshaven, and generally disreputable lot of men. His broken-down actors practicing fencing, his 'Circus Dwarf' . . . are subjects no other artist would have chosen to paint."[8] Hilary Pyle takes a sentimental view of this work, referring to the dwarf looking "meditatively", having a "sad, painted face", with "added poignancy", and the "vulnerability of the performer". The subject of the painting is indulging in no self-pity; he is tough, devious, a survivor. His face is neither painted, nor is it sad. Jack clearly identified the painting as his own major exhibit for the New York Armory Show, that historically important event in twentieth century art.

Jack Yeats recovered from the breakdown. With his growing accomplishment in the painting of oils there came the courage to tackle the aftermath of the First World War and the setting up of an independent Irish state. It moved him inexorably towards the centre of the stage as an Irish artist of national significance. His alliance with the Dublin Painters, a group established to promote modernist, especially continental, ideas, was an important act, even if his involvement was short-lived. He was in fact to remain always a solitary figure in art. But by the early 1920s, when he was already in his fifties, he had become a central voice on behalf of Irish art.

It was Jack Yeats who gave the lecture on Irish art at the important Race Conference in Paris, early in 1922.[9] It was there that he came into contact with Eamon de Valera, and found himself increasingly allied to the Sinn Féin, or Republican side, in Irish

---

[8] *Star* newspaper, 16 July 1912, article by A.J. Findberg entitled "Art and Artist' Life in the West of Ireland". The other works shown by Jack in the Armory Show were *The Political Meeting, A Stevedore, The Barrel Man, Strand Races* and *The Last Corinthian*.

[9] J.B. Yeats, *Modern Aspects of Irish Art*, Dublin, 1922. The booklet, one of an extensive series concerning Ireland, carried an introduction by Eamon de Valera. He claimed that their purpose was "to expose current first principles and to bring exact knowledge concerning current problems into every home in Ireland. A carefully thought out scheme of study is proposed."

politics. All the things that Orpen mocked, Yeats took to his heart. He valued the national spirit in painting more than the exercise of the craft. Indeed, it could be said that he never mastered the craft in any conventional meaning of the words. He was self-taught in the handling of oils. He used them to begin with as an illustrator might, laying down colour within a linear frame. And his sense of the making and mixing of colour is undoubtedly open to quite severe criticism, since all too often he ends up with shades of mauve in default of better contrasts, higher tonal values. Similar criticisms may be levelled against his control of composition and form. But he had a magical reading of the national character, and was able, in many paintings, to translate it into a breathtaking expression of the drama of Irish life. By the mid-1920s he had established a number of major works which count as foundation-stones in Irish art in the twentieth century.

Then came a break with even the limited traditions in his art of the first fifty years. Throwing all caution to the wind, Yeats began to paint with thick impasto, using fingers and a palette-knife as well as brushes, and with the wide use of primary colours, brilliant reds, yellows, blues and greens. It brought fire, sun, light, into unconventionally high-flown antagonisms and juxtapositions which verge often on the extraordinary, and are always challenging.[10] He expressed for those around him how to be liberated in what they painted, and in how they executed their work. No one followed the lead he gave. He presented Ireland with a series of stages on which its own history was enacted. The life of the ballad-singer, the public-house performer, the theatrical entertainer, the political speech-maker, the jockey at a country race meeting, the circus clown, the story-teller, the poet, the soldier, the emigrant, the old sea captain, all became emblematic and symbolic. He built a

---

[10] His early work, technically, presented one set of problems. The late canvases, as Brian Kennedy has perceptively shown, present us with a totally different range of technical problems. See Brian Kennedy, "The Oil Painting Technique of Jack B. Yeats", in *Irish Arts Review Yearbook*, 1993, pp. 118–23.

tapestry around the nation; the unending presentation of the life of Ireland, no longer constrained by that original title, did more to create the cultural blood and tissue of the nation than almost anything else produced by Irish writers and artists.

It was both a pure and a mature expression of Irish nationalism in art. There was innate sensitivity and subtlety in what he did. It was never obvious. Understanding what he was saying was not easy. Nor did it always work. There are paintings that simply mean nothing at all, and there are paintings which technically, compositionally, are disasters. But the general thread of his composition is a reflection of his life, and in his life through its art he sought to reflect and create the life of the country, making credible and acceptable its diverse and rugged nature.

It is questionable how far he was accepted. He was never successful in the Orpen sense of success, not even at the end of his life. Recognition of his potential greatness as a painter came in England more than in Ireland. Ironically this happened only with the National Gallery exhibition in London, which took place as a result of Kenneth Clark's involvement. Dublin responded with a measure of comparable enthusiasm, and began working towards the 1945 retrospective exhibition which duly honoured the doyen of Irish art, who was by then in his early seventies. But the hidden lessons of his life had been spread through the nation, among painters of course, but also among ordinary people who equated Irish art with Jack Yeats in ways that no other artist inspired.

There is a negative side to this. Jack Yeats achieved a preeminent position in Irish art in spite of, rather than because of, his qualities as a painter. He transcended imperfect technique with visionary capacities that at times are overwhelming. No one doubts the poignancy and compassion, for example, of *The Blood of Abel*; yet as a painting it is ill-conceived, its composition without discipline or internal structure, its colour and tone weak.

It is a form of critical suicide, in Ireland, to raise fundamental questions about this problem confronting us over Yeats's art.

Worse still, bound up within it is the more widely spread difficulty over the extent to which bad art in Ireland gains endorsement from the existence at its very heart of so complex, so unique, so instinctive a figure. He swept aside the very idea of a worthwhile academic tradition. He belittled not just the idea that good art came from European cities like Paris, against which he had the strongest of prejudices, but that good art could be defined in such terms. Like de Valera, whom he greatly admired during a substantial part of his life, there was a tendency for Jack Yeats to look into his own heart and discover there what art was about, and why painting should be done in one way and not in another.

He is a giant in Irish art of the twentieth century, perhaps flawed by imperfect technique, but a giant figure nonetheless. He stands proud and solitary as the creator of a unique landscape. He peopled it with men and women who frequently come in from the fringes of society, from the bogs, the fairs, the circuses and the markets, and yet are able, through the power of his presentation, to take centre stage positions with pride and confidence. They become, under his hand, substantial and haunting figures representative of a sad and violent history, of mythic values, powerful tales, apocalyptic achievements. He pushes them forward, transforming their human state into artistic statements that are breathtaking.

The nationalist agenda is a wide one, however, and in no sense exclusive. In *About to Write a Letter*, for example, a patrician view is given of the unexplained episode. And the great painting *Now* draws its inspiration from a visit made to a newly opened London theatre at the turn of the century, recreating from memory the excitement and flurry of a stage entry. The whole vast performance, spanning more than half the twentieth century and adding up to some 1,100 oil paintings and innumerable drawings and watercolours, holds together as a cohesive, complete expression of the man's imagined reality for Ireland. Nothing compares with it in Irish art.

ॐ

Jack Yeats defied the very canons that mattered so centrally to William Orpen. And he was a sceptic towards another, and quite different seminal figure in Irish art of the twentieth century, Mainie Jellett.[11] Mainie Jellett was a product of the art tradition to which William Orpen had belonged, and for a short period was his pupil at the Dublin Metropolitan School of Art before moving to London, and studying there with Walter Sickert at the Westminster School of Art. Accomplished in draughtsmanship, in composition and form, in the painting of beautiful portraits and nudes, Mainie Jellett eventually turned her back on the English art school tradition. She followed French artists; first André Lhote, from whom she acquired the basic principles of Cubism, then Albert Gleizes, who taught her the principles of abstraction. By the mid-1920s, when Ireland was beginning to flex its cultural muscles in exploration of modernism, she was ready to carry out a signal and unique service through teaching and artistic practice in the city of her birth. She believed, in sharp contrast to Jack Yeats, that the key to art in the future derived from Paris, and more specifically was contained within abstraction. This was the natural outcome of Cubism, and offered a key, not just to the future of painting, but to all the arts. Einstein, Stravinsky, Pound, Proust, Eliot, Joyce were all part of her artistic heritage. She read and lectured on abstraction in music, had a competent grasp on Einstein's scientific theories, attended Stravinsky concerts in Paris in the early 1920s. She read works by Joyce as they were published, and more widely was well-read in the modernist literature of the period through which she lived.

Second only to Orpen, among Irish artists, she was an outstanding painter of the female nude, from the period of study under him, through the Sickert period at the Westminster School and

---

[11] See Bruce Arnold, *Mainie Jellett and the Modern Movement in Ireland*, New Haven and London, 1991, for biographical details and a general discussion of the evolution of modernism in Ireland during the first half of the twentieth century.

then with André Lhote, as in *Seated Female Nude*. This accomplishment was not revisited again until late in her life, when she reverted to naturalism for a period.

She believed in the importance of transmitting her knowledge and views about international modernism to the newly independent Ireland, and she brought to this task the skills of a teacher and a considerable ability as a writer.[12] For the country to survive and flourish, culturally, in her view, its artists needed to be international in their outlook. They needed to be aware of world trends, and not confined, either by a local authoritarianism based on lifeless academic painting, or by a nationalism which subscribed to an equally local set of myths and symbols in art, designed to trigger off predictable, safe public reactions. To a remarkable extent, Mainie Jellett reconciled the two quite different traditions deriving from Orpen and Yeats. She was technically a brilliant painter, and a fine draughtswoman. She admired the best in the academic tradition, so long as it had life. At the same time, she shared with Jack Yeats a desire for novelty and experiment, a determination to shock and challenge, a belief in the unique capacity of the individual artist to occupy a territory of influence and expression entirely his, or her, own. They were members together of the Dublin Painters Group, and remained respectful of each other during the comparatively short period of time Mainie Jellett lived in Dublin, from her return from France in the mid-1920s to her early death in 1944.

But while Jack Yeats was essentially static as an artistic influence, aloof, isolated, solitary, Mainie Jellett was the undisputed leader of the Modernist Movement in Ireland, active, aggressive, confrontational.[13] And it really was a movement. She taught,

---

[12] Full details of her largely unpublished writing, mainly for lectures and addresses, but also for publication in journals, are given in *Mainie Jellett and the Modern Movement in Ireland*, op. cit.

[13] Both came to their positions through controversy. Yeats was gregarious by nature, and spoke freely about art in the early years; but adverse criticism made him increasingly taciturn with newspapermen and with the public generally. His

argued, debated, challenged on issues of cultural direction, artistic philosophy, and on all the arts, including architecture. Above all, she painted, with great passion and inspiration, and produced a body of work very much ahead of its time. She engaged in pure abstraction, on the Cubist model, and painted a number of religious works, of which *Virgin and Child* is an outstanding example. Towards the end of her life her work became more naturalistic, as in *Achill Horses*.

She campaigned on the need for young painters to form themselves into a society or group able to take on the Royal Hibernian Academy, and create an alternative venue for the display of modern paintings, which were regularly refused by the selection committee of that august body. This gave birth to the Irish Exhibition of Living Art, an annual show of modern artists' work which was crucial to her contemporaries, though she did not herself live to enjoy the fruits of her work in setting it up. By the time she inaugurated the movement, in 1943, she had already led a generation of painters, many of them women, to find themselves artistically. They included her lifelong friend, Evie Hone, Mary Swanzy, whose art Jellett greatly admired, May Guinness, who had studied at the same time as herself and Evie Hone in Paris, Nano Reid and Norah McGuinness. And she had supported and encouraged younger artists, including those who exhibited with the White Stag Group, among them Pat Scott, Kenneth Hall, Basil Rakoczi. Louis le Brocquy, whose mother, Sybil, was a close friend of Mainie's, came under her influence and was encouraged by her; and she helped the painters in Dublin who associated with Gerard Dillon, whose first solo exhibition she opened.

---

gregariousness became increasingly limited to trusted friends and to those they recommended to him. Mainie Jellett had a more limited circle of friends, but was outspoken about art and fearless in the face of controversy. Sources, published and yet to be published, for these important aspects of her character, have already been cited.

Unlike Orpen, who surrounded himself with students whose work he admired and whose company he enjoyed, Mainie Jellett's relationships with fellow artists were more egalitarian, more cerebral, perhaps more formal and more rigorously concerned with theory and practice of a profession for which she had unlimited time and respect. She did not need to like what an artist did in order to support the determination to do it.

Nationalism, for her, resided in the exercise of freeing painters from constraint and fashion, and allowing them, indeed encouraging them, to express themselves in language which had currency throughout the modern world. This, she believed, was how Irish artists would best serve any reliable concept of "Irish" art, and not by the representation of national life in terms of event or character set forth in panoramic tableau. Hers was a revolutionary view. She did not teach abstraction except to a tiny group of painters who specifically wanted to understand its principles. She taught a disciplined freedom for the artist at a time — the late 1930s — when authoritarianism and nationalism were both tending to stifle independence of artistic thought and freedom of expression.

She gave to Irish art an international frame of reference. Yet she never lost the respect of the academic painters, such as Dermod O'Brien, with whom she enjoyed a strange relationship, based at times, it seemed, in fundamental disagreement and conflict. She was similarly at odds with Seán Keating, the doyen of nationalist artists, whose stamp on Irish art teaching was a reflection of his devotion to William Orpen.

Inescapably, what Mainie Jellett foreshadowed in her teaching, and even more significantly in her espousal of the Living Art idea, was her own desire to lead succeeding generations away from the concept of an identifiable Irishness in art. Irish painters, after the Second World War, began slowly, uncertainly, to take their place within art outside Ireland. They had shows in London and New York. Some lived and worked abroad. They had moved forward and had lost any sense of obligation, as Yeats and Jellett had felt, an obligation which William Orpen sensibly denied in the earlier decades of the century.

Uniquely of their time, these painters defined and advanced concepts of what it meant to be Irish artists, what painters should be doing, how they should do it, in both the technical and visionary sense, and where it would lead. They charted a road, by example, by teaching, by writing, and others followed.

They were markedly different in approach. William Orpen, perhaps responsive in a somewhat negative way to the historical events of the first two decades of the century, placed the emphasis on technique, and excellence of performance.[14] A truly egalitarian person in human terms, he was elitist professionally, choosing the company of students who shone in their art, and ignoring the second-rate. In his teaching and in his painting, he summarised the period through which he lived in a series of masterpieces that rank as high as any works of art produced by an Irish painter.

Yet there is a question mark over using the term "Irish art" to describe the major part of his output: the glorious nudes, the genre scenes, the portraits, the domestic interiors and the glowing landscapes painted at Howth or in the west of Ireland. And in his writing he betrays his position as that of a man who had limited belief in the collective, national purpose to be served by developing art in Ireland as an extension of life in Ireland, and the life of Ireland.

Jack Yeats was the opposite. He believed in the concept, and followed it for himself. But he promulgated nothing, he taught no one, his writings are deliberately obscure on art, and his only lecture on

---

[14] He refers, both in *Stories of Old Ireland and Myself* and in *An Onlooker in France*, to his involvement as a war artist with the senior officers, up to and including Field Marshal Earl Haig, and to the process of personal alienation, attributing it at one point to a supposed or actual threat to his own personal safety in Ireland. For whatever reasons, apart from a brief, one-night visit in 1918, he never returned to the country between the end of the First World War and his death in 1931. The officers with whom he had contact, and whose portraits he painted, were the enemies of Irish independence, and had been responsible for the oppression after the 1916 Rising and the years leading up to independence in 1922.

Irish art is consistently paradoxical, from beginning to end. He cared little for technique, he invented his own compositional rules, he developed a palette which is eccentric, and he plucked from the air some of the most handsome, vital and witty titles for works of art we know. In terms of the national identity and the extent to which it derives from the work of artists, Yeats occupies a uniquely central position that few have ever been able to explain.

Mainie Jellett both believed in, and practised, an art which she related to the life of the country, and to the generations of painters who followed her. The major part of her work consists of abstract paintings, and they belong to a French tradition that she deployed in the education of artists in Ireland. The tradition did not, in practical terms, catch on. No school of Irish abstraction developed under her guidance. The best that can be said of Mainie Jellett's influence is that it opened hearts and minds to the world outside Ireland, and sowed the seeds for the internationalising of Irish art during the final quarter of the twentieth century. The concept itself, "Irish art", is rendered redundant in the wake of what we have seen in our lives.

These were not the only figures to carry out this largely self-appointed task. Of course the academic painters, the traditionalists, the overtly nationalist artists, were engaged in something similar. But none, in my view, have that indefinable characteristic of greatness that I unquestionably associate with the three artists dealt with here. Each in his or her fashion made a prodigious impact on art in Ireland during the twentieth century. Each was entirely different in what they achieved. Taken together, the range of their accomplishments, as influences and as artists, is incalculable.

Essay for the catalogue of *When Time Began to Rant and Rage*. This exhibition, mounted by James Christen Steward, then chief curator at the Berkeley Art Museum in California, opened at the Walker Art Gallery in Liverpool, October 1998. It moved to Berkeley in February 1999, and then to the Grey Art Gallery, New York, in May 1999.

28

IRELAND'S PAINTERS

Ireland's Painters 1600–1940 has a long and interesting history and may truly be regarded as the life work of two distinguished scholars, Anne Crookshank and the Knight of Glin. Both had museum backgrounds, the former in the Ulster Museum, the latter in the Victoria and Albert Museum. It gave them a taste for the particular, an interest in detail, familiarity with primary resource material and generally an eclectic taste. Anne Crookshank went on to become head of the Fine Art Department in Trinity College and the Knight of Glin to be the representative of Christie's in Ireland for many years. He has also been a collector of distinction with a particular interest in Limerick, where his ancestral home, Glin Castle, stands.

Intellectually they have been partners for more than three decades, and they first published their joint book on Irish art, *The Painters of Ireland*, in 1978. It was a well-researched and thorough chronology of the subject. It was conversational in style, eclectic in judgement, wayward and discursive in manner, seeming to leave no stone unturned.

In fact they did leave stones unturned. They took only limited interest in the broad sweep of Irish history, and how it related to art, and they largely ignored the social, cultural and nationalist arguments that many regard as essential to the definition of such a subject. They concentrated instead on a broadly inclusive summary of as many painters working in Ireland over two and a half centuries as they could discover. They earned from Ellis Waterhouse, the distinguished art historian who succeeded Thomas Bodkin at the Barber Institute in Birmingham and has written superbly about English art, this definition of their book: "A general survey on traditional lines." And they seem pleased enough to quote this in their new edition, adding a plea that the complexities of Irish history preclude a broader approach.

Ireland's Painters 1600–1940 comes twenty-five years later, but in its essentials, and in many of its words and phrases, is the same work revised. It has a new title, one that still avoids the issue of whether or not there is Irish Art. It has more chapters, and many more illustrations — this time the vast majority in colour — and a number of new artists. The colour is a mixed blessing; a number of images are dark and "hot" and there is some unevenness in the clarity. It is a good deal more expansive. In its immense detail it is a splendidly rich and varied examination, by far the most substantial we shall ever have and vital to the serious student of the subject.

Moreover, where the judgements have changed, and there is much greater knowledge, we are provided with the fruits of this. Thomas Pooley is given the significant attention he deserves, largely the result of Jane Fenlon's researches, aided by Toby Barnard. And the broad sweep of eighteenth-century portraiture is handled with a certain grandeur, artists such as James Latham, Charles Jervas, Anthony Lee and Thomas Frye coming under generous focus.

But the design remains as it was a quarter of a century ago and this is a major fault. It was possible to argue, in 1978, that the approach was proper because "a reasonable foundation of knowledge" had not been assembled. But the current work renders this argument no longer valid. If the authors cannot stand over what they have written and use it more adventurously than they have, then this represents a major limitation on what they have achieved. Ireland's history, the vigour and inequality of its social life, the uneasy relationship between the two neighbouring islands, have all been reflected in Irish art and literature. It is obscurant and obtuse to argue that this reflection cannot be used to move on the subject matter of *Ireland's Painters* from the Waterhouse definition of "a general survey on traditional lines". It is as though the authors still say, after quarter of a century of further research: "Here are the ingredients, you make the pudding." The ingredients are excellent, the best yet in terms of Irish art. But putting them together still lies, regrettably for these writers, in the future. This puts them in a league that is inferior to the great tradition represented by Gombrich, Wilenski, Schama, Fry, Levy, Pevsner, Rothenstein, Clark and Blunt.

Definitions still remain uncertain. Were all these painters really "Ireland's painters"? Or were they, until the twentieth century, British artists who worked in Ireland, lived in Ireland, honoured the commissions they got as part of their living, but also owed artistic debts elsewhere?

Only one artist has a chapter to himself, the great James Barry. Endlessly fascinating as a subject, with huge ambition, great talent and the imagination of a genius, he was flawed because of his Irish obsession with conflict. Barry is something of a pivotal figure. His career coincided with a rich period of Irish landscape painting and with the climax of the relative independence in politics and trade that made the end of the eighteenth century such an exciting period.

Irish art in the nineteenth century is solid, professional, quite extensive, quite dull. It has no great shape and few outstanding painters. It is as if we are waiting for Irish nationalism to give birth to the excitement of the twentieth century.

It may have been this that persuaded the authors not only to engage again with the twentieth century, but also to expand their observations up to 1940. It is a mistake. This last part is not in the same class as the first sixteen chapters. The authors use the same discursive, even quaint, approach to what has become the best researched period of all, with major publications and full-length biographies to which they refer hardly at all.

But these reservations should not detract from a prodigious achievement, full of intelligence and wit, enlivened by the authors' strange duet-like approach to the craft of writing, a conversation piece in itself.

Reviewed in the *Irish Independent*, December 2002

29

IRISH ART IN THE 1950S

Irish art went through a watershed during the Second World War. Throughout that devastating holocaust, Ireland remained neutral, and in many aspects, social and economic, ideological and intellectual, was in a backwater. But art, particularly the art of painting and sculpture, enjoyed a remarkable period of activity backed by much original talent. The first wave of Irish Modernism ended with the death in 1944 of Mainie Jellett. The first Irish Exhibition of Living Art took place the year before. This was to represent the new Modernism, and it did produce much good work in subsequent years.

Much of the most exciting work in those war years was being produced by a number of artists who worked in association with the White Stag Group, including the young Patrick Scott, Kenneth Hall, who was probably the finest of them, and Basil Rakoczi. They were expatriate Irish, irreverent and anti-national in their thinking, bohemian in their beliefs, liberal in their habits. They came like a breath of fresh air in 1939–40; they left with relief in 1945. The torch passed. Mainie Jellett, who had opened his first exhibition, saw in Gerard Dillon a substantial talent for the future. She knew and admired the work of Louis le Brocquy. And from those early exhibitions of Living Art, a movement established to challenge the heavy hand of the academics in painting, may be drawn the substance of the first decade in the second half of the twentieth century.

Grace Henry, for example, Harriet Kirkwood, Cecil ffrench Salkeld, belonged to the earlier group of Modernists, Henry herself having been involved in the foundation of the Society of Dublin Painters in the early 1920s. But the main group was cohesive and essentially post-war in its artistic outlook. Gerard Dillon, Patrick Collins, Colin Middleton, Norah McGuinness, Elizabeth Rivers, Father Jack Hanlon, George Campbell, Doreen Vanston, Thurloe Conolly, Dan O'Neill, Louis le Brocquy and Patrick Swift represented the central core of painting at the time, while the key sculptors were Oisín Kelly and Hilary Heron, and the principal stained-glass artist exhibiting was Evie Hone.

At the heart of all this was the doyen of Irish Art, Jack Yeats, more modern in technique and effect than painters half his age, more courageous perhaps than most of them would ever be. He was busy enlivening the life of art with paintings such as *Left, Left, We Left our Name on the Famous Road, on the Famous Road of Fame,* which he exhibited at the Living Art show in 1949. The atmosphere of the time was imbued with his spirit. The main dealer, Victor Waddington, was pre-eminently his dealer, lived, breathed and laboured for him, and in due course was to carry off his spirit in a parcel of paintings and drawings to London, where Waddington had already given Irish painters an airing, in London group shows which he organised.

The substance of what was being done was frail enough. The bravery of it, the sense of partnership and collaboration in a Modernist experiment was not altogether matched by strength of artistic purpose or the power and brilliance of individual works. The idiom was remotely "Cubist", angular, surreal or primitive. Quite powerful works were also being exhibited at the Royal Hibernian Academy summer show each year, to which Jack Yeats, an academician, also sent, and where other painters not attached to

Living Art, like Christopher Campbell, showed powerful canvases which were inspired by his solitary, introspective vision.

While the impact of the Irish Exhibition of Living Art was a particularly significant one during the first ten years of its life, it is instructive to look at the work of the "Opposition". At the end of the 1950s the Royal Hibernian Academy, against whose standards Living Art had been established, frequently exhibited works by Living Art artists. Louis le Brocquy and Norah McGuinness were also part of the RHA, and artists such as Beatrice Glenavy, W.J. Leech, Letitia M. Hamilton and Patrick Hennessy, who were academicians anyway, showed their work as well.

One wonders how much was sold, how confident the artists themselves were about what they were trying to do, how many of them would last. Thurloe Conolly pulled out, so did Ralph Cusack. These were residue figures from the White Stag Movement, which itself had really ended in failure. Victor Waddington, as we now know, spent the first half of the decade of the 1950s losing money in his attempts to bring modern art to the Irish people, and by the time Jack Yeats stopped painting, around 1955, had decided to give up and move to London. His assistant earlier on, Leo Smith, had his own Dawson Gallery, giving exhibitions to artists and also dealing in Jack Yeats paintings on his own behalf. But anyone who remembers that quintessential Dublin man will recall the bitterness with which he viewed the city and its people, as far as their response to Irish art was concerned.

In a city now full of galleries, it is hard to conceive of the desert of those years, both for painters, a rare breed, and for collectors, a far rarer breed. The climate was a depressed one. Victor Waddington gave up because he lost a fortune of money supplied by Mabel Waddington, who came from a family which had made its money out of laundries and dry-cleaning. That was the measure of life. And it was a remarkable event when, towards the end of that decade, David Hendriks established the Richie Hendriks Gallery, in St Stephen's Green, first on the corner with Grafton

Street, later midway along the side of the Green going towards the bottom of Harcourt Street.

Between them, by the end of the decade, these two men had carved up modern art in Ireland and were exhibiting the painters who mattered, David Hendriks arguably more "contemporary", though this reputation derived mainly from his strong and stylish introduction of international artists, group shows, and the like.

But I am slipping out of one decade into the next, and allowing the change of temper and style, which to a large degree reflected the economic recovery at the end of the 1950s, to influence judgement. The 1950s were focused on painting, not on wealth. They were years when artists worked, but often did not sell. The galleries were disposed to show works, but then return them to studios. There was surprisingly good critical writing about art, both in the national newspapers and in magazines. *The Bell*, while it lasted, gave prominence to art, as did *Horizon*, in England, which turned some attention on what was happening in the arts in Ireland.

The powerful figures dominating the decade in the Modernist mode, who by their work were trying to address new visual challenges and give a leadership to younger painters, included Louis le Brocquy, Colin Middleton, Norah McGuinness. All of them changed their style quite radically during this decade. The most revolutionary, in this respect, was probably le Brocquy. The humanism which inspired his semi-realist treatment of Mother and Child and Family themes gave way, at the end of the decade, to semi-abstract "Beings" and "Forms" of a quite different kind, must richer in pigment and colour, despite the predominance of white.

Though he seems to have been increasingly detached from other painters and from involvement in art as a "movement", Dan O'Neill probably painted his best work in the 1950s.

The choice made for the decade is in two parts. Jack Yeats was a dominant figure for all artists. He was at the end of a long life and had been exhibiting regularly since the closing years of the nineteenth century. His prodigious output and his gigantic presence as a voice and an exemplar of Irish art demands separate treatment. And it was not hard to discover the remarkable representation of this in magnificent canvases from his old age. That a man in his eighties could perform in paint on canvas as he did is an astonishing feat, and deserves a presentation of its own.

For the second part of this representation of a ten-year period, the choice inevitably becomes personal. However, I have sought to be guided by the degree to which the decade was important in the span of the life of the painter. While I think Dan O'Neill and Gerard Dillon were at their best, I personally regard Louis le Brocquy's best work to belong in the 1960s.

Without way wishing this to be seen as prejudicial to the interpretations of others, which in any case will redefine the idea of Irish art, the 1950s seemed at the time, and seem much more so in retrospect, to be a "confined" period of Irish art. Almost by definition, what came after was a dismantling of the coherence and unity of an Irish nationalist spirit in the arts through the impact of international art, ideas, exhibitions, and knowledge generally. Jack Yeats was a climactic figure. His colleagues, both in his own last decade and earlier, were breaking new ground, determining new avenues for art, actively bringing in work and vision from the outside world. It changed everything.

Shifting Ground was the title of an exhibition at the Irish Museum of Modern Art held in the autumn of 2000. Five critics chose it: Dorothy Walker, Oliver Dowling, Medb Ruane, Caoimhín Mac Giolla Léith and myself, each choosing work to represent a decade. The essay appeared in the catalogue.

30

JACK YEATS: WRITING THE LIFE

We see Jack Yeats through the rose-tinted glass of posterity, and imagine him always to have been loved and admired. We think he enjoyed the fame which now pours down upon his pictures in a golden shower of cupidity. Everyone would love to have a Jack Yeats. The rich buy him for gilt-edged stock. The wise sell him to buy houses for their children. And the world looks on in wonder at this artist who occupies so special a place in Irish hearts.

He expresses the life of the nation in an entirely unique way. He goes to the heart of it because he captures the personality and the actions of its people. The works are drawn from history, from the peasantry, from Irish myths and their heroes. They are taken from men who love horses and from horses which love men. They are inspired by his own love for circus clowns, singers, pavement artists, trick-o'-the-loop men and three-card-trick-men. Jack Yeats has painted the life of Ireland into a thousand canvases and more. And because of this he will live for ever.

But recognition that this was so, in his work and in his life, came late and slow. It is *we* that have transformed him into a success, posthumously, because he is one now. He was hardly that, through the greater part of his life. Well into his sixties he almost lost his way as a painter, virtually giving up for a period of time and devoting his energies to novels and plays. In his seventies came recognition, but not the sale of his works. Almost into his eighties, when he sought to move onto a world stage, with a travelling exhibition in the United States, and his first solo show in Paris, he seemed dogged by the perversities of fortune, recording no great success abroad, and confined to a narrow following in Ireland. All his life he was admired by a small, trusting group of close friends. But world recognition in any wider sense came late.

Disentangling this story has for me been a remarkable personal journey into the heart and soul of a country and of a man. What I discovered there confounds most of what we think we know about his life and about what he experienced. We can take easily enough a revised view of his supposed "success". He had an iron will, and he painted what he painted because he believed in it. Late on, when his pictures failed to sell, and when the economic climate was against him anyway, one might have expected an output from the artist which at least took some cognisance of the world around him. Not so with Jack Yeats. When his fortunes were low, and he faced the bewilderment of critics, and a regular tide of mockery, he turned to painting the largest canvases of his career, huge works which never sold, and were not intended to sell. They were his robust answer to posterity's neglect.

His nationalism is another example of misunderstanding. It has been shaped latterly to fit the country's view of itself, irrespective of the facts. Jack Yeats had strong political opinions. He knew de Valera at an early stage, participating with him at the Celtic Race Conference in Paris, in 1922, and supporting him later. Jack Yeats turned his back on the W.T. Cosgrave-led administration over the execution of Erskine Childers. But he did not let any overt political expression enter his art, and it is wrong to see paintings like *Bachelor's Walk, In Memory, The Funeral of Harry Boland,* or *Talking with Prisoners* as "nationalist" statements. His purpose was always to seek out the suffering of the human heart, and to set it above any deliberate myth-making or the clothing of history with visual memento.

He loved the colour and pageantry of the past. During the 1798 Rebellion centenary celebrations, both in County Sligo and elsewhere, he painted the re-living of the ideals of liberty, and inspired them with the excitement of the occasion. But the statements were human; he was, as it were, coming to his own personal understanding of a country he yearned to rejoin, after a mixed upbringing, partly spent in Sligo, partly in London.

He has been seen as a "Yeats" in the sense of critics pointing to his father, the old reprobate John Butler Yeats, as an artist who gave birth to a greater artist. And this indeed is so. But the other side of his family, the prudent Pollexfens, millers and shipping merchants in Sligo, diligent, hard-working and interested in world success, were more important to him. They have been noted, if at all, for the strain of madness and for their dogged, dull mercantile stability. To Jack Yeats, the Pollexfens and Middletons represented the life of the sea, the adventure of the waves, the magic of piracy and privateering in which their ancestors may well have engaged. But they represented also an engaging commitment to the community, great courage in the face of adversity to Sligo, for example during the cholera epidemic of 1832, and a public-spiritedness which is wholly admirable.

In this sense of feeding the imagination, Jack was more a Pollexfen than a Yeats. He took after his mother, on whom he doted until her death. And he loved his grandparents, William Pollexfen, the fiery, brave, indomitable head of the family, and his gracious, articulate and wise grandmother, Elizabeth. They embodied Sligo to him. And Sligo remained his lifelong passion. He said a bit of it was in everything he did, as an artist. And it certainly infuses paintings, poems, novels, plays and drawings. To understand this, we need to look to the town and the countryside around Sligo. Ben Bulbin is not just a mountain, it is an experience. There is a sweet vulnerability in the isolation of Knocknarea. Dark forces from the south seem to come towards us over the Ox Mountains, their deeper blue emphasised by the sun shining beyond them. They are autumn mountains. Jack loved the Garavogue river. He knew Rosses' Point and the Metal Man as a youthful playground. And the sweep of Sligo Bay up to the coast of distant Donegal was a setting for races on the strand in the sunshine of his youth. We will never capture the essence of this strange and haunting figure without acknowledging how much of a part Sligo played in his life.

He painted into existence the character of this country. He clothed it in people, in landscape and in life. He did so in a careful, deliberate and considered way. All his early exhibitions, with the single exception of the first, held in London, carried the title, roughly, "Life in the West of Ireland"; and they were a presentation, and then a development, of a vision he had, which was to match the literary life of the country with a visual counterpart.

It carried a much shorter distance. The magic of words, whether poetry or theatre, prose or polemic, is the property of everyone. And the impact of his brother, and of the other writers in the early years of the twentieth century, was infinitely greater than his own, which was circumscribed by the small numbers of people who saw his exhibitions, bought works, or had a casual knowledge of them through prints and reproductions.

Jack Yeats himself made even this more difficult, by rejecting the idea of his paintings being reproduced. And though for a time he supported his sisters by making prints for their Cuala Press, even this became a burden to him, and was seen as somehow belittling of his true nature as an artist. So there was an isolation. And, among other things, it meant that Jack Yeats spent nearly the whole of his life under the shadow of his brother's far greater fame.

He admired his brother, and thought that those awarding him the Nobel Prize had taken rather too long about it. This admiration was echoed by Jack's wife, Cottie, to whom W.B. Yeats inscribed copies of his work, and who had a clear understanding of the older brother's poetic genius. But she rated Jack's artistic talent much higher, and often said so.

The brothers remained comparatively distant from each other, their paths diverging in youth, manhood and in their later years. This meant that William Butler Yeats's children, Anne and Michael, hardly knew their Uncle Jack. Fortunately, there was a reconciliation before William's much earlier death. But the record of it, found in the Houghton Library at Harvard, in a letter from Jack to William Rothenstein, reproduced in *Jack Yeats*, comes almost as a mild shock, making one realise that a problem existed for all those years.

Jack was radical in his outlook, always on the side of the underdog. One would know this from so many of his paintings. In time, it affected his political views. His early admiration for de Valera changed, and, though he concealed it, he made references to "that man from 42nd Street" which indicate disillusionment.

Jack Yeats had a great capacity for friendship. The parts of his life that I most enjoyed writing were those concerned with his friendships with John Masefield, John Millington Synge, Samuel Beckett, Thomas MacGreevy, Niall Montgomery, and above all Victor Waddington. They were all different in character. The friendship with Waddington was that of an old man, wise in the world's capacity to neglect and slight him, and conscious of the need to organise his "children" — which was how he viewed his paintings — for posterity's sake.

The friendship with Masefield was wonderfully light-hearted and self-indulgent. They literally played like children, making model boats and sailing them on the river which flowed below Jack's house in Devon, passing the veranda of his studio, which was down the hill beside the water. Their model boats were serious affairs, and Jack wrote a book about them, with designs as illustrations, and advice to all those who are young at heart.

Jack loved Masefield's poetry, his sea shanties, his world wisdom. Masefield was for Jack a surrogate who had actually sailed the world on five-masted sailing vessels, and told the kinds of stories which his grandfather had told him as a child. Masefield admired hugely Jack's ability to draw and paint, to realise the verbal dream in a living, breathing visual way.

Jack's friendship with Synge was all too brief, and very moving in its closing sadness. They enjoyed together an unforgettable month in the west of Ireland in 1905, working for *The Manchester Guardian*. Jack helped Synge with *The Playboy of the Western World*. They collaborated on Synge's book *The Aran Islands*. There was even talk of further collaboration, but Synge's life was cut short, to Jack's dismay, by Hodgkin's Disease, Jack writing a fine memorial essay about his friend.

Both Beckett and MacGreevy feature in Jack's life over many years. The two younger men were at loggerheads over Jack. Beckett disapproved of MacGreevy's attempts to interpret Jack as overtly nationalist in his views. It is possible that MacGreevy had a reason for this, wanting to present himself as a "good" nationalist, and using his writing about Jack to achieve this end. Whatever the reason, Beckett took exception to it, and voiced his own feelings in quite strong terms. But Jack liked and needed the company of both men, and the friendships developed into important and richly rewarding aspects of their lives.

Above all, Jack found and sustained lifelong happiness with his wife, Cottie. She sacrificed her own not inconsiderable talents as an artist — they met at art school in Chiswick — to dedicate her life to his work. And he enjoyed her company and was hugely dependent on her love for him. Her death, which occurred eight years before his own, left him broken-hearted.

Jack Yeats was not a worldly success, but he was that much more important thing, a success within his own heart and mind. He was a completely integrated creative spirit. His technique as a painter was imperfect. Many artists and restorers today shake their heads over his work, his colours, his thick impasto, the darkness of the dark tones, the sometimes erratic compositional approach. But the sheer power of his hand and eye, working rapidly on canvases which flowed from his studio, at times in an abundant torrent — half his huge output was produced after the age of seventy — marks him out as a figure of genius.

I would have felt humbled in his presence, fixed by his sharp eye, energised by the penetration of his mind, his questions, his silences, his strange, elliptical remarks. He stands proud at the threshold of the century, as far as Ireland is concerned, and his shadow was over it at the end. That is a great and lasting achievement.

This account of writing the biography of Jack Yeats was published in September 1998.

31

WILLIAM ORPEN

I

William Orpen in Love

Evelyn St George was undoubtedly the most important person in William Orpen's life. She gave him happiness and she gave him love. She inspired him as an artist, and was the first person to make him recognise that he had within his spiritual makeup the seeds of greatness. She told him what a great painter should do, what sort of pictures he should paint, how he should view the world and how he should respond to it.

They had a love affair. It began some time after their first meeting, which was in about 1906, and was lively and adventurous. As it progressed, she created a uniquely magical "cover" for their extended holidays together in the early summers at Mrs St George's Screebe Lodge, near Maam Cross, the gateway to Connemara, in the west of Ireland. This she did by commissioning an annual portrait of her daughter, Evelyn, known as Gardenia. In reality, the grand design of recording the young girl's growth into womanhood concealed a greater purpose: that of the growing love between her mother and the painter. Orpen was therefore working on this regular commission as well as enjoying the happy times the couple had together in the west of Ireland.

Gardenia, who, as Lady Gunston, later showed me the paintings with a great deal of pride, and with the kindest memories of the artist, came gradually to realise that her mother was having an affair with Orpen. The recognition of this emotionally disturbing discovery was, she said, hard to date clearly, but came after the early portraits of herself, one of the finest being *Gardenia on a Donkey*, painted by Orpen in 1910 at Maam Cross.

Orpen's mother, the former Annie Caulfield, was related to Howard St George, an Irish land agent. He was the grandson of Sir Richard St George of Woodsgift, County Kilkenny. Mrs St George was an American, the daughter and eldest child of George F. Baker, president of the National Bank of America, and a man of immense wealth. She was eight years older than Orpen when she met him. She had grown tired enough of her husband and was looking for a lover. Orpen was of a similar disposition emotionally. Their love affair, which probably started in earnest in 1908, was on a grand scale. It was of huge significance to both of them. The coming together of wealth on the one hand and genius on the other had an electric effect.

Mrs St George had commissioned a number of portraits of herself which are rightly recognised as masterpieces in the genre. In them she was of course indulging her beauty, her love of style, her wealth and the sense of drama which was an inescapable product of her background. But there is evidence of much more in the sometimes severe expression on her face, the faint look of tragedy. The truth was that she was not only bored, she was lonely, despite the frequent presence of her husband and children. This interpretation is confirmed by her youngest child, Vivien, who was Orpen's child. Her account of her mother is a narrative of frustrations and dissatisfactions.

Mrs St George collected in the American way: houses, paintings and furniture were followed by people and reputations. Orpen was an ideal "possession". To the benefit of posterity she saw in Orpen a wonderful opportunity to mould, refine and encourage his enormous talent as a painter, and she set about the task of encouraging him to recognise and fulfil this greatness as an artist which she felt she had defined.

It was true. His Irish background, his innately modest sense of himself, had to some extent limited his development. He had no private means, and work itself was a motivation without allowing him the freedom to indulge his creativity. She set him "tasks". In the portrait of herself wearing the jade bracelet, for example, she had imposed on him the obligation to paint entirely without the use of primary colours, as an exercise in artistic brilliance. She also insisted that a great painter should paint his parents. All great portrait painters do that, she told him. The product was the double portrait of his parents, Arthur Hugh Orpen and his wife, Annie, which is in the National Gallery of Ireland.

Mrs St George did not like Ireland; she found it wet and cold and could not understand the Irish mind. But she loved Orpen, and wanted to be with him. She made him happy. She went to the house in Connemara as part of their adventure together.

As the relationship developed, it took on a life in Dublin and in London, and became the source for gossip and eventually scandal. Orpen's first contact with Evelyn St George had been at the family home, Clonsilla Lodge, outside Dublin. But Evelyn St George also had a flat in Berkeley Square, and the lovers met and stayed there, appearing with increasing frequency in London society. This was commented upon in the press. Evelyn St George was more than six feet tall. Orpen was just over five feet tall. They became known as "Jack and the Beanstalk". Orpen enjoyed the humour of this immensely, and made witty drawings of the pair of them enjoying themselves at Claridge's or the Ritz, or skating together in winter. They always emphasised his small, dynamic figure totally overshadowed by her slim, tall and statuesque appearance, made even taller by the exotic hats she wore.

Gardenia was the closest witness of these events. In 1910, the year *Gardenia on a Donkey* was painted, Orpen was at the height of his powers. In that year he produced several remarkable master-pieces, though it is hard to think of any that carry quite the same intimacy of feeling and subtlety of expression than this work. For her part, Mrs St George was exercising considerable influence over the artist, encouraging in him above all a sense of his own greatness as a painter. Under the influence of her mind and her passion, he flourished and grew in stature.

Gardenia, who in time was to become as forceful and deter-mined a woman as her mother, imitated the influence she wit-nessed. In his work on *Gardenia on a Donkey*, according to herself, she taught Orpen how to draw a donkey's leg — he had never done it before — and she discussed with him other difficulties in the composition. Like many of Orpen's greatest works, the glow-ing impact lies in part in the originality, even the eccentricity, of the pose. This gangly adolescent girl, with her mixture of inno-cence and assurance, is balanced precariously on the rump of the patient beast. From under her bonnet, with its peacock feathers, she fixes the artist with her direct, uncompromising gaze. Her slight authority over the animal is represented by the wand of leaves in her right hand. The painting is a uniquely daring state-ment by an artist whose capacities are repeatedly breathtaking.

He makes of the donkey a bucolic festive creature, swathed in flowers. The beast is a comic reminder of other animals in art, no-tably the white, decorated bull painted by Titian in some ancient scene of sybaritic celebration. The donkey is both comic and seri-ous. The portrait is a double one, the donkey's nature as well as his physical reality just as important to the painter as the pensive, youthful girl.

The golden summer's day, the beautiful, subtle sky, the silver reflection on the sea and the radiation of compositional lines from the girl's head, the donkey's ears, the legs and shadow of the group, produce a remarkable contrast and balance between what is near and the wide space beyond. Orpen managed it several times in canvases painted at Howth, with Grace as his model, but as an epitome of his finest achievement in the genre, recording the happiest period in his life, *Gardenia on a Donkey* is hard to beat.

The truth is that no portraits in William Orpen's career, save those of his wife Grace, come closer to the essence of the man, both in his professional and personal capacities, than this series of Gardenia. They present us with two narratives, one of them quite open, for public consumption as it were, the other private, intimate, secret. And of the series, for which there is no comparison in Orpen's life, except in his self-portraits, the painting of Gardenia St George dressed in a theatrical costume and carrying a riding crop in her hands, painted two years later than *Gardenia on a Donkey*, is pivotal.

Something of the earlier innocence is lost. There is a change in her expression. In addition to her own growing up, so magically rendered in the work, there is the even more poignant perceptions we gain of the invisible artist, hidden behind his easel, working away at the mind's construction in this face, and revealing himself through the expression in her eyes.

Though Lady Gunston claimed that her knowledge of her mother's affair with Orpen came at a slightly later stage, there is, in her expression in the painting, a remarkable mixture of emotions. There is evident knowledge of the relationship she is witness to, though not full understanding of its extent. The solemn regard, incorporating misgivings mixed with personal confidence, is profoundly compelling; much more so, it must be said, than in the earlier paintings of Gardenia, and undoubtedly more so than in the sad features revealed in the final canvas.

It is a work containing the breath of life, the magic of the moment, the thrill of costume drama of a very special kind. And the happiness that her mother and the painter were enjoying inspires the direct and serious gaze of this young girl, whom Orpen had painted earlier, now on the threshold of womanhood, the understanding of herself and her position evident in the expression in her face and her eyes. It is for this reason particularly beautiful for its human appeal and the depth of understanding Orpen has brought to it. It is perhaps challenged for beauty only by *Gardenia on a Donkey*, painted two years before. But then beauty, in portraiture, is never the whole of the story.

Gardenia St George with Riding Crop, almost certainly painted in the summer of 1912, coincided, approximately, with the year of the birth of Vivien, the child of Orpen and Evelyn St George. The moment of birth is itself shrouded in some mystery, since she was born on New Year's Eve, unexpectedly, in the middle of a party, and no one checked the time. It was her mother who decided on the date of 1 January 1912.

What Cyril Connolly said generally about the painter is profoundly the case in this work: "Great artists like Epstein and Orpen know how to provide for the public the bewilderment it deserves." Yet for three people, Gardenia herself, William Orpen and Evelyn St George, there was a world of truth and of emotion, of deep feeling and of eventual tragedy in the art cycle to which they all contributed. Neither before nor since, in his rich and varied career as a painter, did Orpen tackle so wonderfully the subtle and moving narrative of feelings which we see in a series of works in which he meets brilliantly great intellectual, emotional and creative challenges. It is this, above all, that raises the picture to the greatness it enjoys.

Gardenia gradually became aware of the love affair between her mother and Orpen and was distressed by it. When I interviewed Lady Gunston, in the late 1970s, she said that her own realisation of what was going on had occurred before the later and last of the series of portraits of herself by Orpen. This was painted in 1916, when she is depicted in an evening dress looking far from happy. Gardenia told me that when she did come to learn of the affair, she was the instrument for its dissolution. She made some comment to her grandfather, the American banker, George F. Baker, and he intervened and put a stop to his daughter's relationship with Orpen. In any case, Orpen was considering his own involvement in the Great War, and the possibility of becoming a war artist.

For the sake of his own child, Vivien, Orpen remained friendly with the mother. His deep attachment to his daughter is evident from letters long after the love affair with her mother was over.

But while the affair was going on, Mrs St George and her lover had explored, in terms of his career, the elements of greatness that she demanded of him. She encouraged his self-examination through self-portraits and pointed to the great artists of the past who had done the same. She was his muse and had chosen him with masterful authority. This emerged in the growth of quality and range in his work during the years between 1908 and his becoming a war artist in 1916, the year their affair ended.

Gardenia, like her mother, was immensely tall. In old age, even in the beautiful drawing room of the house in Pelham Crescent where she lived, she stalked about with long strides as one might imagine her mother doing. Looking intently at the paintings by Orpen which filled the room, Lady Gunston, as one so often does about childhood, recalled with absolute clarity her experiences at that time. Above all she remembered the intensity of being painted by Orpen. There was the grave seriousness with which they discussed detail. They had done the same for the earlier portraits, some of them painted in the boathouse at Screebe Lodge, and, she conceded, all his works done for Mrs St George were subtle expressions of the love that inspired her mother's liaison with a great artist.

Two articles were written for *Christie's Magazine*, one for each of the two portraits at the time of their sale. They have been rewritten into one article here.

ॐ

II

William Orpen at War

There is a story of William Orpen which is not contained in *An Onlooker in France*, and has in fact never been told, until now. It concerns the artist and Lady Rocksavage, later Marchioness of Cholmondeley. She was a Sassoon, and her brother, Philip, was personal secretary to Field Marshal Haig, the commander-in-chief of the British Army in France during the First World War. Orpen had known the family since well before the outbreak of war. Though socially he did not enjoy the same level of privilege, they provided him with one of several points of access to the kinds of people who sat for him, and in time made him rich and success-ful. He was said to have been in love with Sybil Cholmondeley. His wife, Grace, was certainly jealous of her, and asked pointed questions. Keating remembers being present when Orpen came back from the Park Lane house owned by the Sassoons (this was before Sybil's marriage) and Grace said: "And was she nice to you?" in tones which were undoubtedly sarcastic.

But the story I have to tell belongs to a later period, during the last year of the war. Sybil Cholmondeley, out of daring, or be-cause of a wager, or in order to impress friends, conceived of the idea of getting to the Western Front and seeing the fighting at first-hand. Women of course were barred from the war zone. She had then been married only a few months. She picked on Orpen to assist her. He lived a charmed existence, travelling where he wished, with special passes, a chauffeur-driven car, and all his painting equipment. Though only an honorary major (on account of his life as a war artist), he had stayed at the Front since arriving there in 1917 — most of the war artists did much shorter terms, and then went home — and he had established "commander-in-chief" status among all the other painters.

He agreed to her proposal, that he should bring her secretly through the Allied lines, to the Front, and packed her underneath blankets in the back seat of his open car. His chauffeur then drove them up towards the Front Line. It was to be a short trip, done in the space of a day, with some drawing or painting of "The War", and then back to Paris. But Sybil Cholmondeley became ill, and they had to take shelter in a bombed-out farmhouse. She was in fact pregnant. They stayed overnight, and she miscarried of twins. Orpen was practical, careful, sensitive and efficient during this episode, and probably saved her life. She thought so, and said as much to me. With the help of his chauffeur, he got her back to safety and hospital care the following day, with no one knowing. The wager was won; the price of it substantial.

It showed two sides of Orpen's nature. Always fun-loving, he was on for any prank. This particular one was momentous. Yet when confronted with the serious business of life, he became responsible, caring and concerned. The different aspects of his character multiply. The more one knows him, the more rich and diverse he becomes, both as man and as artist.

Nothing brought this out more clearly than the First World War. He approached it, to begin with, in a light-hearted way. He had, at its outbreak, a growing practice as a portrait painter, and was already an established figure in London. He had a teaching job in Dublin, which took him to the city of his birth twice a year. He was in love with an American heiress, Mrs St George, who helped to refine his talent, and enlarge his ambition as a painter. His studio assistant was Seán Keating. When compulsory conscription — the Derby Scheme — was introduced in 1915 (Ireland was excluded), Keating decided to go home, and urged Orpen to do the same. But Orpen felt that he owed a debt to Britain, and stayed on to help in whatever way he could.

The War Artists' Scheme was ideal for him, and he threw himself into with his customary enthusiasm, and with that light-hearted, even light-headed abandon, which saw "Painting the War" as an exotic interpretation of the gilded view which was already being given to the British public by the war machine, and by the propagandist press.

The Front transformed his understanding. The experiences on the Somme were shattering. Orpen found himself in the presence of death and decay. A broken and destroyed world lay at his feet. The landscapes were a mixture of Hieronymous Bosch and Jacques Callot. The cadavers in the trenches, the waste of machinery and weapons, the skeletal foot rising out of the mud with a boot on it, and all this seen in winter, and then in the brilliant sunlight of the summer of 1917, transformed Orpen's life.

He developed a way of dealing with the vast scale of human tragedy. It was to treat with flippant irreverence those around him; and the more senior they were, the less he minded giving offence. With his mind and heart he was penetrating, more and more deeply, into the realms of horror. The paintings of his first year in France are simple and direct statements of what he found. He sat out in the open, and set down, on canvas after canvas, the upturned earth, the fresh growth of green grass and weed, the shattered trees, the broken evidence of the passing of terrible warfare. The colour in these works is brilliant. The sunlight glows. The skies are blue, flecked with scudding cloud, the ground baked yellow, with patchy green where the grass is growing again.

But in the second and third years, a darker vision came upon him, and the simplicity vanished into a more complex, more frightening series of pictures. The women who came as camp-followers of the army, the drunkenness, the insanity, the disease and wretchedness visited on hundreds of square miles of France and Flanders, he sought to evoke these things, in a growing mood of pity and rage. His palette is more sombre, the colours and tones reflective of despair.

When it was over, and the pity still there, and the anger even more intense, he turned his attention to the Peace. This, too, he painted, but with a fearful sense of the symmetry of politics, its ability to paste over the human tragedy and provide easy answers and shallow remedies. It is an astonishing achievement in an artist to be able to capture that. Yet Orpen did it. In his portraits of those attending the Peace Conference, in his great canvases showing the actual signing of the Peace at Versailles, he not only captured history; he interpreted and revealed it. Rarely if ever do painters do this. Goya, Velázquez, Rubens — he is to be numbered among that group in the canons of art over the centuries for what he did during those apocalyptic years of 1917 to 1919.

What he painted was deadly serious, the total expression of a passionate spirit, confronted by unimaginable horror, and equipped with a lifetime's abilities as draughtsman and painter. No one can understand the sheer power and authority of that work without seeing, in the flesh, those many canvases produced during those years. The vast majority are in the Imperial War Museum, in London. Most, regrettably, are in storage. And no English institution, in the sixty and more years since Orpen's death, has seen fit to do anything about showing his work again.

What he wrote is a different matter altogether. *An Onlooker in France 1917–1919* is a book filled with secrets, for which one needs the key, and the key lies in the paintings and drawings. They explain the reality; the words give it a gloss. And the gloss is essentially flippant. This was in keeping with the times. But it was also in keeping with Orpen's outward nature. He protected his feelings with jokes, verbal shorthand, and a crisp, off-hand manner. It got him into trouble. He led his own charmed life, favoured by the powerful, a friend of generals and those with titles, and this exonerated him from the normal, dutiful behaviour of a temporary major. Something of this shows through, but by no means all. The full story of the artist's curious path through the territory of war, that territory of orders, authority, rank, hierarchy, stubbornness, stupidity, rather than the poignant landscape of battle, will probably never be told. It is hinted at in Orpen's own book.

Essentially, he came, through direct experience, to admire the fighting man. And he did so almost to the point of idolatry. The closer he got to power, the more he discovered ineptitude and callousness, self-seeking attitudes and stupidity. And this went on, not just through the period of the war, but into the Peace Conference at Versailles, where he was horrified to see, at first hand, crude self-interest, short-sightedness, ignorance, and an almost total absence of compassion or feeling.

He had his heroes, and it shows. Field Marshal Sir Henry Wilson was one of them. Orpen had known him in Blackrock, and always revered him. The portrait reveals the admiration for this man, subsequently assassinated by Sinn Féin. He had a high regard for Marshal Foch, for Air Marshal Trenchard, and for individual soldiers and airman. But he found it virtually impossible to translate such feelings into words. When painting them, his view is direct and true, but when writing about them he all too often sounds either trite or sentimental.

It should be read, however, in the context of the flow of Orpen's experience. This holds true through the pages of *An Onlooker in France*. The chronology is straightforward. The innocence, in the opening pages, is enchanting, soon to be overtaken by the first real hints of war, when Orpen reaches the Somme battlefield. He saw the trenches initially under snow. Then came the first horrors: the hand lying on the duckboarding, the stench of unburied bodies, the skeletons, the rats. The living horrors outstripped the dead ones: shell-shocked figures, the infestations of lice, fear, terror, madness. Then the redemption, blind acts of courage, the bonhomie, the humour and warmth and affection. Orpen, who often characterised himself as not particularly literate, writes with great pace and vividness, quoting people, giving colourful record of scenes, developing a picture of how events ran together into the close tapestry of war.

No one will encompass it completely as a subject. Neither poets, like Wilfred Owen and Siegfried Sassoon, nor artists like Muirhead Bone, Paul Nash and Orpen himself, can ever explains the enormity of what went on. But it is through art that the recollections last.

And *An Onlooker in France* is the diary record of a truly great painter, who viewed his work during the First World War as of supreme importance. He had this view, not for the sake of the War itself, but in honour of the fighting man, who became, to Orpen, an emblem, a godlike figure, representative of humanity: noble, sacrificial and ultimately sublime. All else was dross. And the greatest feature of the book, recording events of which no one, now, has first-hand experience, is the tribute it pays to the fighting man.

In 1996 Parkgate Books, an imprint of Parkgate Publications, brought out a new edition of William Orpen's First World War masterpiece, *An Onlooker in France*. This is the Introduction I wrote for it.

ॐ

III

A Mere Fracture

The arrival of one of William Orpen's early masterpieces in the market place just at this time is a wonderful event for Irish art. *A Mere Fracture* was one of a small group of paintings which confirmed the artist's audacious and inventive skill as a young man. In it he displays his masterly command of composition, light and colour; and in the originality of design he breathes into a sombre subject emotional tension and excitement.

The painting fulfilled those expectations expressed about English art in the late nineteenth century by George Moore, and particularly in his essay on the New English Art Club, published in *The Speaker*, of which he was the art critic in the 1890s. It was later republished as an essay in *Modern Painting*: "Nothing counts with the jury but *l'idée plastique*", Moore wrote in his spirited attack on English philistinism about art, and his admiration for the new NEAC vitality which Orpen among others represented. Moore's views were known to the painter, who owned a copy of the book, and mutual admiration led to the two men becoming friends. Indeed, the figure on the right in the painting was thought by some people to be Moore. It was in fact an old army pensioner called Haywood, who was the caretaker of the house in Fitzroy Street where Orpen painted this and several other works.

Orpen's conception of the painting can be exactly dated to 4 February 1901, the day of Queen Victoria's funeral. Coming back from watching the procession to the house in Fitzroy Street with fellow students, Orpen asked one of them, William Crampton Gore, to inspect the leg of another as though looking for a fracture. Gore, who went on to become a doctor, did so, and Orpen stopped him as he knelt on the ground with a typically enthusiastic "Stay like that! That's magnificent!"

The painting was shown in the April exhibition that year of the New English Art Club and was bought by Colonel Swinton for £100. It was the largest sum received by the twenty-three-year-old painter up to that time, but led to commissions, two of them from Swinton himself, who was March Poursuivant, and got Orpen to paint him in his official dress for this ancient office. Swinton also commissioned a large family group.

The other figure, in striking profile, with her hand on Carr's shoulder, is Emily Scobel, a well-known and popular model with whom Orpen had been for a time in love. She sat for *The Mirror*, now in the Tate, for *The Bedroom* (private collection) and for *The English Nude*, which is in the Mildura Art Gallery in Australia. She is dressed in the same bonnet and shawl she wears in *The Mirror*, and the appeal of her full throat, fine facial bone structure, and relaxed ability to pose, are all obvious.

But it is the composition of the work which is so exciting. During its development, Orpen found he needed to add to the canvas (the line of the join runs down through Emily Scobel's shoulder). This allowed him to build up the high structure of bookcase and model galleon on the left, the galleon itself becoming, in the extended canvas, a vital focus point in the work. By so doing he created a curving sweep down through the composition, from top left corner to bottom right, and running through the three inter-related figures in the centre. This harmony of movement is pinned in place, as it were, by the vertical line of mirror and elaborate clock above the fireplace, and by the fine dramatic pose adopted by Haywood.

Fitzroy Street was a wonderful artistic establishment. Orpen himself had a humble studio in the basement, with an earth floor, an old four-poster bed which features in several works, and the devoted attention of Haywood and his wife, who both adored him, and supplied regular meals of roast meat and puddings.

Herbert Everett, another Slade student and friend of the painter, who became a fine marine artist, was the occupant of an-other upstairs room in the house, if anything grander than the one in which *A Mere Fracture* was painted. He was the owner of the galleon model on the bookcase which he used in paintings and drawings of marine subjects. Both he and Augustus John were painted full-length by Orpen in the house. Everett in his portrait is elegantly dressed in top hat, holding cane and gloves, against the dado of his own upstairs room (Maritime Museum). In contrast, the scowling Augustus John in black overcoat is seated in the gloomier basement in front of Orpen's four-poster (National Por-trait Gallery).

These paintings, of which *A Mere Fracture* is an outstanding example, were all great works. They are the early masterpieces by a young genius, quite the most outstanding Irish painter of his day. Beyond that, however, and like so many others of his coun-trymen, he made a far wider contribution. Arguably, one might say he changed by what he produced both the course and the quality of English art in the early years of the century.

Christie's Magazine, May 1998

32

THE GOOSE GIRL CONTROVERSY

The Irish artist W.J. Leech has been associated in the public mind for the past quarter-century with a single, highly popular painting, *The Goose Girl*. This picture, which is in the National Gallery of Ireland in Merrion Square, shows a young girl, in profile, wearing a white bonnet, and walking with her geese through grass and bluebells, and among birch trees.

The painting is the most popular in the gallery's collection, and was regarded as so quintessentially Leech that it was planned to put it on the cover of the catalogue for the forthcoming exhibition of his work in the National Gallery, later in October. Yet now it is being relegated to limbo-land, either of doubtful work by the artist, or not his work at all, and is likely to provoke an increasingly bitter controversy between those who know it is not the work of the artist, and those who hope it might still be acceptable.

The controversy is such that the gallery is guarding its own position on the work and will possibly distance itself from the views of the author of the catalogue and the organiser of the exhibition, Denise Ferran. The gallery is nevertheless including the painting in the exhibition, and it has had cleaning and restoration in preparation for this.

The inclusion is unacceptable practice. The normal procedure, with a major exhibition of this kind, unless it is deliberately exploring associations, influences and derivative works, as well as possible forgeries or mistakes, is to exclude any work of art where there is serious doubt as to its authenticity, lest the inclusion distorts the main thrust of the show.

The inclusion of *The Goose Girl* is despite Denise Ferran's clear advice that, in her opinion, the work is by another painter. The Gallery is going even further, and either bringing in or cataloguing in the Leech catalogue other works by the alternative artist, apparently giving options in order to allow the public to arbitrate on the disputed picture. This is because for some time now a complex and increasingly bitter row among art historians, dealers, and experts has raged around *The Goose Girl*.

Much of the detailed groundwork and research on the painting was carried out by the *Irish Independent*'s Fine Art Correspondent, Ian Baird. For a number of years he has been convinced that *The Goose Girl* is not by Leech, but is the work of Stanley Royle, an English painter from Sheffield, who was roughly Leech's contemporary, and died in 1971, just three years after the Irish artist. This view is shared by several other art experts. Baird is responsible for unearthing evidence of Royle's style and habits as a painter, and also important details about his canvases.

The inclusion of *The Goose Girl* is likely to detract from the undoubted merits of Leech as a painter. It will also undermine the otherwise intelligent and careful presentation of Leech's work which has been a lifelong interest of the leading authority on Leech, Denise Ferran. She has worked for many years as education officer in the Ulster Museum in Belfast, to where the exhibition is also to go.

It will do more than merely detract, however; Leech is not well known in Ireland, and does not enjoy the kind of clear profile as a painter which Orpen, Yeats, Osborne and Lavery have. His style and development is badly in need of clarification and critical enrichment.

The balance against the painting has grown steadily in recent years. Denise Ferran has prepared the catalogue, and is anxious that the *Goose Girl* controversy will not eclipse the other great merits of Leech, which she regards as far more important.

She believes that *The Goose Girl* is not by Leech. She accepts the re-attribution of it to Stanley Royle, who certainly knew and admired William Leech's work, both during his days in Brittany and later, when Leech exhibited in Derby. But she is in the difficult position of having to defer to the publisher of the catalogue in London, Merrell Holberton, who in turn is answerable to the National Gallery of Ireland.

The director of the gallery, Raymond Keaveney, is aware of her views, and has also had presented to him the full researches of Dominic Milmo-Penny, an art dealer in Dublin who has written a substantial paper on the work, pointing out certain serious doubts. His substantive researches cover paintwork and other questions of style. Strongly reinforcing his views, and of critical importance in such art historical research, is the fact that the canvas came from an art supplier in Sheffield named Hibbert.

The firm, which is still in existence, supplied Stanley Royle with his art materials, and the *Goose Girl* canvas is so stamped, as are other paintings by the English artist. This detail was discovered by the National Gallery's chief restorer, Andrew O'Connor, during restoration work. Details of more than a dozen Stanley Royle paintings which have gone through the salerooms in recent years indicate that he repeatedly painted one size of picture, and it is the same as *The Goose Girl*. His dealer has confirmed that this was "his size". Furthermore, he acquired the frames for his paintings from Bouilet of London, and they are of a particularly design.

A further piece of evidence is that another Irish art dealer has seen a print of the disputed painting, probably dating from between the two world wars, but showing the English artist's signature in the canvas in a position which is now blank. The painting is not now signed. The dealer in question is Mrs Elizabeth Guinness, who in April 1995 wrote in a letter published in two newspapers:

"The *Goose Girl* print . . . was signed within the body of the paint."
And the signature was "Stanley Royle".

When first catalogued by the National Gallery, the painting
was not even called *The Goose Girl*, but *A View of Quimperle*, and
indeed on the back, on a piece of paper pasted on, it is inscribed
"Quimperle WL". Leech never painted in Quimperle, though he
did work in Quimper, nearby. There is no evidence that he and
Royle met, though they did know of each other's work.

In style the work is undoubtedly close to other Royle pictures,
and has no technical or stylistic association with Leech. It does not
fit into the development of his style, and is in fact a confusing
work, belonging, as Brian Fallon points out in his book on Irish
art, to a Bastien-Lepage tradition, with soft light and colour, and
much more impressionist than the harder, post-impressionist style
of Leech.

In composition, its work is essentially "horizontal", with all its
lines running across the canvas. Leech, in marked contrast, was a
"vertical" painter, as was Orpen, whose influence is clear in his
work. The main compositional lines run up through the canvas,
and not across.

The painting was acquired by the gallery from the Dublin
dealer James Gorry in 1970, when James White was director. On
the board of the National Gallery at the time was Terence de Vere
White, a collector with a good eye, but an amateur, and he encouraged the purchase. The gallery is unable to give a provenance
for the work, beyond saying that it came from "a collection which
contained other Leech paintings". It is thought to have been
bought at an Allen and Townsend house auction, but there are no
clear details.

Other dealers are seriously concerned about the possibility
that the work might be taken away from Leech, and assigned to
the Sheffield painter Stanley Royle. This, it is argued, would undoubtedly have an adverse effect on the Leech market, which has
grown strongly in recent years, and is currently more dependent

on his looser, more impressionistic style than on the hard, decorative paintings which in reality are among his key works. These include *A Convent Garden, Brittany, The Sunshade,* and *The Cigarette,* all of which differ hugely from *The Goose Girl.*

The reality is probably quite different: that Leech, freed of the millstone of *The Goose Girl,* would emerge as a more coherent artist, his line clear-cut and modern, almost to the point of belonging stylistically with the Charleston and among the "Flappers" of the inter-war years. This might not suit those with a romantic view of Leech, but could be closer to the truth.

The director of the National Gallery of Ireland, Raymond Keaveney, has said several times that the October retrospective of William J. Leech will "address" or "resolve" the question surrounding the controversial painting. Yet it is not known how this will be done, and its very inclusion has little relevance, as the case against it grows in magnitude and conviction.

If the gallery is unhappy about the view taken by its own chosen expert, Denise Ferran, why then did it choose her? Has it alternative expertise to present to the public when the show opens in less than a fortnight? Why is it prejudicing the genuine work of revelation and explanation of this little-understood artist, by putting in a work with a controversy weighted against it?

There is one significant alternative view, coming from one of Leech's first champions, Alan Denson, who published a monograph on the artist in 1968, the year of Leech's death. Denson did not include the painting in his book, nor did he mention it. But in a letter to an English newspaper last year he referred to *The Goose Girl* and asserted that he had discussed it with Leech, and that it was certainly Leech's work. Yet the painting did not come into the National Gallery collection until two years after Leech's death, and was then known, and catalogued by the gallery, as *A View of Quimperle.* It was only later that the painting acquired the new title of *The Goose Girl,* under which it is known so popularly today.

No scholars in the field of twentieth-century Irish art have been able to show any convincing argument in favour of the original attribution. There is a consensus that it deserves the popularity it enjoys. And many thousands of the reproduction of it have been sold in various forms and sizes. But the owners also deserve some consideration, including an explanation of what it is they now have on their walls. The popularity of the work has an unhappy irony to it. Imagine the Irish people nominating as their favourite work in the country's main art collection a picture by an Englishman from Sheffield!

Postscript

On the opening day of the William John Leech exhibition in the National Gallery of Ireland, 22 October 1996, I attended a press preview, and, in the light of controversy over *The Goose Girl*, I inspected the bottom corners of the painting in search of a signature. I discovered remnants of two names, including the letters, "EY" and "LE". These are part of the signature of the man who is now widely regarded as the author of the work, Stanley Royle. The leading authority in Ireland on the work of Stanley Royle is Dominic Milmo-Penny, and I informed him of this finding. Following discussion, Milmo-Penny inspected the canvas in detail, using a powerful magnifying glass, and extended what I had found.

His statement, made last Wednesday, a week after the show opened to the public, is as follows:

> On the 29th October at the National Gallery of Ireland I examined *The Goose Girl* painting to determine whether or not it carries a signature. The examination was carried out using an eye glass of 2.5 magnification. The ghost of the following letters was clearly legible. All of these letters were entire. "LEY . . YLE." In front of "YLE" were the remnants of two other letters. There is no doubt that this is the remains of a signature of Stanley Royle (1888–1961). In every respect the signature

conforms in style with all other signatures of the artist which I
have examined.

The first discovery of evidence of a signature was followed by
numerous investigations of the canvas. Bernard Williams, of the
London auction firm Christie's, said there was no doubt of the signature; it was the remnants of Royle's name, and in his style. The
firm has handled several works by the painter. The Fine Arts
Correspondent of the *Irish Independent*, Ian Baird, also examined
the signature and endorsed this view. For a long time he has had
serious doubts about the Leech attribution.

Their view was further supported by James O'Halloran, Stuart
Cole and Brian Coyle, all of James Adam and Sons, and all professionally engaged in the authentication and checking of paintings.
They had not previously been involved in the controversy. They
now expressed no doubt about the existence of the signature. Several Dublin dealers have confirmed the same identification of the
signature, among them David Britton, of the Frederick Gallery, in
South Frederick Street.

Having checked the painting, Dominic Milmo-Penny immediately wrote to the gallery director, Raymond Keaveney, to insist
that public interest would be best served by an immediate statement to the effect that the gallery now regarded the painting as
Royle's work. Furthermore, he suggested that it should be so labelled in the exhibition. Following this, the director decided to
have the painting taken down and examined.

What is astonishing in all this is the fact that, despite restoration
work carried out on the picture by Andrew O'Connor, it appeared
to have been done without a proper inspection of the surface of the
painting. And this was during the many months in which controversy has surrounded it. It was not, during that time, available to
outside experts. Yet a long and painful dispute has taken place, involving the author of the catalogue, Ms Denise Ferran of the Ulster
Museum, the two partners in the Merrell Holberton publishing

firm, Hugh Merrell and Paul Holberton, the latter of whom also edited the catalogue, and various members of the National Gallery's staff, including those concerned with conservation and preservation.

The view of the gallery, all along, has been a casual one. The director expected, in some way, that the public would resolve the matter, and made no attempt himself to sort out a long-standing problem on which many experts had expressed opinions, nearly all of them attacking the "Leech" attribution of *The Goose Girl*. Dominic Milmo-Penny had himself lodged with the director a scholarly paper on the picture, with his detailed arguments. Yet this was ignored, and even in the final stages before the opening, the entries in the catalogue were only casually amended, so that in one part *The Goose Girl* is by Leech, and on another page it is "possibly" Royle's work.

When the exhibition opened, both the chairman of the gallery, Mrs Carmel Naughton, and the Minister for Arts, Culture and the Gaeltacht, Michael D. Higgins, treated the controversy over the painting as a piece of light relief. They did, however, support the idea of *The Goose Girl* being flanked by other Royle works. For various reasons this was not done. The Minister suggested that "a degree of controversy is not necessarily a bad thing and if this debate encourages any additional interest in art and art history it will have been welcome". He went on to say that the idea of hanging the picture beside Royle's work "would have allowed you the public, as jury, to compare and contrast the varying styles".

Such an idea might have been stimulating, were it not for the fact that the painting carries a signature which no one had noticed until I discovered it during the week of the opening. The professional staff of the gallery, who should have known better, had either themselves not noticed, or were looking the other way. This makes the Minister, and the Chairman of the Board of Governors and Guardians, both of whom are dependent on the gallery for professional back-up on detail, look a bit silly.

It is, as was predicted long ago, bad for Leech and bad for the gallery. The primary obligation of a national institution responsible to the people for the proper guardianship of its possessions is the absolute rigour of authentication and integrity. This was of particular importance with Leech, a little-known Irish artist, whose style and status needed establishing. Getting people in to see an exhibition, having it talked about, using controversy as a bait to entice the public, is inexcusable in such circumstances, and runs a very poor second to the requirements of scholarship.

Leech's posthumous reputation will survive. He has been the victim of exaggerated claims and distortions, and the particular distortion attending this individual work, which even without the signature or other factual details, is an unlikely candidate to anyone with a half-civilised eye for a painting, is now deservedly relegated to the dustbin of false claims. But the reflection on those responsible is serious, and requires some kind of explanation.

Two *Irish Independent* articles from October 1996 have been joined together.

33

Paul Henry: the Loving Apprenticeship

In his Foreword to Paul Henry's autobiography, *An Irish Portrait*, the Irish writer Seán O'Faoláin describes the book as "the story of a loving apprenticeship as long as life itself". The lyrical alliteration reflects the affection with which one significant Irish artist of the twentieth century viewed another. They collaborated, Paul Henry painting a series of small, very distinctive canvases to illustrate O'Faoláin's *An Irish Journey*,[1] and O'Faoláin occupying a significant position as writer and working colleague. They knew each other from the 1930s, when O'Faoláin was a neighbour in Achill. "He is a . . . great asset to my little circle" Henry wrote to Richard Campbell in America.[2] But the collaboration took on a new significance in the summer of 1939 when the two men travelled together around Ireland in order to produce the book and illustrations that appeared the following year as *An Irish Journey*.

There are interesting parallels between this writer–artist association, and two associations that Jack Yeats had. The first of these was with John M. Synge, when the two men wrote and illustrated a series of articles for *The Manchester Guardian* in 1905, and the second, later, in 1913, when Yeats collaborated with James Owen

---

[1] Seán O'Faoláin, *An Irish Journey*, London, Longmans, Green, 1941.

[2] Cited in S.B. Kennedy, *Paul Henry*, New Haven and London, 2000, p. 117.

Hannay, the author, as "G.A. Birmingham" of *Irishmen All*. Henry and Yeats came to know each other in later years, when Henry moved to Dublin, and there are many other parallels between their careers, some of them considered here.

O'Faoláin's remark about Paul Henry's lifelong apprenticeship is deceptively benign. The word "apprenticeship" suggest unfinished business, a career of learning that was endless. And this interpretation of the descriptive phrase, whether meant in that way by O'Faoláin or not, contains the seed of doubt about the ultimate grandeur of the artist's design and its fulfilment. This in turn bears upon Paul Henry's place in Irish art of the twentieth century. He is described in the publicity for the major exhibition put on in the National Gallery of Ireland in the spring of 2003 as Ireland's "greatest landscape painter". Yet this view, disputed for example by the art critic Dorothy Walker, is an uncertain accolade. Nathaniel Hone the Younger would be an obvious alternative claimant.

Paul Henry had a grandeur of design but a narrow compass. There is a design component that overwhelms the particular and deprives us of the real. He is overwhelmingly a painter of skies. People, the men and women of Achill, who featured in early works, were subsequently eliminated from this grand design; in part perhaps this was because they were reluctant sitters, but mainly, it must be said, it was because they were presented by him as rather wooden, artificially statuesque symbols of the difficulty of the working life in the west of Ireland.

He was left with a limited range of foreground features — the white painted cottage of the West of Ireland, the dark peat stack at the door — the occasional cart or donkey, as evidence of life. Then came lake or sea water and the blue hills or mountains that made up the middle ground. All this was to give a warmer perspective to the magnificent painting of clouds that are the abiding feature in his art.

৪০

Paul Henry is an enduring monument to the integrity of artistic vision. He saw Ireland in the settled state of the early years of the twentieth century. To an extent this gave the country a magical allure for many people, when contrasted with the turbulent history elsewhere. Henry identified the simplicity of colour and understood the broad strength of the basic landscape details of mountain, sea and sky. He made the picturesque real and gave reality to the evidence of a hard life and of much striving against the elements.

Henry peopled the early paintings with the figurative expression of toil. Yet it was toil redeemed by companionship and by the collective work of peasant communities. Groups gather to mourn the dead, to draw curraghs up from the sea or to launch them, to gossip at market. His heavy-limbed couples strive against the challenge of the earth, the pitiless and awesome spread above their heads of an ever-changing sky. Their bony hands grapple through the dark soil for potatoes. And in one memorable image, *The Potato Diggers*, an old couple, bent with perpetual toil, strive together over the sod. The implacable sky and sea and mountain and earth are locked together in a carefully designed pattern of work and movement.

Paul Henry became enchanted with his own discovery. He fell in love with his representation of landscape and saw it as the representation of life, particularly of life in the west of Ireland. Paintings poured from him, their essential ingredients common, their capacity to be always different built in, just as the light and the wind in the west of Ireland maintains an inexhaustible differential of experience.

When posters and prints were added to the oil paintings, the apotheosis of the artist into a mythmaker for the country was complete. Paul Henry represented to the world of his time — which in a sense meant the world of these islands — the best vision of the country. It was single-minded, and it was simplified. He largely eliminated the human form. His landscapes cease to be peopled by the peasants whose work and life is so clearly depicted in the turf stacks at the cottage doors, in the fuel gathered across the bogs, and in the cherished order of limed cottage walls and the thatch that gave the inhabitants their protection.

What the National Gallery exhibition achieved is a considerable and enormously valuable widening of the Paul Henry we all thought we knew. The artist has provoked a mixed reaction over the years, his reputation somehow diminished by the transition of what he depicted. What started out as a straightforward representation of the simple life of peasants in the west of Ireland became for many people a theatrical and increasingly unreal recollection of the past. Other forms of art took over. His wife, Grace Henry's work, which has great value in its own right, was seen by many as superior to his work.

We needed to see a richer and more diverse Paul Henry. Through the adroit and intelligent choice of paintings, many of which come from private collections or little-known public collections abroad, the exhibition is enriched by urban scenes, dock subjects, some lovely studies of trees, and a remarkable series of paintings of towns like Kinsale, New Ross, Athlone, Kilkenny.

These have had a profound effect. People were made to look again at an artist's work with which many thought they were sufficiently familiar. The result was to find in it a richer and more composed rigour. The view of Kilkenny from the river is a particular case. This, together with the other townscapes, were done in association with Seán O'Faoláin when he was writing *An Irish Journey*. They were meant as illustrations and indeed were so used. Their very shape, that of vertical rectangle, indicates this. But they imposed on the painter a new sense of environment, a new way of looking at his surroundings.

In the Kilkenny picture, the dark cloud behind the Tholsel tower in the city emphasises Henry's sure command of chiaroscuro, his clever use of contrast, his essential skill within an almost monochrome representation of light. He uses greys and creams so richly. His trees are like people, leaning and crawling in a particular direction.

The 2003 show at the National Gallery was divided into two parts. There was the main exhibition of oils in the Millennium Wing. In the Print Room his graphic work was displayed, his sketchbooks, his London, Midland and Scottish Railway posters, his book illustrations and his often quite intimate portraits of family and friends, which give an inner sense of the artist. There is that very welcome capacity demonstrated here to see behind the large works in oils and find the deliberative man at his desk planning what he might do, and the scale and shape of how he will do it.

In Irish art it is the exception rather than the rule to find painters working together in schools or studios. The great figures of the twentieth century were solitary in their creativity, an inescapable necessity of true vision. William Orpen certainly was, so was Jack Yeats. Walter Osborne worked on his own, so did Nathaniel Hone. There was some collaborative energy with the White Stag Group, with Mainie Jellett and her followers, with Gerard Dillon, Colin Middleton, Dan O'Neill and George Campbell. But the true working of energy with the painter is a solitary exercise, exemplified by Paul Henry, both in his output and in the strange, silent, satisfying world that he chose to paint, over and over again. It is surprisingly attractive and it escapes being boring through the loftiness of Henry's wonderful skies, the huge arching environment he clearly loved better than anything else.

ॐ

Paul Henry's life has an inspiring quality to it. There was the austere childhood, the unpromising early years, the interest in art handicapped by the difficulties of study, the classic period in Paris, the difficult apprenticeship as a draughtsman, designer, illustrator in London, and then the Damascus road conversion of Achill. One is compelled by circumstance to begin with this. He saw Achill, and was both lost and found. He was lost to all other artistic endeavour. He was found by his subject. The scenes that engaged him were to be inexhaustible and lifelong.

When he came to write about it, in later years, Achill is where he begins. In his first chapter, headed "Give me Liberty", of his autobiography, *An Irish Portrait*, he describes the train journey across Ireland, the drovers and cattle jobbers travelling with him to the great cattle fair in Mullingar. This was in 1910 and he was heading for County Mayo. To the south-east, as he set out, were the Wicklow mountains, seen distantly, dominated by Lugnaquilla, bathed in morning sun.

His memory is vivid. He was writing forty years on from the event. He recalls, as he probably did countless times for friends in the twenties and thirties, the cattle men leaving the train at Mullingar. In the early morning flurry of people at the station they were replaced by even more colourful men of the west who were heading home after drinking all night at the fair. They brought into the carriage the whiff of the farmyard and devoured breakfasts of porridge, egg, ham, fish, even steaks of beef, drank quarts of tea and finished with bread and butter and marmalade.

As one so often does in the west, he drove himself on towards the setting sun, having made no arrangements, having no special destination. He and Grace — though Grace is never mentioned in *An Irish Portrait* — stayed a night in Dooagh, but then moved on. By chance he picked up a jaunting car outside a hotel, its driver from the south side of the island, who recommended that as the best Achill could offer. As a result, Paul Henry arrived at the place of his destiny, Keel. "As I wandered round and through the village, and out on the road that led through Pullough, and looked down on Dooagh and to the noble cliffs of Achill Head, I felt that here I must stay somehow or another."

He describes Keel as a tiny village, and the embarrassment of arriving there without having made any arrangements. This embarrassment was real since there was nowhere to stay. He focused

his attentions on the postmistress, Mrs Barrett. She and her husband are the subject of a small oil painting in the Ulster Museum,
exhibited in the spring 2003 show, donated to the museum by
Mervyn Solomon in 1994. It is a crude work, virtually mono-
chromatic, yet with a sensitive treatment of the characters of the
couple, particularly of the man. Paul Henry appealed to him
when Mrs Barrett was unable to accept his pleadings to be allowed to stay.

The sun rose in the morning. The clouds assembled in the sky.
The distant mountains turned pale blue, the near ones were
darker. There were boats with sail. There were people engaging in
toil. Paul Henry had his life spread out before him and he began
to paint it. The exhibition is the record.

This is an altered and expanded version of an article on the exhibition
which was published in the *Irish Independent* in April 2003

34

THE PAT SCOTT RETROSPECTIVE

Patrick Scott is in his eighty-second year. He has the looks and attitude of a much younger man. Relaxed, supple, invariably gracious and witty in his attitude to others, he has been an adornment of the art world of Dublin for more than half a century. He has somehow managed, throughout this long period, to disengage himself from fame. He has never sought publicity or critical attention. He is often at other painters' exhibitions, commenting, sometimes sharply, sometimes with encouragement, but more interested in gossip and reminiscence.

He has generally avoided labels, and has not been rated in the hollow pecking order of artistic importance, at least not in the assiduous way that does more damage than help to an artist's reputation. And now, suddenly, we are confronted with a truly splendid show of his output since the early days of his art at the time of the Emergency.

He was a product of a brilliant and underrated period in Irish art. I would take mild issue with Yvonne Scott (no relation) writing in the excellent Hugh Lane catalogue of the show, when she says of the "Art Establishment" in the 1940s that it was "notoriously conservative, insular, repressive". By "Modernist" standards, in fact, Dublin was frequently ahead of London, particularly in the field of pure abstraction, during the 1920s and 1930s. The painters led by Mainie Jellett were way ahead of Ben Nicholson and

Barbara Hepworth. And recent researches have revealed that Matisse in his "Fauves" period had an Irish friend and working colleague who shared his studio and painted "Fauves" works as early as 1906.

The truth of the matter is that Patrick Scott, shortly after leaving St Columba's College in Rathfarnham, became aware of a new and original group of painters, the White Stag Group. It is conventional to claim that they had moved to Dublin simply to avoid having to fight in the Second World War. This was partly true, but an oversimplification. In London, where they had been formed in the early 1930s under the patronage of Christopher Wood's brilliant dealer, Lucy Wertheim, they had already become familiar with the work of "Modernist" Irish artists such as Nano Reid and Norah McGuinness, and when the nucleus of the group arrived, they associated with Mainie Jellett and her followers. The White Stag painters were artists both of abstraction and of surrealism, and their vibrant and dramatic art had an immediate impact, not just on cultural and artistic life, but because they came under Special Branch suspicion as possible enemy agents!

Their work and their social and intellectual irreverence appealed to Scott, whose own early work was rapidly at the centre of the movement. Indeed, some of the earliest of his paintings belonging to this period have been part of an important White Stag exhibition in London at Theo Waddington's Galleries. His father, Victor Waddington, an art dealer in Dublin during this crucial period of the 1940s, was an early promoter of White Stag Group work.

This brilliant early period is well represented in the Retrospective Exhibition, giving a powerful sense of purpose in paintings done in his very early twenties. There is an interim period of work, coinciding with a profession as an architect and designer. He joined Michael Scott's (no relation) architectural practice in 1945, and by the early 1950s was involved in design work with the Signa company, working both in Dublin and London. This period in his work consists of spare, architectural paintings, landscapes of an almost constructivist style. They lead to the explosive and seminal *Bog Sun*, one of the first of his works that I saw in Leo Smith's Gallery in Dawson Street forty years ago.

He painted remarkable large unprimed canvases in the 1960s, based on bog images, the sun often a central thematic expression of unity and power. Then came gold. Its enamelled shining intensity contrasted with the limp comfortable linen softness of the background and the delicate touches of colour.

There is a symphonic quality about his work, in marked and wonderful contrast with his wayward and appealing character. Disarmingly shy, with his slight hesitation of speech, Pat Scott has been an enduring and increasingly impressive contributor to Irish painting. The Hugh Lane Retrospective is a fitting celebration of this.

Pat Scott's Retrospective was held in the Hugh Lane Gallery, Parnell Square, Dublin, early in 2002. This review appeared in the *Irish Independent*.

beautiful works of art which both they, and other members of the Gleizes Circle, painted.

Visiting France always contained an element of pilgrimage; to see a Gleizes painting — and they are rare enough in public collections in his own country — was an important part of travel. And going to Gleizes's houses — Méjades at St Remy-de-Provence, Moly-Sabata, Serrieres — recreated a world of substance and experience, of human energy and philosophical insight.

The man himself became palpable. There was the small, slight figure. He had a permanently brooding expression on his faintly pinched and worried face, that of a nervous man, which he was. His appearance contrasts with the calm and graceful figure of his wife, Juliette, in a cloche hat, standing behind him in photographs that he sent to Mainie Jellett. His mind and experience were used to enrich my own biography of the Irish artist; but as is the nature of biographical writing, the story unfolded into other lives, and of course it went on.

It goes on, even now, in the text of these lectures given by Gleizes in 1931, and which Peter Brooke has translated with such a wealth of understanding, both of their thought, and of the background. They are statements of astonishing vitality and relevance. In "Art and Production", for example, he takes Man and derides him: "men prefer their habits to their lives". He cautions us for our predisposition to think "that everything can be fixed by the economists". He examines the change which progress had wrought: "In the past we produced in order to live; now we live in order to produce."

He was particularly concerned, in the text of that lecture, with Man's distortion of nature. Yet his words of 1931 lodge in our lives at the end of the twentieth century with a compelling force.

> I want to emphasize the importance of thinking seriously about all those things that appear in our specialist shops, those things whose origin is questionable, whose composition is suspect and whose seasonableness seems unlikely; about those

masses of tinned foods which have spread all over the earth
and whose use and abuse is clearly not unconnected with the
spread of the deficiency diseases, of tuberculosis and cancer,
whose microbes, with such great earnestness, are being sought
in the laboratories . . . Man has mechanized the earth itself,
and the seed. He has changed it, both in the spirit and in the
letter. Natural fertilizer was necessary to the earth: it was the
food which replaced the energy lost through the work of ger-
mination and ripening. There was never a lack of it in the past,
nor was there any reluctance to make use of prudent and judicious improvements.

Mechanization and technology have interfered with this
process which, like the agile tool in the craftsman's hand, operated on the basis of a scale of proportions proper to itself.
Now it is uncontrollable, a blind mechanism, which disturbs
the product, robs it of its vitality, and has completely changed
its nature.

Gleizes, in this line of thought, though it does not predict genetic
modification, predicts the psychological and emotional approaches by which mankind would consciously and deliberately,
under the eyes of popular politicians and wise economists, set
about the destruction of the planet.

I dwell at length on this singular aspect of Gleizes' thought, as
expressed in the third of these lectures. I do so because of his own
direct and personal involvement, both then and in later years, in
life and work detached from his urban origins and from the supposed singularity of the life of the arts. I also follow this line of
thought because it was one that brought Gleizes close to his followers, including Mainie Jellett.

In many respects she followed his method. Like him, she was
intellectual, with a formidable mind by which she grasped his
teaching and his thoughts, and added to them with her own. Like
him, she spread what was really a gospel and a belief through lectures and articles which related art to ordinary life. At the time of
these three Gleizes lectures, the experiment of Moly-Sabata, an art
commune founded by Gleizes, at least in its first phase under the

direction of Mainie's friend Robert Pouyaud, had come to an end in rather bitter circumstances. Though Mainie Jellett had been hugely sympathetic towards the project, and intensely interested in it as a practical expression of Gleizeian ideas, she held herself aloof from it, as did her friend, the Irish artist Evie Hone. Nevertheless, in the period leading up to Gleizes' visit to Poland to deliver these profound observations upon twentieth-century art and life, the two women spent a good deal of time with Albert and Juliette Gleizes.

Ironically, their visits deprive us of the content of the exchanges that took place, and the letters from this period are not numerous. It seems that Mainie was certainly instrumental in extending Gleizes' knowledge and understanding of Celtic life and art. Through her mother, she was related to one of the more significant scholars on the subject, Margaret Stokes. Mainie had a detailed and educated knowledge, not just of the evolution of Celtic art in Ireland, but of the wider Celtic culture which in its essence is centripetal rather than centrifugal, egalitarian rather than hierarchical, and committed to the idea of art and life being combined.

Moreover, the Ireland from which Mainie Jellett in the first instance had travelled to Paris, and met Gleizes, and from which she and Evie now presented themselves as participants in Gleizes' philosophical and creative world, was attempted to fulfil in the newly created State some of the principles which are set forth in these lectures.

There may have been no connection. There is no overt reference. But in "Art and Religion" the intellectual and spiritual perceptions come very close indeed to her life and thought. And Gleizes could almost be writing with reference to Ireland when he makes the apt observation about the trap into which the historian falls when he judges "everything by the way of thinking of his own age".

Once again, as with agricultural production and food consumption, Gleizes suddenly electrifies us by the seemingly obvious yet fundamental observations he makes about the way we see the past. The historian, looking at the period up to the thirteenth century in Europe,

> . . . has failed to understand and appreciate these ages in the light of their own state of mind. Is that not why they are generally thought to be barbarous? Those Merovingian and Carolingian centuries in which the Latin, the German and the Celt were fused together in a human synthesis, rough and tumultuous as all healthy youth must be, did not think of themselves as simply preparing the way for us. They had enough to do living their own life. And it was to organize their own life that they adopted views which are not the same as ours. These included federation based on the freedom of localities, a collective conception of property, elites living according to the rules of monasteries, where they set men an example of the vigorous practical application of the evangelical principle — cultivation of the spirit; discipline of the senses through physical work and intellectual meditation.

Mainie Jellett, in her teaching practice in Ireland — she was both a teacher of the young, and a lecturer and inspiration for her contemporaries — had a sense of the "clean sheet" represented by the new Irish State. Its people were there to be led and instructed. It was open to the kind of inspiration which art might offer. And it was an intensely spiritual and an intensely intellectual, even argumentative society.

Her notes and her lectures reflect and draw upon those of Gleizes. And this is the case in each of the subjects he covers. She was interested in science, and had read Einstein. She was practically concerned with the human realities of production — no one living in Ireland through the 1920s could have avoided this. Most profoundly of all, she had travelled with him the road of understanding about abstraction, which inspires the early part of the first lecture of these three, and the manifestation of spirituality in art which is its central theme.

I was both electrified intellectually and profoundly moved spiritually by reading this first text. It was almost incidental how it reflected upon my own starting point, in Mainie Jellett's career. This was an important and pivotal period for her, the beginning of the 1930s, a point of departure, when she painted some of her most wonderful and inspiring religious works. But in a much more abstract way I found myself spellbound by the immediacy and the simplicity of Gleizes, reaching out across seventy years and arresting my own sense of artistic purpose and worldly direction by what he said all those years ago. He writes:

> It is impossible to understand artistic activity independent of its union with religion. And, while recognizing that art is the servant of religion, it is equally impossible to understand religion independent of its union with art. Religion provokes artistic activity and stimulates it. It gives it the duty of maintaining among men a consciousness of the purpose of their existence.

This thought, which some would argue belongs centuries back in time, seems to float, in terms of the these three Gleizes lectures, uncomfortably adrift in that period of *entre deux guerres*, with all its extremes and uncertainties. Remote from the past, towards which Gleizes looks with an admiration which increases the further back he goes, it seems equally remote from us today. Yet his words take on an immediacy, a relevance, a life, a vigour which encapsulates for me much that is wrong in our own world, and inescapably in much modern art. This lacks a relevance to our existence, just as our existence lacks any real contact with the spirituality which inspires so much of Gleizes' thought and work.

The words that are offered here are arresting and dynamic. They are intensely modern, of our time, and suited to our own intolerable world dilemmas. He reaches across two-thirds of this confused and chaotic century with answers that are so wholesome, so simple, so direct, so inspired. He offers a spiritual argument, an artistic argument and a religious argument; and in the end they are all the same argument — about the need for modern man to confront his role and purpose in the western world and in the world as a whole.

The geography of thought and concern has widened somewhat since 1931. The ability to know, if not to understand, has been dramatically speeded up by modern technology. But the problems remain the same. We are governed by economists, and this should not be the case. Religions have multiplied, and religion has disappeared, taking with it spirituality and artistic enlightenment. And art, the flux and catalyst that Gleizes applied to all these problems in his wise and penetrating words delivered all those years ago in Poland, has lost its way. He offers here so many stimulating answers. Reading him is like finding a gospel for the new century.

Written as the Introduction to Peter Brooke's edition of three essays by the French artist Albert Gleizes, with whom Mainie Jellett worked in the early 1920s. The book is given the title of the three essays: *Art and Religion, Art and Science, Art and Production*.

NORA NILAND AND SLIGO

My association with Sligo dates back to the late 1950s. I first went there in the summer of 1958 and stayed at Glen Lodge on the shores of Ballisodare Bay. I was married in Sligo the following August, and from then on spent Christmas, Easter and summer holidays on the shores of the Bay with Knocknarea Mountain rising behind the house. It was said that Yeats used to visit the Jamesons there in Glen Lodge and there were stories of the boatmen rowing to the house, candles on the gunwales. Apocryphal or not, the stories were a welcome part of those years. There were copies of his works in the bedrooms and inevitably the close proximity of scenes from his writing made each visit a kind of pilgrimage. The high point of this was August, when the Yeats Summer School brought many visitors. We knew Tom Henn, the first director of the school, who was related to our oldest friend in Sligo, Dermot O'Hara. And over the years I contributed to the school.

By the winter of 1961 I was employed as a journalist with *The Irish Times* and involved in feature writing and book reviewing for Terence de Vere White, the Literary Editor. The following year I became editor of a small literary magazine, *The Dubliner*. I met Nora Niland early on during many of my visits to Sligo and we formed a bond of friendship that was coloured by professional need and interest on both sides. Journalists invariably move

35

Albert Gleizes and Twentieth-Century Mankind

Albert Gleizes set himself and the fellow-artists of his own time on a course of collision and conflict with the western world. It was a course which he intended should be productive and beneficial. His outlook was benign and compassionate. But he saw and solved some of the major problems of his time from the standpoint of the artist, and his thoughts are brought together in these three lectures. He challenged the western world's view of history, its denial of religion, its use of science. His philosophical thought represents a profound critique of its view of material things, of its principles of manufacturing and marketing, of its use of knowledge. He redefined the way it saw, felt, heard and responded.

Of the relatively small number of artists who saw and were aware of what he was saying, few agreed, fewer still followed him. One of them, the Irish abstract-cubist artist Mainie Jellett, has been an abiding interest in my own life since the late 1950s. I came to know Gleizes through her, read their correspondence, examined the master–pupil relationship and how it operated, saw it in terms of their rigorous studies of abstraction, and her involvement in his profound redefinition of the laws of painting. Above all, I admired that friendship and collaboration in the powerful and through life with their professional qualifications like a knapsack on their backs. Librarians may be the same, never entirely free from the obligation to know about books, literature and the life of the writer. Without doubt, from the beginning, our friendship was so coloured. Nora knew things that would make stories for me. I wrote in newspapers and could be of help to her.

I remember her as rugged and strong-willed. She had fought for most things in her life. She fought certainly for the library in Sligo and for the collection of Yeats paintings, drawings and watercolours that are one of the town's outstanding glories. Until very recently, Sligo and its people knew, only as in a glass darkly, how good a collection of the artist's work it has. Small in number, chosen by a gifted and brilliant series of judgements, the works contain Jack Yeats at his very best. They represent something of the heart of the man, his love of the town, his love of the west of Ireland, his love of history and of sacrifice. He was, of course, political. But his politics have been grossly misunderstood and misrepresented. He saw always the human dimension in the making of a national spirit, and he loved the marginal and minor key occurrence.

Nora Niland appreciated this in the painter. While on the one hand she grasped after major works, like *The Funeral of Harry Boland* or *Talking to Prisoners,* she was also wise enough to see the absolute and perfect charm of a tiny watercolour like *G'Morrow, Strawberry.* This 1903 picture, only five by three inches in size, carries with it the kind of story that appealed to Nora and made her laugh. The picture was shown first in a show called *Sketches of Life in the West of Ireland.* The writer Seumas O'Sullivan reviewed the show and wrote of "the glee, the sheer childish glee", emphasising how much Yeats managed to see his subject through the eyes of a child. Years later, when O'Sullivan (his real name was James Starkey) was the editor of *The Dublin Magazine,* he hosted a PEN Club dinner for Jack Yeats and proposed the toast of honour, mentioning the earlier occasion. Yeats went back to his studio and found the drawing, still in his collection. He sent it round to O'Sullivan as a gift. In 1971 it was lent to the Sligo Library and Museum, later becoming a gift, no doubt with Nora Niland's careful persuasion.

Nora Niland saw the point of things. She saw what paintings meant and why having them and looking at them needed ownership and a place of safety. She had feelings for art and she had a good eye. An eye for art is worth much more than academic qualification. It is a priceless gift in someone who works for the public interest.

Nora had a shrewd appreciation of how things were in her own day in Sligo, a difficult time for getting anyone to appreciate anything. And she predicted instinctively what the future held. This made her visionary and gave her direction and purpose. It meant inevitably that she had a solitary disposition. She had to think and act for herself, and she occupied a world of competition and cupidity even in those distant days.

I met her often and I wrote about what she achieved. I liked being on the fringes of Sligo life, coming and going for holidays, never fully involved in the artistic or literary activities but watching them, often with amusement at their transience. I felt more permanent, knew the town in winter weather, experienced other aspects of it, the history, the politics, the seafaring.

Returning is always a pleasure, and no part of it more redolent of the past than the art in the Niland Gallery, one of the finest art galleries on this island. I know that Niland is only part of its name, but it is the important part and the lasting part, and it is a fitting memorial to a great benefactor. Nora Niland did Sligo proud, and she did not find her actions always easy to carry through. The gift of time and love is often the hardest to assess and the hardest to accept. She made it exceptional.

Written in July 2002 as a contribution to a pamphlet on Nora Niland edited by Jim McGarry of Collooney.

37

DOROTHY WALKER

Dorothy Walker died from cancer in December 2002. She was an uncompromising modernist in her pursuit of Irish art. Her mentor was Michael Scott, the architect, whose partner, Robin Walker, was Dorothy's husband. She was part of the executive committee of the first Rosc, in 1967, over which Michael Scott presided, and that experience may be said to have shaped her critical stance.

The decade of the 1960s was a time of critical turmoil. A good deal of this derived from the autocratic control of the Modernists in Irish art by Father Donal O'Sullivan , who was Director of the Arts Council, and who had a close association both with Michael Scott and with Louis le Brocquy. It meant a particular interpretation of what Modernism was about, and it caused the exclusion rather than the inclusion of many Irish painters.

This was made manifest in particular with the first Rosc exhibition, a huge show at the RDS of foreign artists. Through diffidence, cowardice or uncertainty, Irish painters and sculptors were excluded, leading to fierce controversy. Some critics, including myself, attacked the concept and the execution. Dorothy was its most fervent defender.

In her book, *Modern Art in Ireland*, published in 1997, she pays due respect to the earlier traditions of Modernism, going back to the 1920s. But it is a retrospective view designed to introduce her real point of departure. This was based on the belief in an artistic explosion deriving in part from the economic miracle of Seán Lemass and in part from the post-war artistic liberalism of the 1960s. It was an entirely tenable position and she occupied it bravely and with considerable intellectual resourcefulness and determination. I disagreed with it entirely, but that was part of what made art coverage so entertaining in those years.

The star in her firmament was Louis le Brocquy, about whom she wrote the best general account of his career, coupled with a good interpretation of his work. Irish art from le Brocquy to the present, largely excluding the figurative image, the academic school of painting, the Royal Hibernian Academy and the basic traditional skills in painting that were favoured by an increasingly detached "other half", were her preoccupation. The second half of her *Modern Art in Ireland* reflects this selective view.

She was unrepentant when faced with challenge or criticism. Over many encounters we enjoyed our differences and got a great deal of amusement out of them. She liked to experience the simmerings of disagreement, and they brought to her lips a smile of anticipation as she gathered herself for the inevitable fray.

We shared one exhibition, covering the last fifty years of Irish art, as joint curators, both of us uncharacteristically on the same side, in effect, choosing works of modern art, but modern art that had already become history. She had Patrick Collins and Louis le Brocquy, among others; I had Derek Hill and Gerry Dillon. We no longer stood opposed. We were on the same side of the fence, broadly in defence of paint on canvas, broadly against the more eccentric extremes of conceptualism.

In this chronological and fashionable sense I happily gave way to the force that drove her forward, always hunting for the new, always espousing the frontier figures who were writing their increasingly strange messages in the sand. She was at times remarkably forthright.

She described Seán Scully as "the most important Irish painter of the eighties and nineties, abstract or otherwise". It is a categoric judgement, of course eminently open to rebuttal in any context, including that of the personal choice from which it came. But it did have an impact and it did lead, as much of what she said always led, to argument and dispute.

This made the art of painting far more exciting and central than its following or its practitioners merited. But there was no harm in that. She was the figure in a Dylan Thomas poem, enigmatically forcing splendour out of obscure material.

Was she right, or was she wrong? Few critics in Ireland over the past forty years have managed to provoke, in a serious and argumentative way, such a central criticism about the purpose of art and the kinds of messages that were being sent.

It is largely deserted territory now, with each new intervention or direction somehow preordained as an inevitability. We cut our teeth on a different inventiveness, and with Dorothy at exhibition openings it was never dull.

She was a discriminating collector and owned fine examples of artists, including Mainie Jellett and Pat Scott. She made a vigorous and at times explosive contribution to the careers of painters and the judgements of their critics.

Dorothy Walker died in December 2002. We had known each other from the 1960s, often crossing swords over art criticism, and very different in our outlooks. This obituary appeared in the *Irish Independent*.

38

DEREK HILL MEMORIAL ADDRESS

The important thing about Derek Hill's life was that he made a vocation out of promoting love and friendship between England and Ireland. Transcending all that he did, and inspiring most of his actions, was his belief in bringing together two countries and their people. He expressed it as one does one's faith: hard to explain, easier to demonstrate by actions which are inspired by love and affection.

It became something of a political act. While Derek was in no sense political, and vowed that he did not understand politicians, he nevertheless pursued his vocational task on behalf of friendship between two countries during a period which progressively got worse. Starting out, fifty years ago, he could not possible have known what was going to happen. Lives were to be lost, violent acts were to be perpetrated on people in England and in Ireland, and this would lead to unimaginable animosities between the people in the two countries.

What he brought to a highly politicised country was the benefit of the generosity which inspired his acts. I remember an occasion when I was staying with him. I had been extremely critical of John Hume in a number of articles, and Derek had arranged a dinner party to which John Hume and his wife Pat had been invited, as well as Brian Friel and his wife, Anne. I warned him that John and I would not be getting on too well. And Derek accepted this. And so it turned out. To begin with, we hardly spoke. But then, by dint of perseverance and utter charm, he melted the strained atmosphere and made us all happy and then talkative and then friendly. In the end we all sat on a sofa while different people took photographs. It was an achievement which he would simply have put down to good manners and tact.

The Irish "Troubles" never undermined nor lessened Derek's sense of unspoken mission. He simply went on exploring friendship and extending it through all the contacts he had. The instinct he acted on was love. The territory was mainly Donegal.

Everything else about him that I love takes second place to this, except for one thing: his painting.

I think he was a great painter. Few critics believed that in the early years. He was quite often mocked. He was known as "Peanuts" Hill, a reference to the small fees he charged for portrait commissions when other painters were asking a small fortune for the painting of a commissioned portrait. Derek painted people because he was interested in them. He posed them in unusual ways. He produced wonderful landscapes, and lovely, powerful, breathtaking pictures of the sea, particularly of Tory Island.

As a painter, Derek had great technical skill, and was a master of colour, understanding its source and its effect. He had all the essentials of painting. The Golden Section, which magically can transform a painting with its compositional aptness and its invisible magic, flowed through his veins like blood. He primed his canvases well, he sketched in his pictures with an easy, relaxed brilliance.

When he held his second retrospective exhibition at the Royal Hibernian Academy, it suddenly dawned on many people just how good he was.

Derek had a great capacity for friendship, and was the total egalitarian. His range was enormous, from the Tory Islander to the landowner, from the businessman to the gardener. It seemed to make no difference, but in reality Derek Hill would never allow it to make a difference. He applied his own peculiar kind of authority.

He was privileged and did not have to work. He pursued interests, and became richly endowed with a natural, inbred scholarship. He knew his subjects, his love of Islamic art, painting, opera, music generally, gardens, architecture, biography. He had a brain as sharp as a razor.

He was a wonderful letter writer. He was a master in the difficult art of writing postcards. I have a box full of them, and take great pleasure in their possession. They possess you, not you them. That is what correspondence does. Keeping in touch was awfully important to him. He would write, and his letters contained anxiety about not hearing, not getting news, not being praised or thanked or asked for help. All his friends heard him from time to time wailing down the telephone about being neglected.

He was the victim of funny tricks and practical jokes. On one occasion we all went across for dinner to Glenveigh Castle, where Derek's friend Henry P. McIlhenny, known as "the Sauce King", was in residence, with an eccentric house-party. McIlhenny liked to tease Derek Hill, and there was great rivalry between them. Others teased him as well.

At that time, in the early 1960s, the telephone was still quite a prized possession, and beside it, on the table, was a select listing of Derek Hill's friends in the county, less than twelve as I remember. He was not anxious that people should know he had the telephone installed, and this prompted one practical joke, the brainchild of Desmond and Marega Guinness. They went to a local shop and borrowed one of those signs which said YOU MAY TELEPHONE FROM HERE and then put it up outside the Glebe House where Derek Hill lived, to his obvious embarrassment.[1]

He was a great supporter of the Wexford Opera Festival, and he served on the Council of the Friends of the National Collections of Ireland for forty years.

---

[1] I learned subsequently that it was not Henry P. McIlhenny, but Marega and Desmond Guinness who were responsible for this particular leg-pull.

I was privileged to share many days with him. They were always happy and stimulating occasions, always focused on things he loved, and always enriched by his extensive mind, his wit and understanding, and his openness to the opinions of others. He was gentle in manner and this showed in his conversation. But he was, and always remained, very English.

I remember vividly the occasion on which he received the Freedom of Letterkenny. I went up especially for it, as indeed did other friends, and stayed the night in Churchhill, not with Derek but in a place in the village. The celebration of all he had done for Donegal was most pleasing to him. But I can't help thinking that he was not entirely happy when, in the course of a speech, a local politician more or less took possession of Derek, maintaining that he had "become one of us", and was, from now on, to be regarded as an Irishman. Acceptance of this idea, either by Derek or by anyone else, would really have negated his whole purpose in life, and transgressed an innate sense of who he was and where he came from. Of course, he said nothing, and even as the words were uttered, he simply gazed out, with a smile of contentment on his face.

He was the quintessential Englishman, relaxed, mannerly, gentle, easy with all types of people, gracious, quick to learn, slow to teach, but always ready to do either.

One day above all others stands out. This was when he received honorary Irish citizenship from President Mary McAleese in the presence of the Taoiseach, Bertie Ahern. In a short speech, he described it as the happiest day of his life. The happiness derived from being recognised for the benign affection in which he had held this country for half a century, the gifts he had given, the kindness shown. But above all it derived from being true to himself as well as being true to us. That is how we should remember him.

The Derek Hill Memorial Service in St Patrick's Cathedral, Dublin, was held on Tuesday, 10 October 2000. This was my address.